Harvey Wasserman's
History
of the United States

Harvey Wasserman's History of the United States

by Harvey Wasserman

Four Walls Eight Windows, New York

Copyright © 1988 Harvey Wasserman.

Revised and updated edition of the 1972 book.

First Four Walls Eight Windows edition published September 1988 by:
    Four Walls Eight Windows
    Post Office Box 548
    Village Station
    New York, New York 10014

Library of Congress Cataloging-in-Publication Data
Wasserman, Harvey.
    Harvey Wasserman's History of the United States/ by Harvey
Wasserman.
        p.   cm.
    Reprint. Originally published: Harper & Row, 1972.
    Includes bibliographical references.
    ISBN 0-941423-10-7 (pbk.): $6.95
    1. United States—History—1865–1921.   I. Title.
E661.W33   1988   88-16508
973—dc19   CIP

Manufactured in the U.S.A.

This is dedicated to the two-eye love.

Prologue

I was born upon the prairie, where the wind blew free and there was nothing to break the light of the sun.

I was born where there were no enclosures and where everything drew a free breath. . . .

Parra-Wa-Samen (Ten Bears)

I could see that the Wasichus did not care for each other the way our people did before the nation's hoop was broken.

They would take everything from each other if they could, and so there were some who had more of everything than they could use, while crowds of people had nothing at all and maybe were starving.

They had forgotten that the earth was their mother. This could not be better than the old ways of my people. There was a prisoner's house on an island where the big water came up to the town. We saw that one day. Men pointed guns at the prisoners and made them move around like animals in a cage. This made me feel very sad, because my people too were penned up in islands, and maybe that was the way the Wasichus were going to treat them.

In the spring it got warmer, but the Wasichus had even the grass penned up. . . .

Black Elk

Contents

Introduction

Why should we read Harvey Wasserman's history of the United States when we can read a regular and respectable textbook written by some regular and respectable historian? Because his book is a beautiful example of people's history, when libraries and homes all over this country are clogged with dull and orthodox history. Also, because high school students, college students, and almost everybody will find it utterly refreshing and educational in the deepest sense.

What is "people's history," and why do we need it? To begin with, we would expect a people's history to be written in such a way that we can all understand it, free of that pretentious vocabulary which the professional scholar often uses to disguise the ordinariness of his ideas. Harvey Wasserman writes simply and bluntly. We are astonished—because we have developed such an awe of complex terminology—when a book begins a discussion of the late nineteenth century in the United States like this: "The Civil War made a few businessmen very rich." The sentence is terse. It is true. And it promises to tell us much more.

That sentence makes a suggestion crucial to any people's history of the United States: that behind the politics, the wars, the diplomacy stressed in conventional histories of this country, there is something more basic, something the political scientist Harold Lasswell once described as "who gets what, how, and why?"

Bold historians in the early part of this century did search below the surface of political conflicts for more fundamental motives in human behavior. Charles Beard's *An Economic Inter-*

pretation of the Constitution, written just before World War I, tried to dispel that fog of romantic nonsense spread through our school system in which the Founding Fathers who drafted the Constitution were depicted as selfless patriots, concerned only with the welfare of their countrymen. He informed us that most of these men were masters of slaves, owners of property, and holders of bonds, whose economic interests and political philosophies made them want a strong, conservative government that would prevent rebellions by the propertyless.

It is unpleasant, going even further back, to think that the Puritans and pilgrims and settlers of Jamestown had gold, land, and fortune on their minds and that they were willing to enslave blacks, shoot Indians, and hold their white brethren in servitude to increase their wealth. We would much rather think of them as the founders of Harvard College and the creators of representative government through the House of Burgesses in Virginia. It is a bit unsettling to think that George Washington was not just a good general but a wealthy slaveholder and that his chief adviser, Alexander Hamilton, as one of the first acts of the United States, created an alliance between the government and the wealthy class which has persisted down to this day. We have too often preferred history books which avoided these uncomfortable thoughts.

We seem to think that a book is unbiased if it repeats the bias of all the books that went before it. Generation after generation of writers and readers have seen the Civil War as a sectional battle between North and South or a political conflict between Democrats and Republicans, with Abraham Lincoln always representing the moral struggle against slavery. Therefore, we suspect a historian of lacking "objectivity" if he points out that the Northern politicians and business leaders were much more interested in land, railroads, tariffs, banks, and political power, than in the plight of the slaves. This interpretation explains why the country's leaders were willing to leave the black in semislavery after the Civil War, once they got what they wanted. In the same mood of telling it like it is, C. Vann Woodward's book *Reunion and Reaction* explains how the greed for railroads was so important in the betrayal of the Negro during Reconstruction.

The *New York Times* back in 1917 considered Charles Beard's ideas "dangerous to the community and to the nation." It called his book on the Constitution "grossly unscientific . . . not based upon candid and competent examination of facts." I suspect some people will call Harvey Wasserman's history "unscientific" because it has a clear point of view, one which points, disturbingly to who gets what and how.

You never hear a fat, fact-filled textbook referred to as "unscientific," because there is an assumption that fatness and fact-fullness, in a book where no point of view is obvious, makes that book scientific and objective. That is a great myth. Every history book has a point of view; every historian is subjective. No matter how thick a book it is, it is extremely thin in relation to the mountain of complex facts in the past. The historian had to pick a few rocks off this mountain of reality, and, depending on which rocks he picks (whether he picks seven or seven hundred) he can create one impression or another.

These impressions which history books create are not just of academic interest. They have a powerful effect on the present situation. Every historian has a choice which he exercises, either deliberately or subconsciously, to select from the past so as either to make us satisfied with the record of our national behavior or to make us critical of it. Whether we are satisfied or critical affects our attitudes and our behavior today.

Harvey Wasserman is clearly not pleased with what he finds in the past, and so he reminds us of what more complacent historians underemphasize: our brutality towards the Indians, our statesmen's and industrialists' dreams of empire, our aggressiveness in beginning to build that empire around the turn of the century. He stresses the power of the Vanderbilts, Carnegies, and

Morgans, because he knows that power is not just a fleeting historical fact. Today, just as in those days, very wealthy corporations dominate American life. They are the great forces behind political events, and they determine the everyday lives of most Americans. Giant conglomerate businesses manipulate our policy in Chile; sugar companies make us hostile to Cuba; armaments industries lobby for big military budgets. In their thirst for profit they have wasted national resources and destroyed the beauty of the countryside. They have ravaged the earth's coal and iron, stripped the forests, ruined the beaches, polluted the air and water, and sucked the energy, the health, out of generations of working people.

To know that this has been true for a long time, that it is a persistent fact of American history, is important. It means these conditions do not belong to one period of the past. Here we find a use in history. If it shows conditions as continuous and deep-rooted—in this case, the power of corporate wealth behind politics, behind everyday life—it suggests to us that more radical measures than electing another president or passing another program in Congress will be necessary to change these conditions. It suggests that we will have to dig to the roots—to change our thinking, our relations with one another, to transform our institutions, our economic system, our day-to-day existence.

We do not find, in the pages to follow, the customary respect for the political leaders or the industrial leaders of the country. Theodore Roosevelt is shown for what he indeed was, not the athletic, heroic idol of youth we find in so many of our school textbooks, but an aggressive nationalist and expansionist, a believer in white, Anglo-Saxon supremacy. John D. Rockefeller is not a clever businessman turned kindly philanthropist, but a lord over the lives of many people who uses wealth and position ruthlessly.

Again, our vision of the past affects the present. A historian, by his picture of the powerful figures of the past, can leave his readers in awe of leaders and trusting in their wisdom, their honesty, their good will. Or, he can leave us suspicious of the motives of the mighty, critical of their actions, and persuaded that if the country is to fulfill its promise, the citizenry must have faith in their own wisdom and make use of their own power. In our time we have plenty of evidence to support such a critical attitude; in the failure of national leaders to solve the crucial domestic problems of this day, in the record of their deception of the American people about the war in Vietnam, in their disregard for the lives and liberties of so many people here and abroad.

In order for the American people, disillusioned with leadership, to trust in themselves, they need to know something which history knows: that people, facing the enormous power of the Establishment and apparently without power themselves can create power by determining not to be controlled, by acting with others to change their lives. We have seen such examples in other countries; we need to know that in the United States, too, there have been great popular movements for change. The textbooks pass lightly over these movements. Harvey Wasserman tells us about them in a way that will make it hard for us to forget. He tells us about the farmers in revolt against the railroads and banks and industrial combinations, about the labor movement and its struggles against the giant corporations. These movements only had small successes; they did not take the power away from the business and military interests in the country. But they did keep alive the spirit of resistance and unity against arbitrary power. If we keep their story fresh in our memories, perhaps we can pass on that spirit to whatever generation will make a new America.

How exciting those struggles were! How marvelous those men and women who organized farmers in Iowa and Minnesota and Kansas in the 1880s and 1890s, the Populists of the Great Plains who followed the suggestion of Mary Ellen Lease to "raise less corn and more hell!" We wonder how could our orthodox his-

xviii *Introduction*

tories have ignored for so long the violent railroad strikes of
1877, the Haymarket frameup of anarchists in 1886, the great
Pullman strike of 1894, the textile strike of women and children
in Lawrence, Massachusetts, in 1912? The same issues are with
us today. In the Ludlow Massacre of 1914 the National Guard,
paid by Rockefeller, machine-gunned women and children and
burned down the homes of striking miners. We think of a more
recent event at Attica prison in New York, when another Rockefeller allowed soldiers to attack rebellious prisoners and kill both
inmates and hostages. The massacres of the helpless go on and
will go on until history and anger overflow, until we have had too
much and insist that it stop.

The United States, much as we talk proudly proudly about its
"progress," has not changed very much from those days that
Harvey Wasserman recalls for us in such shocking color. The rule
of force, the rule of wealth, and the rule of law still hang heavy
over the lives of Americans, sending their sons to die in far-off
ventures for power and profit, gobbling up the wealth of the
country for private gain, wasting the immense resources, the
labor and talent of over 200 million people. We are more tech-
nologically advanced, we have more gadgets, there are more
reforms on the books, but our basic problems remain the same.
The recollection of what happened fifty or a hundred years ago
sharpens our perceptions, helps us understand how deep are the
roots in the soil we must turn over.

History should not leave us with a dark and hopeless vision.
There is too much of that already. There are too many pessimists,
too many cynics, and too many hard facts to support the pessimists and cynics: the recurring wars, the political prisoners, the
nuclear weapons stockpiled everywhere, the lies of national leaders. We need also to see how courageous men and women in
their time stood up against those hard facts and began the soft-
ening process, the creative process, that we can continue. And so
in the last fifty or so pages of this book, there is the good feeling

of standing alongside people who fought back: the irrepressible Mark Twain pointing his finger at the American imperialists, the adventurer and story-teller Jack London arguing for socialism, W. E. B. Du Bois pioneering the fight for black people, Charlotte Gilman telling of the economic and sexual exploitation of women, Emma Goldman speaking magnificently for anarchism, against war, for our freedom to love and to live our lives as we choose.

In the American past, these were years of suffering and brutality, and only days of magic. But we can have more of those days, Harvey Wasserman tells us in his own peculiar, magical way. It is up to us.

Howard Zinn

Boston, Massachusetts
1988

Author's Preface

HARVEY WASSERMAN'S HISTORY OF THE UNITED STATES
is a child of both the 1960s and the 1890s. It grew out of a Woodrow
Wilson fellowship to the University of Chicago, 1967–8.

The University that year was part of a city being torn apart by
hostile preparations for the Democratic National Convention, at
which Hubert Humphrey would be nominated. Amidst racial upheaval and bitter conflict over the Vietnam war, a generation of
students was experiencing its first serious violence. In October,
100,000 of us surrounded the Pentagon. That march also hosted the
formation of the Liberation News Service, an "Associated Press of
the Underground" aimed at remaking the media.

The politics inside the University of Chicago reflected the strife in
the streets. Within the history department a battle raged over what
was to be taught, and by whom. The noted Yale historian Staughton
Lynd, an outspoken critic of the war, was denied a job despite his
superb qualifications. Hans Morgenthau, the legendary political
scientist, drew tremendous flack for his own principled anti-war
stance. Virtually every student I knew at the U. of C. was expelled
in 1969 after occupying the administration building.

The lightening rod within the history department was Jesse
Lemisch, a young maverick whose particular focus was on the masses
of working people so little mentioned in mainstream histories. His
"bottom up" scholarship emphasized—at least as I understood it—
that the American Revolution was made by the sailors who fought
and died in the Boston Massacre, who tossed the tea into Boston
harbor, and by the farmers who shot from behind the trees at

Lexington and Concord, and then composed the bulk of the Revolutionary Army. Franklin, Jefferson, Washington, Adams all had their special genius. But the context for their roles were created by the raw, mass power of the sailors and farmers who bitterly resented the imperial British and then, later, felt much the same way about the new American ruling class.

Lemisch also analyzed and categorized the political slant of all the major American historians with whom I was familiar, including many then teaching at the U. of C. His lectures, along with those of Staughton Lynd, who had taken a job downtown at Roosevelt University, forced me to rethink everything I thought I knew about the study of history.

That winter I re-read virtually every history book I had studied as an undergraduate, and was introduced to a wide range of "new" scholarship from historians such as Howard Zinn, Charles Beard, Vernon Parrington, Herbert Apthekar, W.E.B. DuBois, Matthew Josephson and even Brooks Adams, Theodore Roosevelt's intellectual mentor, whose view from the far right was piercing and revealing. With all the humility common to one in his early twenties, I resolved to re-write American history.

After a year of teaching elementary school in New York city, I found myself in the garage of a communal farm in western Massachusetts, doing just that. The Liberation News Service had split in an infamous ideological dispute just before the Chicago convention. The explosion landed our faction on sixty acres of rolling hillside between the towns of Amherst and Greenfield.[1]

From August of 1970 through the winter of 1972 that little garage was crammed with the great books of our past. Many came from the fabulous Brattle Bookshop in Boston, America's oldest antiquarian

---

[1]Montague Farm has since played a very magical role in the development of the organic gardening and farming movements, and in the effort to stop the spread of nuclear power plants. Raymond Mungo's FAMOUS LONG AGO and Steve Diamond's WHAT THE TREES SAID tell much of the story, as does my own ENERGY WAR: REPORTS FROM THE FRONT.

bookstore, then run by George Gloss, now by his son Ken. George allowed me to buy for pennies some of literature's most fabulous treasures and to make them a part of this historiographic odyssey.

Among these books was William Appleman Williams' *Contours of American History*, which dissected our national story into three cycles, each with five parts. The idea of historic cycles made basic, natural sense, and provided a vital framework around which to organize the rhythms of our national story.

While reading about the period between 1860 and 1920, I was deeply moved by the intense battles of the populist farmers and of the urban working class to win a human definition for the Industrial Revolution. It seemed a travesty that so little about these powerful movements appeared in our mainstream survey texts.

Inevitably, the Captains of Capital, who receive such favorable press in so many of those same books, began to appear in a different light. And I was enchanted by the early movements for black power, feminism, ecological preservation and Bohemianism, all of which bore such clear kinship with the campaigns still bursting all around us.

In essence, the forces that struggled to control the era between the Civil War and the First World War seemed to express with astonishing clarity of language and action all the basic issues that are still tearing modern America apart. As the Vietnam War dragged on, and as we entered the 1970s amidst profound chaos, I found myself writing about that earlier, unresolved cycle of our history.

Since 1972, it has unfortunately become necessary to add a few dates and target nations to the map of armed U.S. interventions abroad. Little else is changed from the original edition except the concluding section, 'Third Heartbeat from the Sun.' The title comes from a theme by Jimi Hendrix. The changes were made to accommodate Cheif Seattle, whose words so succinctly define much of the crisis we continue to face on this planet today.

Much has happened since this book's first publication. But the issues of social justice and ecological sanity raised by the populists and socialists, blacks and feminists, Wobblies and Indians, anarchists, Bohemians, ecologists and so many other rebels and radicals at the turn of the century remain largely unresolved.

Their story remains one of the hidden keys to our national spirit . . . and to our future.

Howard Zinn's early support made publication of this book possible, and his comments and introduction have helped shape it. Shaw Livermore, Jr., Bradford Perkins, Robert Sklar, Marvin Feldheim, Marlene Dixon, Herb Klein, George Kateb, Marty Jezer and numerous other scholars at Ann Arbor, Chicago, Amherst and elsewhere made important contributions. The Amherst College, University of Massachusetts, Harvard University, Labadie, Boston, Jones, Forbes, Greenfield, Columbus and Bexley Public Libraries provided vital resources and assistance. Peter Irons compiled the original maps.

Other friends, supporters and inspirations are far too numerous to mention, but thanks as always to Studs Terkel, Ben Spock and Mary Morgan, Doug Parker, Andrea, Peter, Ronnie and Willie Simon, Mariana Cook, Melody Moore, Sara Price and her fine family, Kitty Axelson, Anne B. Khalsa, Walter Hursey, Hugh Van Dusen, Sharon Cooke, Irv Levy, Kataoka Yoshio, Edna and Irving Levine, M. Mogie, and all the good folks from LNS, the Fellowship of Religious Youth, the Montague, Wendell and Packer Corners Farms, Green Mountain Post Films, the Allen Farm Sheep and Wool Company, South Mountain Woodworking, the New Alchemy Institute and EcoLogic, the Clamshell and related Alliances, MUSE, the Progressive Magazine, New Age Journal, Harrowsmith, the Advocate Newspapers, the Nation, the Utne Reader, Greenpeace, Shobun-Sha Publishers, Greater Talent Network, the Conference on World Affairs, the Wasserman Uniform Company, the NAUMD and the LYJC, the Blue Mountain Center, the Social Venture Network, the American Business & Professional Association, Euclaire Avenue, the Styron, Matross-Doctoroff, Wainer-Watts, Chilewich, Saks, Shapiro and Wasserman clans, Angie Bennett, and, of course, Susan, Rachel and Annie & Abbie, the Fabulous Bugettes, who are the two-eye loves.

To Marshall Bloom, Oscar Smilack, Jack Wolf and Fred Zapinsky, whose inspiration remains so strong, a fond hello.

And hello, again, to you, too.

Harvey Wasserman's
History
of the United States

part one

---◆◆◆---

The Machine

The Robber Barons

Gold is the most precious of all commodities; gold constitutes treasure,
and he who possesses it has all he needs in this world,
as also the means of rescuing souls from purgatory,
and restoring them to the enjoyment of paradise.

Christopher Columbus

God gave me my money.

John D. Rockefeller

The Civil War made a few businessmen very rich.

The North and the South both gave army deferments to the
rich. The Confederacy exempted owners of more than fifty slaves;
the Union let those who had it buy their way out for $300.

Among those who paid their $300 were J. Pierpont Morgan,
John D. Rockefeller, Andrew Carnegie, James Mellon, Philip
Armour, and Jay Gould. Mellon just listened to his father, who
told him in a letter that "a man may be a patriot without risking
his own life or sacrificing his health. There are plenty of lives
less valuable."

Accordingly, young Mellon bought his way out and joined a
few thousand men like J. P. Morgan and Jay Cooke in the business
of war profiteering.

To Cooke the war meant about $3 million a year in commissions
alone. A wealthy banker and speculator, he wormed his way
into the government as official promoter of Union bonds. After
four years of war the national debt had skyrocketed from $75
million to almost $3 billion. Cooke became a multimillionaire and
the most powerful banker in the country. The national debt, he
announced, was "a national blessing."

3

J. P. Morgan, son of a millionaire banker, took his cut dealing gold and guns. Through a middleman, the 24-year-old Morgan bought obsolete carbines from the War Department at $3.50 a-piece. His partner then resold them to Union General Fremont at $22.00 each.

Meanwhile Philip Armour supplied the Union Army with beef. Jay Gould speculated gold and securities while Cornelius Vanderbilt dealt rotten hulks to the Navy and began putting together a railroad empire. Jim Fisk ran contraband southern cotton through the Union blockade, and John D. Rockefeller piled up profits as a Cleveland merchant and invested them in oil refineries.

America's first crop of "war millionaires" was taking shape. Mellon wrote his father that there were men starting in business who "continue growing richer and don't care when the war closes."

The War Profiteers Play Monopoly

For the millions who actually fought or who watched the two war machines wreck their farms, towns, and lives, the Civil War meant unimaginable horror, four years of unmitigated slaughter and devastation. Five hundred thousand people died, and the romantic spirit of the thirties and forties was consumed into a mangled, bloody mess.

The economic root of the war was a collision of the rising factory owners of the North against the slave-owning ruling caste of the South. Both wanted control of the federal government and both wanted the land west of the Mississippi, then being taken from the Indians.

Between them were the growing agrarian masses, who wanted free land for homesteading. After four decades of political strife, in the midst of a collapsed railroad boom and a national depres-

sion, the small farmers joined the industrialists to elect Abraham
Lincoln on the slogan "Vote Yourself a Farm!" War over slavery,
union, and control of the Mississippi River and the West followed
almost immediately.

With the slaveowners out of Washington, the farmers and
factory owners speeded construction of the national industrial
machine and prepared to open the West. A homestead act was
passed as well as an immigration act, high tariffs, and a reform
of the national banking system.

Industrial entrepreneurs poured into the capitol for huge
"grants" of money and land. The Pacific Railway Act of 1862
gave the promoters of the Union Pacific and Central Pacific Railways five square miles of land for every mile of track they would
lay across the west.

Two years later, after an amazing round of bribery, the members of Congress decided to up the grant to ten square miles in
addition to the allotment of as much as $48,000 for every mile of
track.

By 1872 a bought Congress had given various industrial con
artists more than $700 million and 200 million acres of public
land, an area roughly the size of Maine, New Hampshire, Ver-
mont, Massachusetts, Rhode Island, Connecticut, New York, and
Pennsylvania. Grants by the individual states swelled the money
and land totals even higher, and by the time land grant colleges
and independent speculators got through, virtually all the homestead land was in the hands of eastern finance.

Actual construction of the railroads was also quite profitable.
The directors of the Union Pacific, which began cross-country
construction in Omaha, hired the Credit Mobilier Corporation to
do the road work. The directors of the Union Pacific also happened to control the Credit Mobilier, which charged the UP
about $23 million more than construction had actually cost,
money which came out of the federal subsidy and the public sale
of worthless stock. The Central Pacific ring of California did even

better, picking up $121 million for $58 million in actual construction.

Thus, with the railroad grants as their key capital base, a few men began to carve giant private empires out of public money and land. Many of them, like Rockefeller, Vanderbilt, Carnegie, and Jim Hill, had begun life in dire poverty. Most were of Scottish or old Yankee descent.

Vanderbilt was one of the few who got his start before the Civil War. He was born to Dutch parents in 1794. As a youth he ran a ferry boat from Staten Island to Manhattan, slowly building capital to buy more boats. By the 1850s he was a full-fledged pioneer in the free-enterprise system, whose methods he perfected. "Whenever his keen eye detected a line that was making a large profit," wrote a biographer, "he swooped down and drove it to the wall by offering better service and lower rates."

Then, with the competition driven out of business, "he would raise his rates without pity, to the lasting misery of his clients."

Vanderbilt slowly collected a fleet of ships, and in the crazed years of the Gold Rush he made a fortune running prospectors from New York across Nicaragua by boat and stage and then on to California. He was at his best in the jungles, where he "drove his men to the breaking point, setting the example by fourteen to sixteen hours a day of sleepless vigilance and labor.

The engineers were appalled but on he went. Sometimes he got over the rapids by putting on all steam; sometimes, when this did not avail, he extended a heavy cable to great trees up stream and warped the boat over. . . . The engineers reported that he "tied down the safety-valve and 'jumped' the obstructions, to the great terror of the whole party."

The tall, gaunt commodore swelled his fortune by carrying the mail, studiously keeping postage rates high through his power in Congress.

During the Civil War he began piecing together a railway system with capital from his fleet, capital he added to by buying boats like the *Niagara* for the Union Navy. Gustavus Myers wrote in *Great American Fortunes* that

Vanderbilt was one of the few men in the secret of the Banks' expedition; he knew that the ships had to make an ocean trip. Yet he bought for $10,000 the *Niagara,* an old boat that had been built nearly a score of years before for trade on Lake Ontario. "In perfectly calm weather," reported Senator Grimes, of Iowa, "with a calm sea, the planks were ripped out of her and exhibited to the gaze of the indignant soldiers on board, showing that her timbers were rotten. The committee have in their committee room a large sample of one of the beams of this vessel to show that it has not the slightest capacity to hold a nail."

As early as 1853 the dour, semiliterate commodore was worth about $11 million, little of which he spent on his wife and nine children, who led a notably sparse existence. His son William, whom he considered stupid, was shipped off to a farm on Staten Island.

One day, however, William cheated his father in a small business deal; Cornelius then considered his son "fit" and brought him into the business, eventually leaving him around $100 million. "Law!" the Commodore once screamed, "What do I care about the Law! Hain't I got the power?"

Vanderbilt's early foe in the railroad game was "Uncle" Dan Drew, a financial manipulator of whom an admirer noted "no hardships or privations could deter him from the pursuit of money."

Like most of his contemporaries, Drew was deeply religious, an avid churchgoer, and a sponsor of cathedrals and seminaries. "He holds the honest people of the world to be a pack of fools," said Henry Clews, a Wall Street contemporary. "When he has been unusually lucky in his trade of fleecing other men, he settles accounts with his conscience by subscribing toward a new chapel or attending a prayer meeting."

Drew got his start as a cattle drover, buying the animals from midwestern farmers and driving them over the Alleghenies to market. It was as a drover that Drew pioneered the practice of "stock-watering."

During the long drive to market Drew kept the cows from getting water and often, in fact, fed them salt. Then, just before selling them, he let the thirst-crazed animals bloat themselves, multiplying their weight and price but adding nothing of value.

Drew perfected financial "stock-watering" on the Erie Railroad, the first trunk line from New York City to the Great Lakes. The road was built at a cost of around $15 million, and its completion in 1851 brought celebrations and "tremendous barbecues" all over the country. The Erie was hailed as a "monument at once of engineering skill and commercial enterprise."

Unfortunately, the rails were made of weak iron which had to be replaced, and the engines and cars were rickety and cheap. Furthermore, $26 million in stock—watered stock—was issued on around half that in real assets. The difference went to men on the inside, like Drew.

In the late sixties Vanderbilt squared off against Drew, Jim Fisk, and Jay Gould for control of the Erie. Vanderbilt wanted to add it to his New York Central; the "Erie Ring" wanted it for their stock-watering games and their thriving business into New York City, which they multiplied by dealing through Tammany Hall and by blackmailing farmers and merchants along the road who had no other way to get their goods to market.

When Vanderbilt tried to buy up the Erie stock the Ring began printing fresh shares like confetti. Certificates flew all over Wall Street, followed by court injunctions which each side got from their own judges.

Suddenly, Vanderbilt took the upper hand—

At ten o'clock the astonished police saw a throng of panic-stricken railway directors—looking more like a frightened gang of thieves, disturbed in the division of their plunder, than like the wealthy representatives of a great corporation—rush headlong from the doors of the Erie office and dash off in the direction of the Jersey ferry. In their hands were packages and files of papers, and their pockets were crammed with assets and securities. One individual bore away with him in a hackney-coach bales containing six millions of dollars in greenbacks. Other members of the board followed under cover of the night; some of them, not daring to expose themselves to the publicity of a ferry, attempted to cross in open boats concealed by darkness and a March fog.

The Erie directors holed up in the Taylor Hotel in Jersey City, which they surrounded with armed guards. When a rumor spread that Vanderbilt was offering $50,000 reward for the return of Drew to New York, "a standing army was organized from the employees of the road, and a small navy equipped. The alarm spread through Jersey City; the militia was held in readiness; in the evening the stores were closed and the citizens began to arm; while a garrison of about one hundred and twenty-five men entrenched themselves around the directors, in their hotel."

But it was a false alarm, and a little later a rumor circulated that Gould had left for Ohio. Soon thereafter he surfaced in Albany with a valise containing $500,000 for "legal expenses." There, said Charles Francis Adams, he undertook the task of cultivating a thorough understanding between himself and the members of the legislature.

Fabulous stories were told of the amounts which the contending parties were willing to expend; never before had the market quotations of votes and influence stood as high.

Faced with an apparently endless expense, the commodore called a truce. He let Drew back into New York and agreed to a temporary settlement. "Vanderbilt allus told me that I acted very foolish in goin' to Jersey City," said Uncle Dan. "I tole him I didn't know but what I was circumstanced in an ockered light."

After the Vanderbilt fight Drew played a smaller and smaller role on Wall Street and eventually died a pauper.

The following year—1869—Fisk and Gould fought Pierpont Morgan for the Albany & Susquehanna, a key link to some rich Pennsylvania coal fields. In a snowstorm of legal paper, Fisk, now known as "the Prince of Erie," sauntered into a stockholder's meeting with a gang of thugs, expecting to take over.

A group of Morgan men (recruited from the Bowery) met him and threw him down a flight of stairs, where he was "arrested" and taken to the local police station. The "policeman" that "arrested" him turned out to be a Morgan man in costume, and Fisk walked out of jail a little later.

Soon Morgan took control of the Albany terminal of the road, while the Erie Ring held the station at Binghamton. With injunctions flying right and left both sides sent out a trainload of thugs. The two locomotives rammed each other at a tunnel fifteen miles east of Binghamton, where "there was a crash and a smash, and the Albany locomotive rolled off the track, leaving the other without cowcatcher, headlight, or smokestack."

A pitched battle ensued, which the better-armed Morgan men won. The Erie Army retreated into the tunnel and regrouped. Morgan's men charged but were afraid to attack in the dark. Night fell, the militia marched in and the battle reverted to the courts, where Morgan eventually won.

That same year Gould cornered the national gold exchange and sent the price skyrocketing. When it peaked he poured his gold onto the open market, taking a gigantic profit and incidentally crashing the entire economy. "Let everyone carry out his own corpse!" yelled the irrepressible Fisk.

THE CRASH OF '73

Four years later eastern speculators noticed their money was drying up again, as it had in 1819, 1837, and 1857. This time the Franco-Prussian War had thrown European money sources into disarray, while the postwar orgy of speculation in the United States put thousands of operators out on a limb, holding paper empires with nothing real under them.

Jay Cooke was sunk deep over his head in the Northern Pacific

Railroad. Morgan, whose father had just arranged a $50 million loan to save the French government, wanted to add the NP to his expanding empire. He began publishing stories in his newspapers aimed at undermining the market value of Cooke's stock.

Under the strain Cooke's cash reserves disappeared. He was forced to duel Morgan on the floor of Congress for a $300 million "loan." Morgan won.

On September 17, 1873, President Ulysses S. Grant visited Cooke's palace in Philadelphia and spent the night. In the morning, while Grant slept, oblivious to what was going on, Cooke rode downtown and closed the doors of his bank. The national money supply disappeared. Millions of farmers and workers were thrown into a desperate struggle for existence. Mortgage money dried up, unemployment skyrocketed, families wandered from city to city in search of work.

For Morgan, Vanderbilt, and a few others with big money, crash meant good times. Labor was cheap. Giant factories stood idle, waiting to be picked off for next to nothing. With Cooke out of the way Morgan became the most powerful banker in the country. Vanderbilt and Gould added property after property to their empires while Rockefeller put the final touches on his oil kingdom. Bit by bit, they took it all.

Just as a number of German barons planted their castles along the banks of the Rhine, in order to tax the commerce between East and West, which was obliged to make use of this highway, so it is with these economic narrows. Wherever they are found, monopolies plant themselves in the shape of "rings," " corners," "pools," "syndicates," or "trusts."

Rockefeller's position was pretty well set by the 1873 depression. Rising as a merchant during the Civil War, he invested his capital in Cleveland oil refineries, taking care as he grew to commandeer all the railroad support he could get. By the early seventies he was the most powerful oil man in Cleveland.

Like Drew, Rockefeller was deeply religious. He read the Bible every night before retiring to bed, where he would discuss the day's business with himself. "These intimate conversations with myself had a great influence upon my life," he wrote in his autobiography.

The Baron of Oil had "the soul of a bookkeeper," kept all his accounts in his head, and was exceedingly taciturn, almost never displaying any emotion of any kind. On making a large profit, however, Rockefeller was known to clap his hands with delight, or throw his hat in the air and yell "I'm bound to be rich! *Bound to be rich!*"

With ruthless precision Rockefeller trimmed waste from his refineries while forcing rebates from the roads that carried his oil, carefully insuring that they charged his competitors more—

Wilkerson and Company received car of oil Monday 13th—70 barrels which we suspect slipped through at the usual fifth class rate—in fact we might say we know it did—paying only $41.50 freight from here. Charges $57.40. Please turn another screw.

In the depression of the seventies Rockefeller consolidated virtually the entire oil industry in his own hands. Dominating the railroads, underselling and, in at least one instance, blowing up would-be competitors, Standard Oil simply strong-armed the rest of the industry out of existence. "I tried to make friends with these men," explained John D. "I admitted their ability and the value of their enterprise. I worked to convince them that it would be better for both to cooperate."

By 1880 Rockefeller refined 80 percent of the nation's oil. Its gigantic capital fund allowed the Standard machine to pile railroads, ore mines, shipping companies, pipelines, state governments, and U.S. senators one on top of the other into a mushrooming empire that was probably the most powerful single organization in the world.

By the 1880s Standard and the other baronies growing with it —Carnegie Steel, the Morgan and Mellon Banks, James Duke's

American Tobacco Company, Swift and Armour Meat Packing, the railroads of Gould, Jim Hill, Tom Scott, and the Central Pacific ring—filled every corner of American life.

THE OCTOPUS

On the West coast the Central Pacific Ring of Leland Stanford, Collis Huntington, Mark Hopkins, and Charles Crocker dominated the economic life of California through their control of "the Octopus"—the state's railroad and steamship system. Stanford, the political arm of the corporation, was governor of California in 1862 when the Central Pacific grant was made, and later represented the Ring as U.S. senator.

In the 1870s the Octopus beat Tom Scott and got a treaty with Gould that secured a hookup with the Southern Pacific, thus insuring its control of all the railroads leading into California.

With that base the Central Pacific Ring extorted a fantastic, bitterly resented tribute from the people of the west coast. San Francisco merchants estimated it was cheaper to send goods around the tip of South America to Antwerp and back again than it was to send them via the Octopus to Redondo Beach.

To the railroads the Ring added the Occidental & Oriental Steamship Company, coal and iron mines, newspapers, gigantic parcels of land, and the government of San Francisco and the state. Huntington bragged that he could travel on his private property from New York to Yokahama. Allied with Carnegie, Gould, and Rockefeller, the California barons ruled the West coast like a feudal manor.

JAY GOULD, RIP-OFF KING

In New York, Jay Gould collected railroads—the Wabash, the Union Pacific, the Southern Pacific, the Denver Pacific, the Texas Pacific, the Kansas Pacific, and the Missouri Pacific—and pieced together a virtual transportation monopoly through most of the

West. He paid $3.8 million for the Missouri Pacific through which $25 million in state subsidies and more than 20 million land grant acres had passed like water through a strainer.

Manipulating the stock market through the Associated Press and the *New York World* (which he bought from Tom Scott), Gould became known as "the Mephistopheles of Wall Street." His favorite tactic was to malign a corporation through the media, driving its price down. Then he would buy it and loot the real assets, and then rebuild its reputation and sell it. He advertised that the charter of the New York Elevated Railway was going to be revoked by the state attorney-general (one of his men). When ⁺he stock crashed he bought control of the company and then imposed a ten-cent fare on the city. "His touch is death" warned Dan Drew.

With a retinue of plainclothed bodyguards the consumptive Gould lived off an empire that employed a hundred thousand people and that made no sense at all except in terms of financial manipulation.

In 1884 a group of Wall Street "friends," one a former partner, created a panic to catch Gould short of credit and ruin him. With his railroad system a joke and his finances in chaos, he admitted he was "beaten" and threatened to declare bankruptcy and crash the entire economy unless his attackers let up.

His conservative enemies agreed and allowed him some breathing room to recover, which he used to manipulate the market in his favor and screw his attackers to the wall.

Gould died in 1892, and his empire, much of which passed to his son George, became the subject of bitter legal hassle.

THE CRASH OF '93

The following year the stock market crashed again for the usual reasons—too much paper flying over too little reality, too many profits taken on too few actual goods. The industrial takeoff

JAY GOULD'S PRIVATE BOWLING ALLEY.

Source: Culver Pictures, Inc.

of the postwar years now ended with 65 percent of the nation's railroads in receivership. The farmers, still not recovered from the last depression, staggered under the blow and turned en masse to radical Populism; the labor movement, already in an advanced state, grew in power and militancy.

One of the corporations hardest hit by the 1893 depression was the United States government. By January 1895, the drain of gold out of the country was set at $43 million, and the standard of basing money on gold was near collapse.

Deeply alarmed, President Grover Cleveland made preparations for the Treasury Department to hold a public bond issue and to call in paper money. Morgan blocked both moves and forced Cleveland to turn to him and August Belmont, representative of the Rothschild's banking house of Paris, to salvage the gold standard. A Morgan-Belmont syndicate then floated $65 million worth of bonds to provide Cleveland with 3.5 million ounces of gold, taking at least $1.5 million in "commission."

The wreckage of the 1893 collapse left three barons in control of the heart of the economy—Morgan, Rockefeller, and Carnegie, the baron of steel.

Morgan was born in Hartford in 1847. Cold and colorless, he studied mathematics in Germany and then settled into his father's banking business. In his old age his face was disfigured by a rare disease that made his nose swollen and red. He had the mind of a computer, the passion of a Swiss watch.

Morgan, in his position as the leading banker on Wall Street, had taken to "reorganizing" as many railroads as he could get his hands on, which by the nineties was about half the track in the country.

After the Erie War of 1869 he worked himself and his father's capital into the role of "peacemaker" among warring corporations. When a major struggle loomed he would invite the directors to his yacht *Corsair* (*Corsair II*, 204 feet long, was sold to the navy for use in conquering Cuba) and preside over a settlement. Any new stocks or bonds that resulted were handled by the House of Morgan and often interlocking directorates were created. A typical settlement occurred when General Electric and Westinghouse threatened to engage in "ruinous competition." Morgan settled the fight, took a directorship in both corporations, and the two companies pooled their patents.

The only man as big as Morgan was Rockefeller. Allied with E. H. Harriman of the Illinois Central, Rockefeller in the 1890s sat atop complete control of the oil industry, a widespread network of controlled or affiliated railroads, huge coal and iron mining interests, and a gigantic yearly income that allowed him to buy properties, ruin competitors, and manipulate national prices and markets at will.

Between Morgan and Rockefeller, Andrew Carnegie held the key. Outgoing, well-read and articulate, the lively Scotsman was known to the world as a philanthropist, to his associates as a pirate, and to the workers in his factories as a killer. An outspoken advocate of peace and human community, Carnegie built an empire on the tools of war and paid other men to use them. He was a pioneer preacher of the gospel of wealth, a leader of men "who invoked the name of the Prince of Peace in their diatribes against war, and who put rifles in the hands of Pinkertons with which to shoot down strikers in their own factories."

Carnegie built his empire of steel from the untiring efforts of a few devoted engineers who helped him cash in on the Bessemer process. Later he brought Henry Frick, the coke king, into his operation as plant manager, thus tying most of his raw materials under one roof. By the nineties he held undisputed control over the nation's key growth industry.

In 1899 friction developed between Carnegie and the Pennsylvania Railroad, where he had begun as an office boy. He threatened to "go to war" and build his own railroad to the Great Lakes, a move that upset both Rockefeller and Morgan.

Rockefeller offered to buy him out but the deal fell through.

In 1900 Morgan told Carnegie to name his price and then paid over $492 million.

Quickly Morgan added his own steel holdings to the Carnegie properties and on April Fool's Day, 1901, the House of Morgan offered the first billion dollar trust—the United States Steel Corporation—for public consumption. *Cosmopolitan* magazine declared it a turning point in American economic history—

The old competitive system, with its ruinous methods, its countless duplications, its wastefulness of human effort, and its relentless business warfare, is hereby abolished.

MORGAN MARRIES ROCKEFELLER

Not quite. Within a month the whole system was almost shaken apart. Morgan had stolen the Chicago, Burlington & Quincy out from under Rockefeller, a move that Harriman termed "a hostile act."

In early 1901 a shooting war raged between Morgan and Rockefeller men for control of a key stretch of right-of-way in Utah. In May, Harriman moved secretly to take control of the Northern Pacific on the open stock market.

Morgan was in Europe and his staff was caught napping. But Jim Hill of the Great Northern, now a Morgan field marshall, discovered what was happening and retaliated. Northern Pacific stock soared from 110 to 1000, brokerage houses collapsed, and the entire economy went into a panic.

The Harriman attack sent a shiver down Morgan's spine. The Northern Pacific, spanning the continent from the Mississippi to Puget Sound, was the key artery linking the House of Morgan holdings from New York to Asia, the mainline of a "commercial expansion greater than had been seen since Venice was in her prime"—

Morgan needed the power to make a low, stable rate for a long haul across the prairies of the United States, over the Rockies, then by ship to the Orient. Thus he began, like some great merchant of Renaissance times, "to reverse the needle of trade," to send a flood of cotton to the Orient via his cars and lines, and to bring back silks to Seattle.

With Hawaii and the Philippines as newly conquered imperial bases and with the American army committed to guarding an "Open Door" to China by force of arms, the frontiers of trade along this route were apparently infinite.

In the shadow of this and of increasing popular anger with Wall Street, Morgan asked Rockefeller for peace. Rockefeller agreed. Harriman and Rockefeller exchanged stock with Hill and Morgan, and the two Houses joined on the board of the Northern Securities Corporation of New Jersey.

The Morgan-Rockefeller truce was the culminating event of the age of free enterprise. In the six years after the conquest of Cuba—from 1898 to 1904—some 234 trusts were formed, the largest being United States Steel and the center of the movement being the House of Morgan.

In 1904, Progressive President Theodore Roosevelt made a loud antitrust attack on the Northern Securities Corporation. The Supreme Court ordered the combination broken up, but the real effect was nil. "Two certificates of stock are now issued instead of one," said Jim Hill. "They are printed in different colors, and that is the main difference."

By 1912 the Morgan-Rockefeller community of interest involved 341 directorships in 112 corporations valued somewhere around $22,245 million and including such affiliated properties as Standard Oil, United States Steel, the Chase National Bank, First National and National City Banks of New York, the Guaranty Trust, Bankers Trust, Philadelphia National Bank, Illinois Trust and Savings, Hanover National Bank and National Bank of Commerce, the Equitable, Mutual, and New York Life Insurance companies, American Telephone and Telegraph, Western Union, International Harvester, International Mercantile Marine (owner

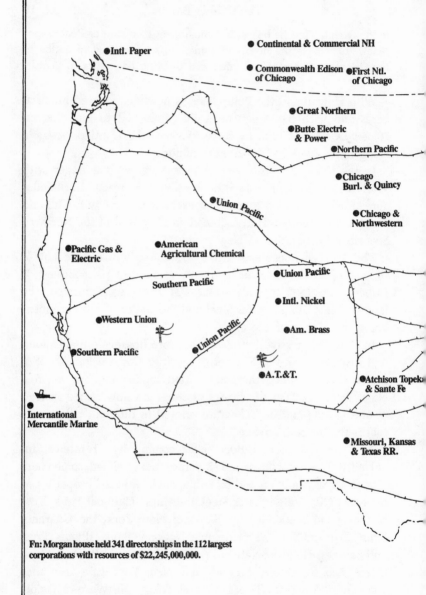

● Continental & Commercial NH

● Commonwealth Edison ●First Ntl.
of Chicago   of Chicago

● Great Northern

●Butte Electric
& Power

●Northern Pacific

●Chicago
Burl. & Quincy

●Chicago &
Northwestern

●Union Pacific

●Pacific Gas &   ●American
Electric   Agricultural Chemical

●Union Pacific

Southern Pacific

●Intl. Nickel

●Western Union   ●Am. Brass

●Union Pacific

●Southern Pacific

●A.T.&T.

●Atchison Topeka
& Sante Fe

●
International
Mercantile Marine

●Missouri, Kansas
& Texas RR.

●Intl. Paper

Fn: Morgan house held 341 directorships in the 112 largest
corporations with resources of $22,245,000,000.

It was involved with more
than 164,000 miles of railroad.

Hanover Ntl.

Equitable Life

J. P. Morgan & Co.

Liberty Ntl.

Mutual Life

N.Y. Life Trust

Chase Bank National City Bank

Banker Trust

Union Trust

Chemical Ntl.

Guaranty Trust

New York, New Haven & Hartford

Westinghouse

Amalgamated Copper

General Electric

NY Edison

Niagara Falls Power

Con. Gas N.Y.

Elevated

Armour Meats

Erie RR.

Phila Rapid Transit

Swift Packing

Baldwin Locomotive

Reading RR.

Pullman Co.

Standard Oil

Penn. RR.

International Harvesters

U.S. Steel

Central

U.S. Rubber

Penna. Steel

Public Service of N.J.

Phelps Dodge

Baltimore & Ohio

Case Machine

Illinois Central

Lackawanna Steel

Chalmers

Cambria Steel

B & O RR.

Westinghouse

Chesapeake & Ohio

K. C. Rail & Light

Louisville & Nashville RR.

Southern Railway

Norfolk & Western

Atlantic Coast Line

K. C. Southern

Tidewater Oil

General Asphalt

American Cotton Oil

U.S. Realty

American Sugar Refining

FRANCINE GERMONO

MORGAN-ROCKEFELLER EMPIRE

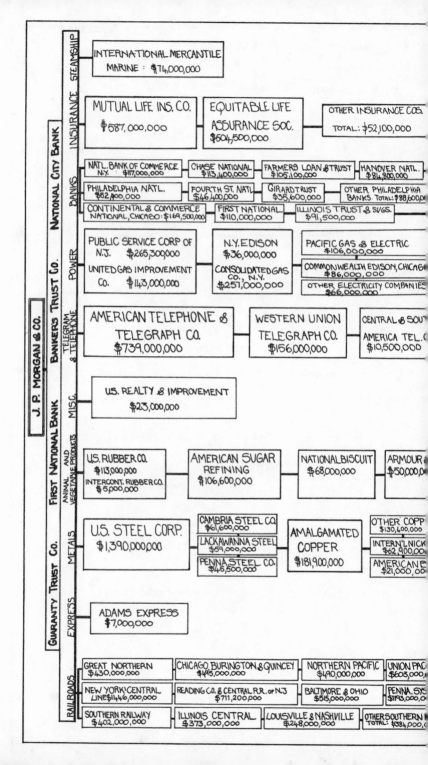

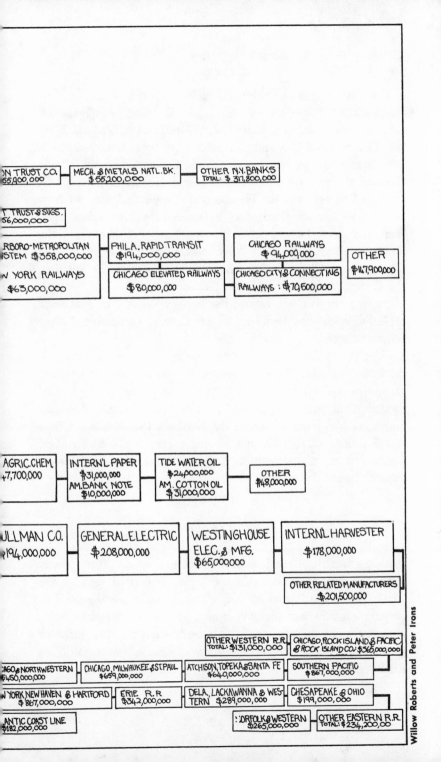

ON TRUST CO.
$65,900,000

MECH. & METALS NATL. BK.
$55,200,000

OTHER N.Y. BANKS
TOTAL: $317,800,000

T TRUST & SVGS.
$56,000,000

RBORO-METROPOLITAN
SYSTEM $358,000,000

PHILA. RAPID TRANSIT
$194,000,000

CHICAGO RAILWAYS
$94,000,000

OTHER
$147,900,000

NEW YORK RAILWAYS
$63,000,000

CHICAGO ELEVATED RAILWAYS
$80,000,000

CHICAGO CITY & CONNECTING
RAILWAYS: $70,500,000

AGRIC. CHEM
$7,700,000

INTERN'L PAPER
$31,000,000
AM. BANK NOTE
$10,000,000

TIDE WATER OIL
$24,000,000
AM. COTTON OIL
$31,000,000

OTHER
$48,000,000

ULLMAN CO.
$194,000,000

GENERAL ELECTRIC
$208,000,000

WESTINGHOUSE
ELEC. & MFG.
$65,000,000

INTERN'L HARVESTER
$178,000,000

OTHER RELATED MANUFACTURERS
$201,500,000

OTHER WESTERN R.R.
TOTAL: $131,000,000

CHICAGO, ROCK ISLAND & PACIFIC
& ROCK ISLAND CO.: $565,000,000

CAGO & NORTHWESTERN
$450,000,000

CHICAGO, MILWAUKEE & ST. PAUL
$659,000,000

ATCHISON, TOPEKA & SANTA FE
$640,000,000

SOUTHERN PACIFIC
$867,000,000

W YORK, NEW HAVEN & HARTFORD
$867,000,000

ERIE R.R
$342,000,000

DELA., LACKAWANNA & WES-
TERN $289,000,000

CHESAPEAKE & OHIO
$199,000,000

ANTIC COAST LINE
$182,000,000

NORFOLK & WESTERN
$265,000,000

OTHER EASTERN R.R.
TOTAL: $234,200,00

Willow Roberts and Peter Irons

of the *Titanic*), Armour Meat Packing, United States Rubber, International Paper, American Sugar Refining, Amalgamated Copper, American Can Company, Westinghouse, General Electric, Consolidated Gas and Edison of New York, Commonwealth Edison of Chicago, the Niagara Falls Power Company, Pacific Gas and Electric, the Philadelphia Rapid Transit, Elevated Railroads of Chicago, and the Interboro-Metropolitan System of New York; the Chicago, Burlington & Quincy, the Milwaukee & St. Paul, the Rock Island, the Atchison, Topeka & Santa Fe, the Southern Pacific, the New York, New Haven & Hartford, the Chesapeake & Ohio, the Erie, the New York Central, the Reading, the Central of New Jersey, the Baltimore & Ohio, the Pennsylvania, the Norfolk & Western, the Lehigh Valley, the Louisville & Nashville, the Southern, the Illinois Central, and assorted other railway systems.

With the frontier gone and the nation crisscrossed with railroads and interlocking directorates, the New York "community of interest" prepared to expand. American investments, backed by American marines, poured into Central and South America. Harriman laid plans to extend the Northern Pacific across China and Russia to eastern Europe, buying pieces of the South Manchuria Railway and attempting to secure rights along the Russian-owned Trans-Siberia.

King Dollar

As the wealth of the barons mushroomed, so did their power. From the days of Jackson the spoils system carried through the Civil War to the "Great Barbeque" of Grant, when the flood of corporate money into the government became a tidal wave. With amazing speed an efficient, loosely centralized political machine grew out of corporate money. "It was simple," wrote William Allen White—

A state boss collected money from the railroads, the packing houses, the insurance companies, and the banks in his state.

This money he sent to his henchmen in the counties, who distributed the largesse to their followers, who controlled the county conventions. The object and aim of all county conventions was to control the nomination of those Republicans who would run for the legislature and the state senate. When they were elected, as all good Republications were, they would follow the boss.

On most matters they were free; but where legislation touched the banks, the railroads, the insurance companies, or the packing houses, they were bound in honor to vote with the boss, and on his candidate for United States senator and for the tie-up he made with a candidate for state printer.

The two united made a winning majority. So, over the United States, our senators went to Washington obligated to the large corporate interests of their states. . . .

The railroad lobbyists and bosses in Washington amalgamated their forces. Thus the plutocracy built its mighty fortress.

In mass elections "votes" equalled "dollars." No candidate could win without a political party and thus real issues were eliminated because "the same monopolies that run the Republican run the Democratic party." A political party, explained Secretary of State William Seward, was "a joint-stock company in which those who contribute the most direct the action and management of the concern."

The parties were essentially rival corporations competing for the spoils of power. The bigger barons usually contributed to both, often supporting candidates against each other to cover their bets.

Washington was a bad joke. Congress was "transformed into a mart where the price of votes was haggled over, and laws, made to order, were bought and sold." In 1877, after troops crushed a bloody national rail strike, President Rutherford B. Hayes looked in amazement at what had become of American government—

Shall the railroads govern the country, or shall the people govern the railroads? . . . This is a government of the people, by the people, and for the people no longer. It is a government of corporations, by corporations, and for corporations. How is this?

At the turn of the century the U.S. Senate—ninety men—included no less than 25 of the country's 4000 millionaires.

At its base the federal government's power rested on a network of city and state machines. Every state had a boss to distribute "contributions," arrange jobs to build up an organization, and in return fight off unwanted legislation and arrange graft-rich "public works" projects to keep the money flowing.

Supported by local life insurance companies and their huge cash reserves, Thomas C. Platt ran the state of New York for twenty years from the "Amen Corner" of the Fifth Avenue Hotel in New York City. In Kansas, George Peck ran the machine; in Ohio it was James Foraker and Mark Hanna; in California it was the Octopus. Pennsylvania passed from Simon Cameron and Matthew Quay to Tom Scott to Standard Oil, which, complained H. D. Lloyd, "did everything to the Pennsylvania legislature except refine it."

The best-known of the city machines was Tammany Hall, whose power in New York dated to the days of Jackson. Tammany often controlled the mayor's office, but like the other city machines, its true power came from key positions in the bureaucracy—zoning commissions, street railway franchises, gas-regulating commissions, water works, the police department, and the treasurer's office. Like the other machines, Tammany was allied with one political party but ruled regardless of which was "in power."

Many of the city bosses were prewar arrivals, often Irish, who grew up in the tenement wards they came to control. The postwar immigrants spoke any of twenty or thirty European languages and dialects and usually no English. They were completely at the mercy of the winds, almost always broke, and in desperate need of food and housing. Machines, like that of "Czar" Martin Lomasney in Boston, filled some of those needs, or at least appeared to—

Is somebody out of a job? We do our best to place him and not necessarily on the public payroll. Does the family run in arrears with the landlord or the butcher? Then we lend a helping hand. Do the kids need shoes or clothing, or the mother a doctor? We do what we can, and since, as the world is run, such things must be done, we keep old friends and make new ones.

Tweed made a well-publicized yearly donation of $50,000 to the poor relief fund. The Timothy D. Sullivan Association of the Bowery staged outings, picnics, and parades and arranged bail and pardons, building permits, railroad passes, and loans, and distributed coal during the strike of 1902. The policy in Philadelphia was "to please the people by an ambitious and spectacular program of public improvements," projects which also allowed the machine to line "their own pockets and those of their friends with the profitable contracts involved."

At Christmas one boss "provided dinner, with turkey, mince pie, and all the trimmings, for all the poor and derelict who presented themselves at his headquarters. . . . Practically every house in the Bowery contained a picture of the boss."

And, wrote John Hicks, if the loyalty of the wards wasn't enough, "wholesale frauds were easily possible, for the election machinery was in Tammany hands."

The city machines completed the structure of corporate rule. Bosses like Abe Ruef of San Francisco, Roger Sullivan of Chicago, Jim Pendergast of Kansas City, "Doc" Ames of Minneapolis, "Iz" Durham of Philadelphia, and Martin Behrman of New Orleans were often amusing picturesque characters.

But behind them were violent Mafia-style organizations that controlled the booming industrial cities for the benefit of the corporations that provided their slush funds. "The existing coalition between the Erie Railway and the Tammany Ring is a natural one," explained Charles Francis Adams, "for the former needs votes, the latter money."

THE LEGAL BACKSTOP

Nonetheless, as early as the seventies popular hostility to the money power was too great to be denied by electoral manipulation. At all levels of government the American people demanded that the corporations be brought under some degree of popular control.

This pushed the issue to the last line of legal defense—the Supreme Court.

After the Civil War, Congress passed the Fourteenth Amendment, guaranteeing the rights of exslaves by forbidding any state to "deprive any person of life, liberty, or property without due process of law . . ."

In 1886 the Supreme Court voided some 230 state laws meant to regulate corporations on the ground that they deprived the corporations of their property "without due process of law."

This insane ruling meant that a corporation—an organization of property—got the same legal rights as a human being. At the same time the corporations were never held liable on a human basis for criminal offenses—maltreatment of human beings and murder, for example, as literally thousands of workers were killed in factories where safety devices were "unprofitable."

In 1874, in *Schulenburg* v. *Harriman*, the Court stopped an attempt to take back a public land grant from a railroad which had not completed its contract. In 1895 the Court ruled an income tax law unconstitutional.

In 1887 Congress passed the Interstate Commerce Act to regulate the railroads and other businesses dealing across state lines. Almost immediately the law became the tool of the corporations themselves. Richard Olney, a lawyer for the Boston & Maine and

Attorney General under Cleveland, advised a railroad president
that

The Commission, as its functions have now been limited by the courts,
is, or can be made, of great use to the railroads. It satisfies the public
clamor for a government supervision of railroads, at the same time that
that supervision is almost entirely nominal.
Further, the older such a commission gets to be, the more inclined it
will be found to take the business and railroad view of things. It
thus becomes a sort of barrier between the railroad corporations and
the people. . . .

The Sherman Anti-Trust Act, passed in 1890, served the same
function. Republican Senator Orville Platt of Connecticut explained why Congress bothered to pass it at all—

The conduct of the Senate . . . has not been in the line of honest
preparation of a bill to prohibit and punish trusts. It has been in the
line of getting some bill with that title that we might go to the country
with.
The questions of whether the bill would be operative, of how it
would operate, . . . have been whistled down the wind in this Senate
as idle talk, and the whole effort has been to get some bill headed:
"A Bill to Punish Trusts" with which to go to the country.

If there was ever any doubt, the Supreme Court wiped out the
Sherman Act's effectiveness against the trusts five years after its
passage. In 1895 it ruled that the E. C. Knight Company, which
refined 98 percent of the nation's sugar, restrained trade only
"indirectly."

But from 1890 to 1897 the Sherman Act was used twelve times
to break labor strikes. "What looks like a stone wall to a layman,"
said the humorist Mr. Dooley, "is a triumphal arch to a corporation lawyer."

The Barrel of the Gun

But if the system seemed to run on money and legalities, there was no mistaking that ultimately it rested on brute force. From the thirties on, federal, state, and local armies, militia, and police were in ceaseless use breaking up demonstrations, strikes, labor unions. In the name of property, law, and order, jails were constantly filled and official violence brought down on those who advocated worker control of factories, the right to organize, a black-white alliance in the South, and a redistribution of wealth and power.

In a pinch the barons also had their private armies of Pinkerton "detectives," professional guards, strikebreakers, vigilantes, and citizen's leagues to handle the untidy work of doing away with rebels. In a nation with a solid unemployment rate and an average income below the subsistence level, a man like Jay Gould wasn't kidding when he boasted "I can hire one-half the working class to kill the other half!"

Atop this flexible tyranny sat the Four Hundred, a group of four to six hundred families centered in New York and including the biggest of the barons and their entourage—a self-proclaimed "nobility of wealth." Frederick Townshend Martin spoke their creed in *The Passing of the Idle Rich*—

The class I represent, care nothing for politics. . . . It matters not one iota what political party is in power or what president holds the reigns of office.

We are not politicians or public thinkers; we are the rich; we own America; we got it, God knows how, but we intend to keep it if we can by throwing all the tremendous weight of our support, our influence, our money, our political connections, our purchased senators, our hungry congressmen, our public-speaking demagogues, into the scale against any legislature, any political platform, any presidential campaign that threatens the integrity of our estate.

One by one they sought titled European aristocrats for inter-marriage and hired geneologists to trace their family trees back to kings and queens of the Middle Ages.

The nineties, so desperately depressed for the farming and working communities, were the "Gay Nineties" for the caste that owned America. A world exposition opened in Chicago; sports—football, baseball, croquet, lawn tennis—came into vogue. The Vanderbilts, Rockefellers, Fricks, and Hills built multimillion dollar palaces on Fifth Avenue and in Palm Beach, Long Island, and Newport with the money they could only make more with or throw away—

At a dinner eaten on horseback, the favorite steed was fed flowers and champagne; to a small black and tan dog wearing a diamond collar worth $15,000 a lavish banquet was tendered; at one function, the cigarettes were wrapped in hundred dollar bills; at another, fine black pearls were given to the diners in their oysters. . . .

Then weary of such limited diversions, the plutocracy contrived more freakish occasions—with monkeys seated between the guests, human gold fish swimming about in pools, or chorus girls hopping out of pies. . . . Diamonds were set in teeth; a private carriage and personal valet were provided for a pet monkey; dogs were tied with ribbons to the back seats of Victorias and driven out in the park for airings. . . . A copper king turned connoisseur overnight and bought a complete museum of art.

As if to put a climax to lavish expenditure, the Bradley Martins in 1897 gave a ball in New York that dazed the entire Western world. "The interior of the Waldorf-Astoria Hotel," according to a member of the family, "was transformed into a replica of Versailles and rare tapestries, beautiful flowers, and countless lights made an effective background for the wonderful gowns and their wearers. I do not think that there has ever been a greater display of jewels before or since; in many cases the diamond buttons worn by the men represented thousands of dollars and the value of the historic gems worn by the ladies baffles description.

"My sister-in-law personated Mary Stuart and her gold embroidered gown was trimmed with pearls and precious stones. Bradley, as Louis XV, wore a court suit of brocade. . . . The suit of gold inlaid armor worn by Mr. Belmont was valued at ten thousand dollars."

The MACHINE

The American industrial machine was clearly becoming the biggest in the world. Each landmark of growth, each statistic of wealth, was hailed by the barons with excitement and pride.

Upon completion of the transcontinental railroad in 1869, Jay Gould could hardly control his delight. "WE have made the country rich," he yelled. "WE have developed the country, coal mines and cattle raising, as well as cotton. . . . WE have created this earning power by developing the system!"

With great national fanfare the Union and Central Pacific lines were joined at Promontory Point, Utah. A gold and a silver spike were to be driven into the final tie by one of the many dignitaries carried to Utah for the ceremony. But none of them could handle a sledgehammer. A construction worker had to be called out of the crowd to knock in the spikes.

By 1888 the American industrial system was killing 100 workers every day—around 35,000 were killed each year, with over 500,000 reported injured.

More than 700,000 American workers were killed in industrial "accidents" from 1888 to 1908. Nearly a million industrial injuries were reported in 1913. The railroads alone killed ten workers a day, the coal mines about the same. If you only get maimed you were lucky—

A brakeman with both hands and all his fingers was either remarkably skillful, incredibly lucky or new on the job.

A substantial part of the work force was made up of children, especially in the mines and in the textile mills of New England towns like Lawrence, Massachusetts, where half the workers were girls between the ages of fourteen and eighteen—

A considerable number of the boys and girls die within the first two or three years after beginning work. . . . Thirty-six of every 100 of all the men and women who work in the mill die before or by the time they are twenty-five years of age.

The life-span of the average mill worker in Lawrence was twenty-two years shorter than that of an owner.

To help guarantee a large work force for their factories, the barons advertised America all over Europe as the land of the rich, where anyone "good enough" could become wealthy in no time. The plains of Montana were hailed as fertile, jungle-like farmland and became known as "Jay Cooke's Banana Belt." Steamship companies and rail lines starving for passengers uplifted entire peasant villages and set them down in the West.

For the immigrants the voyage to America was a journey of hope, an escape from the poverty of Europe's dying peasant culture. America meant a new chance at life.

But for Andrew Carnegie, himself an immigrant, people coming to America meant a "cheap and mobile labor force," as he pointed out in 1905—

Taking the cost, the value of a man, a woman, or a child, in this Republic as low as you put the slave, and that was an average of about $1000, you are getting 400,000 a year and that means $4,-000,000 cash value.

Utterly powerless and confused, piled into the ghettoes of New York, Chicago, Philadelphia, Baltimore, and Boston, or shuttled to the crippled western farm community, the new arrivals were at the disposal of employers without whom they literally could not get food, clothing, housing. The bitter prewar diatribe of a South Carolina senator began to make a perverted sort of sense—

The difference between us is that our slaves are hired for life. . . . Yours are hired by the day, not cared for, and scantily compensated, which may be proved in the most deplorable manner, at any hour in any street of your large towns. . . .

American industry was paid for in the broken backs and dead eyes of men, women, and children who were valued only as fuel. "Men are cheap and machinery is dear," explained Woodrow Wilson. "You can discard your man and replace him; there are others ready to come into his place; but you can't without great cost, discard your machine and put a new one in its place."

THE BLOAT OF THE CITIES

The factory system demanded a centralized population to keep a mass working force and a mass market close at hand. Absentee landlords and bankers tightened their grip on the small farmers of the West and South, devastating the farm economy with high rents, freight rates, and taxes and thus helping to undermine the balance of urban-rural population. William Allan White wrote that "the farmer was beginning to realize that the farm was no longer a way of life but a part of a great agricultural industry."

Sometimes he must burn his corn for fuel; often he cannot sell his grain for the cost of production, even though thousands of persons in the great cities may be hungering for it; frequently he cannot afford to send his children to school, and in a steadily increasing number of cases he is forced to abandon his farm and become a tenant or a wanderer.

Meanwhile the cities spiralled out of control. New York was four times as large in 1900 as it had been in 1860; Chicago was fully fifty-five times as big.

Unplanned, with public funds pilfered, the cities became gigantic hellholes for the system's cheap "manpower." They varied mainly in that "some are built more with brick than wood, and others more with wood than brick." They were literally the worst in the world. In 1894, New York's Sanitation District A included 32 acres on which more than 31,000 people attempted to live—a density of 986 people per acre. The highest density in Bombay, India, was 759 people per acre; Prague had only 485 per acre in what were known as the worst ghettoes in Europe.

DEFOLIATION FOR PROFIT

The cities expressed the second foundation of American industrial growth—destruction of the natural environment.

The money system had no built-in mechanism to account for such "intangibles" as ecological systems or natural harmony.

Nor was there any conception of limiting waste. In fact, the system was built on waste.

"Raw materials," like trees, coal, oil, and rivers, were in apparently infinite supply and of marginal "dollar value." Soil, wildlife, forests, streams—all were "cheap" and, in money terms, their destruction was at best a marginal question.

Furthermore, the natural resources themselves were usually secondary to the operations of extracting, transporting, processing, advertising, and selling them. Natural ingredients went in one end and what came out didn't really matter, as long as the machine kept churning out dollars.

As a linear rather than a cyclical device, the profit system found it better to waste and destroy than to conserve and reuse.

The natural continent went in one end of the money machine a whole entity and came out the other as garbage, with the machine still clamoring for more frontiers to consume.

A perfect indicator of the waste was the railroad system. Usually the roads bore little or no relationship to the land through which they passed. According to economic historians Thomas C. Cochran and William Miller,

Almost all of the land grant railroads were poorly built along the most tortuous paths. Within fifteen years after they were completed almost all of them had to be rebuilt to eliminate needless curves, shifting roadbeds, splintering "sleepers," and spreading rails too light to bear the weight of the engines.

And it was never clear if the roads were being run to carry goods and people or merely to expand the owners' capital. Years of control by speculators like Gould left their mark. Robert Riegel wrote in *The Story of the Western Railroads* that

The effects of his management never wore off entirely. . . . There was never any effort to build up a strong, soundly managed group of roads. . . The roads that he touched never quite recovered from his lack of knowledge and interest in sound railroading.

In general, there was little pattern to railroad construction beyond the location of their land grants, the amount of stock that could be floated on the public, or their blackmail value to the bigger roads. Often, wrote financial historian John Moody, "the builders had no further conception of it than as a line connecting two given points usually a short distance apart. The roads of these began anywhere and ended almost anywhere."

By 1897 the mighty Union Pacific was nothing more than "two dirt-ballasted streaks of rust. The stations along the mountain grades were tumbledown shacks, most of the equipment fit only for the scrap pile."

At the same time the Nickel Plate, the West Shore, and the Toledo, Peoria and Warsaw lines were merely a thousand miles of useless track, built to threaten competition against the big systems who would take them over at fantastic ransoms.

The stock-watering bonanza brought on still more useless construction. According to Charles F. Adams, the New York Central issued $50,000 of "absolute water" for every mile of track from New York to Buffalo, phony stock values that would require dividends paid by the people who actually used the road.

By the 1880s about twice as many railroad lines had been built as the country could profitably employ. . . .

Poor's Manual stated that the entire capital stock of the railroads, then [1884] about four billions of dollars, represented water; all of the share capital, and a large portion of the bonded debt issued in the preceding three years, was "in excess of construction"—pure hopes, sold to the public. Yet unremitting competition in the railway field continued. By 1884, five trunk lines ran between New York and Chicago, and two more were building, though three would have been ample, and most of these were on the verge of bankruptcy.

WHO DO YOU TRUST?

At the turn of the century it was generally accepted that the free enterprise system had finally passed away. It was hoped by many that the "community of interest" arrangements between the banks and the big trusts would help rationalize the economy. Wasteful competition would be eliminated, and professional, "progressive" management would take charge.

But the trusts brought no basic changes. From its very beginning the long-awaited United States Steel Corporation was half water. Morgan floated $1.4 billion in stock over $682 million in real assets and took a $62 million "commission" for handling the issue. By 1903 U.S. Steel stock had dropped from 40 to 8. The price of a ton of the company's steel jumped from $24 to $28 soon after the trust was formed.

As for efficiency, the giant corporations were at best unwieldy, impersonal bureaucracies. And they turned out to be powerful, destructive barriers to technological progress.

For while many of them could and did conduct expensive scientific research, they also used their power to buy up new inventions and bury them in the patent office, keeping them out of the hands of the public.

Small innovations were indeed used to cut short-range production costs. But major changes that might require expensive re tooling or complicated reorganization were suppressed time ar again. "A huge organization," wrote *Engineering News*, "is too clumsy to take up the development of an original idea. With the market closely controlled and profits certain by following standard methods, those who control our trusts do not want the bother of developing anything new."

Woodrow Wilson, before he became President, agreed—

I am not saying that all invention has been stopped by the growth of the trusts, but I think it is perfectly clear that invention in many fields has been discouraged. . . . and that mankind has been deprived of many comforts and conveniences, as well as the opportunity of buying at lower prices.

THE NECESSITY OF EMPIRE

It was hoped by many that trustification would at least help stabilize the economy. The competitive system had suffered five major depressions in the 1800s—those of 1819, 1837, 1857, 1873, and 1893. The thirty-four years from 1866 to the end of the century were half depression; breakdowns covered 1866–1867, 1873–1879, 1883–1885, 1890–1891, and 1893–1897, a total of seventeen years.

In some instances crashes resulted from manipulation by the big speculators.

But at the bottom of them all was the basic structural weakness of the system—it couldn't distribute purchasing power to the people at large because, by its basic nature, it was geared to do exactly the opposite.

The natural function of capitalism was not to supply human need but to insure that capital—money—would multiply itself. This it did quite well. Conservative economist Willard King, cited in a 1916 government report, estimated that 2 percent of the population owned 60 percent of the nation's wealth. The next 33 percent—the middle class—owned 35 percent of the wealth. The bottom class—65 percent of the people—got the remaining 5 percent of the community's resources.

Economist C. B. Spahr estimated that in 1890, 11 million of the 12.5 million families in America had an average annual income of $380, at very best a bare subsistence wage. Most families had to take in boarders to survive.

Since most of the community didn't get enough money to command what it really needed—food, clothing, housing—the economic power went to more of the "safe" investments—railroads, steel mills, oil refineries, and power plants.

The system churned out these capital goods in exchange for money which the rich reinvested in still more capital goods.

The money machine exploded in a self-multiplying spiral. Neither people nor the natural environment had any built-in control.

The barons and their sons became a semiofficial ruling committee, administering the new industrial state for their own private profit and power.

The professional middle class poured into the expanding corporate and government bureaucracies and eased the rhetoric of nineteenth-century laissez faire. The new corporate administrators would use the government as labor mediator, stabilizer of finance, guarantor of at least some general welfare, and organ of social and thought control.

But on the bottom the struggle for survival was still the same. Farmers, workers, and unemployed still had to fight each other for income, housing, and land. The basic social and economic divisions—employer/employee, landlord/tenant, and banker/-mortgagee—remained.

What redistribution of the wealth did occur came in spite of the system. The rising standard of living won by sections of the working class was paid for in blood through decades of constant political confrontation.

And what "prosperity" twentieth-century America enjoyed was paid for by the people of other nations.

For in the nineties the American economy crashed into a crisis from which it never recovered. The Depression of 1893

From "*Puck*," *September* 21, 1904.
"I rather like that imported affair."

From "*The Rocky Mountain News*," *Denver*, 1900.
Uncle Sam: "By gum, I rather like your looks."

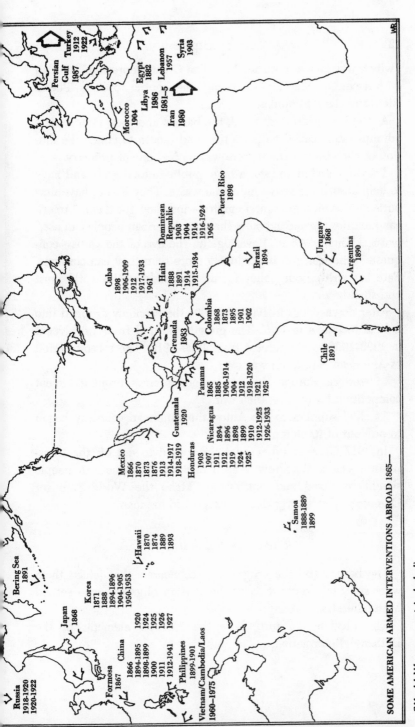

SOME AMERICAN ARMED INTERVENTIONS ABROAD 1865—

(World Wars are not included)

Russia
1918-1920
1920-1922

Bering Sea
1891

Japan
1868

Formosa
1867

China
1866
1894-1895
1898-1899
1900
1911
1912-1941

Korea
1871
1888
1894-1896
1904-1905
1950-1953

1920
1924
1925
1926
1927

Hawaii
1870
1874
1889
1893

Philippines
1899-1901

Vietnam/Cambodia/Laos
1960-1975

Samoa
1888-1889
1899

Mexico
1866
1870
1873
1876
1913
1914-1917
1918-1919

Guatemala
1920

Honduras
1903
1907
1911
1912
1919
1924
1925

Nicaragua
1894
1896
1898
1899
1910
1912-1925
1926-1933

Panama
1865
1885
1903-1914
1904
1912
1918-1920
1921
1925

Grenada
1983

Colombia
1868
1873
1895
1901
1902

Cuba
1898
1906-1909
1912
1917-1933
1961

Haiti
1888
1891
1914
1915-1934

Dominican
Republic
1903
1904
1914
1916-1924
1965

Puerto Rico
1898

Brazil
1894

Uruguay
1868

Argentina
1890

Chile
1891

Morocco
1904

Libya
1986
1981-5

Iran
1980

Persian
Gulf
1987

Turkey
1912
1922

Egypt
1882

Lebanon
1957

Syria
1903

(which was known until 1929 as "The Great Depression") ended with American Marines "extending" the frontier to Cuba, Puerto Rico, and the Philippines.

As the new century dawned, the barons and their middle-class administrators called on patriotism and racism to create the illusion of community where there was no real one of property.

They demanded and got a huge public-funded army and navy to help absorb the heavy industrial waste. They had to have new outlets—colonies, guns, and empire—and they got them. "American factories are making more than the American people can use," warned Senator Albert Beveridge on the eve of the Cuban conquest. "American soil is producing more than they can consume. Fate has written our policy for us; the trade of the world must and shall be ours."

After downswings in 1901 and 1904 the economy dropped into a fitful recession in 1907. The growth rate fell from 7.6 percent in 1902–1906 to 4.6 percent from 1909–1913. The takeoff period of American capitalism was over.

In western Europe the corresponding crisis brought violent competition for empire, then war.

As chief supplier to the Allies, the American economy began to pull out of its slump in 1914.

In 1917 German submarines threatened to cut off the trans-Atlantic trade. Woodrow Wilson decided the American people should be taxed and drafted to "Make the World Safe for Democracy," whatever that was supposed to mean.

The Imperial Religion

The barons and the Progressive technocrats that joined them were spiritual descendents of the Puritan oligarchs who settled Massachusetts.

The Puritans, in turn, bore the harshest elements of the Lutheran Reformation.

Essentially the attack of a nascent merchant economy on Catholic feudalism, the Lutheran Revolution first and foremost asserted that every person carried in the soul, as an individual, the priesthood of God. It followed that one of the pillars of the Reformation was individual liberty, and with it universal education, for every individual had the right and need to read and understand the Bible.

But Luther was at heart a political conservative, and as espoused by John Calvin, a Geneva logician, the attack on Catholicism took the form of a new totalitarian alliance of church and state.

The core of the Calvinist system was the belief that humans were evil, that original sin had destroyed their harmony with the all-powerful Creator and had thrown them into a ceaseless struggle to return to Grace.

That return could only be seen through a life of unending toil and self-denial. God had predetermined those who would gain heaven, and His choice was manifest on earth in the successful labor of an "elect" who attained wealth, power, and standing in the community.

Those who were not chosen were doomed to the fire and brimstone of the Puritan hell, a place vividly and endlessly portrayed by mirthless preacher-magistrates who were driven, apparently, to promoting a new dimension of psychic paranoia. Puritanism became an endless tribute to a single-minded drive to amass wealth and power, to the unhappiness of man, to a petty community consciousness and universe limited by a hard and wrathful divine authority, and to a relentless fear of death and what might lie beyond.

Coming to America just twenty years before the violent Puritan revolution in England, the first wave of Calvinist pilgrims were noted as "active, capable men, excellent administrators rather than speculative thinkers, stewards of the public interests as well as their own, [who] would take it ill to have their matured plans

interfered with by busybodies and incompetents. Their own counsel sufficed them and they wanted no help from outsiders."

As an economic and political unit, the Massachusetts Bay Company was "a joint-stock corporation, organized very much as business corporations are today."

One of its magistrates was John Winthrop, who exercised both political and spiritual power. "There is a twofold liberty," he said, "natural (I mean as our nature is now corrupt) and civil or federal. The first is common to man with beasts and other creatures. By this, man, as he stands in relation to man simply, hath liberty to do what he lists; it is a liberty to evil as well as to good. This liberty is incompatible and inconsistent with authority. . . ."

For the other kind of liberty, the "civil or federal," was maintained and exercised in a way of subjection to authority—

If you will be satisfied to enjoy such civil and lawful liberties, such as Christ allows you, then will you quietly and cheerfully submit unto that authority which is set over you, in all the administrations of it, for your own good.

The authority of Winthrop and the other Puritan oligarchs was that of an "aristocracy of saints" who, like Cotton Mather, would "tolerate all views that were not in error." Puritan dogma forbade theater, drunkenness, and "fornication" even within marriage. "Heresy, Prophaness & Superstition & other Corruptions in Worship" were offenses to be judged and punished by the authorities. The Puritans "projected caste distinctions into eternity." It wasn't just action they wanted to control; it was thought.

So the Puritan community "punished" without mercy—to the point of organized murder—Indians, witches, Quakers, Baptists, Nonconformists, and other deviants on whom they often practised elaborate tortures, as if their own preoccupation with hell demanded the construction of a working model on earth.

One public execution, in fact, brought raptures of divine elation from Cotton Mather, who welcomed as a sign of grace the opportunity to sermonize at a hanging—

The Execution of the miserable Malefactor, was ordered for to have been last Week, upon the Lecture of another. I wondered then what would become of my PARTICULAR Faith, of her condition being so ordered in the Providence of God, that it should furnish me, with a SPECIAL OPPORTUNITY to glorify Him. While I was entirely resigning to the wisdom of Heaven all such Matters, the Judges, wholly without my seeking, altered and allow'd her Execution to fall on the Day of MY LECTURE. . . . For my own part, I was weak, and faint, and spent; but I humbly gave myself up to the Spirit of my Heavenly Lord and Hee assured mee, that Hee would send His good Angel to strengthen mee. . . .

Mather also saw his congregation's gift to him of a slave as a sign of divine favor. One of the most important of the Puritan preachers, Mather's "religious exaltation flowered from the root of egoism. His vanity was cosmic."

SOCIAL DARWINISM

The free spirits of frontier agrarianism, of new immigration, of the Enlightenment, and of the Romantic era drained away much of the totalitarian karma of the Bay Colony.

But the Puritan mind surfaced in the authoritarianism of Alexander Hamilton, John Adams, and the Federalist group, and in the centralized power of the federal Constitution.

And in the late nineteenth century the depressing catastrophe of Civil War and the ensuing triumph of the materialist Victorian culture helped revive it anew.

For now Calvinist theology got a new ally—evolutionary science. In 1859 the British scientist Charles Darwin laid before the world the theory that man, like all animals, had evolved to his present state by a long, violent process of natural selection from which only the "fittest" had survived.

The theory was seized in fashionable circles as a secular ally to the Calvinist belief in an aristocracy of the elect. It was used to "prove" that man was "superior" to all other animals, that the competitive system of economics was the only "natural" one, and that the true state of man was constant struggle.

And finally, it postulated that those with wealth and power ruled by natural right.

The cornerstone of the "Social Darwinist" system was that the pursuit of money was the basis of civilization. There seemed no alternative, for competition was considered a law of life. "Society as created," explained Milton Smith, president of the Louisville and Nashville Railroad, "was for the purpose of one man's getting what the other fellow has, if he can, and keep out of the penitentiary."

The laws of business were both the natural laws of the earth and the divine laws of God, as John D. Rockefeller, one of the elect, pointed out—

The growth of a large business is merely a survival of the fittest. . . . It is merely the working-out of a law of nature and a law of God.

Since Calvinist man was evil, and since natural man was a creature evolved through constant struggle, those who survived, those who crawled out of the sea of strife into the sunlight of Fifth Avenue—those were the fittest of nature and the elect of God, the true guardians of order. Thomas Nixon Carver, a preacher, capsulized the creed of the self-made man—

The laws of natural selection are merely God's regular methods of expressing his choice and approval. The naturally selected are the chosen of God.

At Yale, William Graham Sumner assumed the role of high priest. The problem, he said, was to "get rid of some of our notions about liberty and equality, and . . . lay aside this eighteenth-century philosophy, according to which human society is to be brought into a state of blessedness."

Starvation, alienation, human destruction at the factories—all belonged "to the struggle for existence. . . . Let every man be sober, industrious, prudent, and wise, and bring up his children

to be likewise, and poverty will be abolished in a few generations."

Indeed, he said, nobody ever proved that poverty really existed,
at least not at Yale—

It is constantly alleged in vague and declamatory terms that artisans
and unskilled labor are in distress and misery or under oppression.
No facts to bear out these assertions are offered.

Henry Ward Beecher, a Brooklyn preacher, added in 1875 that
"There may be reasons of poverty which do not involve wrong;
but looking comprehensively through city and town and village
and country, the general truth will stand, that no man in this
land suffers from poverty unless it be more than his fault—unless
it be his sin."

After all, if a person didn't have any money and wasn't good
for business, then what good was he at all? "Niggers," sneered
J. P. Morgan, "are lazy, ignorant, and unprogressive; railroad
traffic is created only by industrious, intelligent, and ambitious
people."

Asa Candler, founder of the Coca Cola company, felt that "the
most beautiful sight we see is the child at labor; as early as he
may get at labor the more beautiful, the more useful does his life
become."

Anybody who tried to change things performed an unnatural
act. "Objections to the foundations upon which society is based
are not in order," ruled Andrew Carnegie, "because the condition
of the race is better with these than with any other which has
been tried."

Those deviants who did fight the system were in for a tough
time. "We shall keep order roughly here, if necessary," vowed
Reverend Joseph Cook, "for all Americans are capitalists, or expect to be."

It seemed that "a divine right to rule had passed from kings
to property."

PROGRESSIVE IMPERIALISM

As the new century dawned, the mammoth eruption of industrial wealth and technological power, of a matured industrial revolution, brought the consciousness of a new order of civilization. Within a few years on either side of 1900 the automobile, airplane, wireless, motion picture, strange new serums to treat disease, and the theories of Nietzsche, Freud, and Einstein became mass realities. Not just society but man was facing transformation. The earth was shaking and the machine was flying out of control.

The outline of the city became frantic in its effort to explain something that defied meaning.

Power seemed to have outgrown its servitude and to have asserted its freedom. The cylinder had exploded and thrown great masses of stone and steam against the sky. The city had the air and movement of hysteria, and the citizens were crying, in every accent of anger and alarm, that the new force must at any cost be brought under control.

Prosperity never before imagined, power never yet wielded by man, speed never reached by anything but a meteor, had made the world irritable, nervous, querulous, unreasonable, and afraid.

All New York was demanding new men, and all the new forces, condensed into corporations, were demanding a new type of man—a man with ten times the endurance, energy, will, and mind of the old type—for whom they were ready to pay millions at sight.

As one jolted over the pavements or read the last week's newspapers, the new man seemed close at hand, for the old one had plainly reached the end of his strength, and his failure had become catastrophic. . . . The two thousand-year failure of Christianity roared upward from Broadway, and no Constantine the Great was in sight. . . .

In the heat of the explosion were powerful farm and labor movements that threatened revolution.

At the same time the industrial barons showed all the characteristics of a dying aristocracy, indulging in an astounding orgy of conspicuous consumption and flaunting their wealth and leisure in the face of an increasingly desperate public.

Caught in the squeeze was the middle class. Theirs was a frustrating position in society. The small towns, once so clearly dominated by the doctors, lawyers, merchants, preachers, and teachers, were disappearing. In their place came the mammoth, boss-run cities, filled with strange peasant immigrants, and the equally impersonal corporations, owned by the barons.

It was a question of individuality, political necessity, economic opportunity, and social power. "The lawyer's place in society as an economic factor," complained one professional, "has been superseded by the corporation, this artificial creature of his own genius, for whom he is now simply a clerk on salary." "Our time," complained one writer, "our talents, our lives, our possibilities, are all the property of the other men. We are intellectual prostitutes."

America was literally a different country. The old way of life had been overwhelmed by forces unknown. "What was it all worth," wondered Henry Adams, "this wilderness of men and women as monotonous as the brownstone houses they lived in?"

The intellectual class floundered, feeling cut off from "reality" and, as Jane Addams expressed it, "absolutely at sea so far as any moral purpose was concerned." Frantically it sought a "new structure of loyalties to replace the decaying system of the nineteenth-century communities" and a new set of values to restore a semblance of order.

Many of the young intelligentsia joined the fringes of the farm and labor movements working for reform. "Working with college men and women who were convinced that the old order was breaking up," Frederick Howe felt he was "living in a world that had confidence in literature and in the power of ideas—

The political renaissance was now surely coming. It would not stop with economic reform; it would bring in a rebirth of literature, art, music, and spirit. . . .

The colleges were to lead it; it was to have the support of the more enlightened business men; it would call forth the impoverished talents of the immigrant and the poor. The spirit of this young America was generous, hospitable, brilliant; it was carefree and full of variety. The young people in whom it leaped to expression hated injustice. They had no questions about the soundness of American democracy. They had supreme confidence in the mind. They believed, not less than I had always believed, that the truth would make us free.

As expressed by Howe, Lincoln Steffens, H. D. Lloyd, Clarence Darrow, Robert Lafollette, and others, the middle-class reform movement was bright, optimistic, and humane in its direction and spirit.

But it was not the core of the movement. In society at large the professionals held the balance of power between the barons on top and the farmers and the workers on the bottom. In 1896 the Democratic party fell to the agrarian movement. William Jennings Bryan, the insurgent candidate, was viewed by the barons as a "dangerous revolutionary." The Republican party defeated him, but not without opening a few doors. "McKinley won," wrote William Allan White, "because the Republicans had persuaded the middle class, almost to a man, that a threat to the gold standard was a threat to their property."

From then until the First World War the "Progressive" middle class rode the wave of popular discontent into power. The barons first fought, then accepted it as an ally. In 1900 the National Civil Foundation was begun, mirroring a movement in local chambers of commerce throughout the country. Chaired by Mark Hanna, the organization joined the big barons with a wide representation of the professional class and the conservative trade unions, primarily the AF of L—"the billions of capital, the millions of wage earners, of scholarship and letters, of the bar, the press, the platform and the church."

In 1901, McKinley was assassinated, and presidential power fell out of Hanna's hands and into those of Theodore Roosevelt.

In Roosevelt, a Long Island country squire, and in Woodrow Wilson, a university president, the Progressives found their messiahs of power; behind them the militant middle class marched to its "revolution from above."

For the new century was chaos. The baronial money-lords were decayed and old; the masses, ignorant, evil, and threatening. What was needed, wrote Richard Ely of Yale, was professional, scientific control—

What we need everywhere in modern society, and especially in the United States, is a natural aristocracy, by which we mean an aristocracy of merit. Provision may conceivably be made for a true aristocracy in the structure of government itself.

In a complex and specialized society, knowledge was power, privileged power. The ascendance of a technological aristocracy, a "mandarinate" of science, had to come, as E. A. Ross pointed out in *Social Control*—

As higher education, claiming more and more years of one's life, widens the space between those who possess it and those who do not, and as the enlightenment of the public wanes relative to the superior enlightment of the learned castes and professions, the mandarinate will infallibly draw to itself a greater and greater share of social power.

The new technological elite would seek "the consent of the governed," but clearly they, not the people, would be the governors.

The definition of democracy had changed from government "of, by, and for the people" to, as Woodrow Wilson defined it in his War message, "The right of the people to have a say in their own government."

The universities, wrote Ely, should prepare to train "a class of office-holders." In economic regulation, in labor relations, in law enforcement, and in education, the learned caste would lead the way to liberal reform and intellectual control. Police power alone was not enough. The technocracy wanted people's minds. Wrote Ross,

A method that, once and for all, moulds character is superior to one that deals merely with conduct. . . . A far-sighted policy, such as the training of the young, is preferable to the summary regulation of the adult. In the concrete these maxims mean that the priest is cheaper often than the detective, that the free library costs less than the jail, and that what is spent on the Sunday School is saved at Botany Bay. . . .

It is, then, strictly scientific to emphasize the ceremonial salute of the flag in the army or navy in order to economize in court martial, to prefer a little reform school for the boy to much prison for the man, and to reform the law breaker rather than to catch and convict him after a fresh offense.

The superior methods of control are inward.

"The administrative mind is the highest vehicle of energy," wrote Brooks Adams. "We need a new deal of men and we need it very badly"—

We must have a new deal, we must have new methods, we must suppress the states, and have a centralized administration, or we shall wobble over.

We are now attempting to produce the generalizing mind. We are attacking administration scientifically. If we succeed in training the next generation right, and their nervous systems do not give way under the strain, we shall, likely enough, pull through and land a big fish. . . .

The change is represented by the steel cage of thirty or forty stories. Everything has to pass into the basis of steel.

"You've got to have better human beings," said a member of Wilson's Commission on Industrial Relations. "The state must invest in human beings in the same way you invest in cattle on a farm."

To the Protestant middle class the basic nature of humanity had not changed. The universe, said William James, was a finite "joint-stock affair," where ideas had their "cash-value" and man's strongest force was his "will to believe." Inferior men were still weak, slothful, doomed to Hell, and the flabby, decadent barons and teeming, uncontrolled masses were ample proof. The building of the new man would be the calling of those with the will to power. "The law of the worthy life," said Roosevelt, "is fundamentally the law of strife; it is only through labor and painful effort and grim energy and resolute courage that we move on to higher things."

The vehicle to that "worthy" life would be the triumph of an intense, uniform, and violent national will. "Let us insist," he wrote in *Fear God and Take Your Own Part*, "on the thorough Americanization of the new-comers to our shores, and let us also insist on the thorough Americanization of ourselves"—

Let us remember that we can do nothing to help other peoples, and nothing permanently to secure material well-being and social justice within our own borders, unless we feel with all our hearts devotion to this country, unless we are Americans and nothing else, and unless in time of peace by universal military training, by insistence upon the obligations of every man and every woman to serve the commonwealth both in peace and war, and, above all, by a high and fine preparedness of soul and spirit, we fit ourselves to hold our own against all possible aggression from without.

Roosevelt occasionally billed himself as the friend of the working-man and put the government into the role of labor mediator for the first time. But when it came to a head between property and life, property came first. "We shall guard as zealously the rights of the striker as those of the employer," he said in 1895. "But when riot is menaced it is different. The mob takes its own chance. Order will be kept at whatever cost. If it comes to shooting we shall shoot to hit. No blank cartridges or firing over the head of anybody."

Bryan had the support of "all the ugly forces that seethe beneath the social crust," he said. "I know the Populists and the laboring men well and their faults. . . . I like to see a mob handled by the regulars, or by good State-Guards, not over-scrupulous about bloodshed."

"This country needs a war," he wrote Henry Cabot Lodge in

1895. In a debate he attacked the president of Harvard by telling him that "the futile sentimentalists of the international arbitration type [promote] a flabby, timid type of character which eats away the great fighting qualities of our race." In 1897, as assistant secretary of the navy, he told the Naval War College that the "great masterful races have been fighting races"—

No triumph of peace is quite so great as the supreme triumphs of war. . . . We of the United States have passed most of our few years of national life in peace. We honor the architects of our wonderful material prosperity. . . . But we feel, after all, that the men who have dared greatly in war, or the work which is akin to war, are those who deserve best of the country.

The conservative barons were hesitant to attack Cuba, but when McKinley finally gave the word the young colonel stormed San Juan Hill with the Rough Riders, a group of "born adventurers, in the old sense of the word."

"I waved my hat and we went up the hill with a rush," he bragged. "I killed a Spaniard with my own hands! . . . Look at those damned Spanish dead!"

"During the past three centuries," he wrote in his epic *Winning of the West,*

The spread of the English-speaking peoples over the world's waste spaces has been not only the most striking feature in the world's history, but also the event of all others most far-reaching in its effects and its importance. . . .
There have been many other races that at one time or another had their great periods of race expansion—as distinguished from more conquest—but there has never been another whose expansion has been either so broad or so rapid.

In 1899 he applauded the expansion of the empire of western Europe, and demanded more of the same from America—

In every instance the expansion has taken place because the race was a great race. It was a sign and proof of greatness in the expanding

nation, and moreover bear in mind that in each instance it was of incalculable benefit to mankind. . . .
When great nations fear to expand, shrink from expansion, it is because their greatness is coming to an end. Are we still in the prime of our lusty youth, still at the beginning of our glorious manhood, to sit down among the outworn people, to take our place with the weak and craven? A thousand times no!

Roosevelt urged American women to have more children and thus help assure the predominance of the Anglo-Saxon race. He sent the "Great White Fleet" around the world for the first time, declared American hegemony over Latin America, and forced to its unpopular, horrifying conclusion the long guerilla war against the people of the Philippines.

The American elect had declared a new world theocracy. The pattern was visualized by Brooks Adams in *America's Economic Supremacy* and *The New Empire*. The speeches and writings of Roosevelt and Progressive senators like Albert Beveridge of Indiana were the war cries of a new Rome—

[Grant] never forgot that we are a conquering race, and that we must obey our blood and occupy new markets, and, if necessary, new lands. . . . He had the prophet's seer-like sight which beheld, as a part of the Almighty's infinite plan, the disappearance of debased civilizations and decaying races before the higher civilization of the nobler and more virile types of men. . . .
And now, obeying the same voice that Jefferson heard and obeyed, that Jackson heard and obeyed, that Monroe heard and obeyed, that Seward heard and obeyed, that Ulysses S. Grant heard and obeyed, that Benjamin Harrison heard and obeyed, William McKinley plants the flag over all the islands of the seas, outposts of commerce, citadels of national security, and the march of the flag goes on. (Long-continued cheering.) Bryan, Bailey, Bland, and Blackburn command it to stand still, but the march of the flag goes on. (Renewed cheering.) And the question you will answer at the polls is whether you will stand with this quartet of disbelief in the American people, or whether you are marching onward with the flag. (Tremendous cheering.) . . .

We are raising more than we can consume. We are making more than we can use. Today our industrial society is congested; there are more workers than there is work; there is more capital than there is investment. We do not need money—we need more circulation, more employment. Think of the thousands of Americans who will pour into Hawaii and Puerto Rico when the republican laws cover these islands with justice and safety! Think of the tens of thousands of Americans who will invade mine and field and forest in the Philippines when a liberal government, protected and controlled by this Republic, if not the government of the Republic itself, shall establish order and equity there! . . .

It is God's great purpose made manifest in the instincts of our race, whose present phase is our personal profit, but whose far-off end is the redemption of the world and the christianization of mankind. . . .

God has not been preparing the English-speaking and Teutonic peoples for a thousand years for nothing but vain and idle self-contemplation. No! He has made us the master organizers of the world to establish system where chaos reigns.

part two

The People

The Revolt of the Farmers

From Martin Luther down all the great social, political, and religious reforms that have ever been accomplished began clear down among the common people and worked upwards, while all oppressions, wrongs, and corruptions began up yonder and worked downward.

Edward Martin,
History of the Grange (1873)

It is a struggle between the robbers and the robbed.

Sockless Jerry Simpson

Democracy in America began with the small farmers, generation after generation of pioneer families moving steadily westward into the forests, clearing their own land, growing their own food, living their own lives.

It is quite immaterial whether he ever becomes the owner of the soil. He is the occupant for the time being, pays no rent, and feels independent as "the lord of the manor."
With a horse, cow, and one or two breeders of swine, he strikes into the woods with his family and becomes the founder of a new country, or perhaps state.
He builds his cabin, gathers around him a few other families of similar tastes and habits, and occupies till the range is somewhat subdued, and hunting a little precarious, or, which is more frequently the case, till neighbors crowd around, roads, bridges, and fields annoy him, and he lacks elbow room.

Self-sufficient and fiercely independent, the pioneer farmers were hostile to anyone, government or otherwise, that threatened

their freedom. "American democracy was born of no theorist's dream," wrote Frederick Jackson Turner. "It was not carried in the *Susan Constant* to Virginia, nor in the *Mayflower* to Plymouth. It came stark and strong and full of life out of the American forest, and it gained strength each time it touched a new frontier."

It was the small farmers that poured out of the woods from Lexington to Boston and Saratoga to wage revolutionary guerrilla war against the imperial British. After the Revolution they fought the native merchants in uprisings like Shays' Rebellion and opposed the federal Constitution as the mercenary, manipulative tool of a new ruling establishment.

It was they, through Madison, who wrote the Bill of Rights as the minimum people's price for a federal government.

It was they who provided the muscle for Jackson's war on the national bank and monopolies, and they also, in large part, backed his violent expansion into the Indian lands of the South and West.

In the 1850s another wave of settlers stood poised to occupy the last farm frontier, the Great Plains west of the Mississippi. The land would be divided among the homesteaders that farmed and built homes on it.

But the South wanted the west for slavery. In 1850 James Buchanan vetoed the Homestead Act, calling it "communistic." A year later Lincoln was elected president and the South seceded.

At war's end the last wave of frontier farmers crossed the Mississippi—

God made this earth to be free to all; and whoever takes wild land, and clears it, and cultivates it, makes it his own—he's a right to it!

The families that poured into Iowa, Minnesota, the Dakotas, Nebraska, Kansas, and later Oklahoma faced different problems than the farmers in the forests of the east. The prairie was hard; the horizon unbroken and endless.

I am looking rather seedy now while holding down my claim
And my victuals are not always of the best;
And the mice play shyly round me as I nestle down to rest.
In my little old sod shanty in the west.

The hinges are of leather and the windows have no glass
While the board roof lets the howling blizzards in,
And I hear the hungry coyote as he slinks through the grass,
Round my little old sod shanty on my claim.

My clothes are plastered o'er with dough, I'm looking like a fright
And everything is scattered round the room,
But I wouldn't give the freedom that I have out in the West,
For the table of the eastern man's old home.

Backbreaking labor, plagues of grasshoppers and disease, drought, vast distances to lumber, supplies, and markets, floods in spring, blistering summers, and endless, stir-crazy winters— the lot of the sod-buster family was often a lonely ordeal that aged and killed those who tried it at a fearsome rate.

But the homesteaders held on, threw down their roots. In 1883 Kansas farmers produced 150 million bushels of corn, more than any other state. Livestock and grain poured out of the "middle border" between the Mississippi and the Rockies in huge quantities.

But the homesteaders found that farming skills and financial solvency were two different things. The titles to the land had been stolen. Railroad grants cut huge swaths through the western states. Speculators swarmed into the homestead territories, and by fraud and extortion took hundreds of thousands of acres for private sale. Grants to state governments and land grant universities further decimated the free areas. Only one out of every ten families that went west after the Civil War actually got free land. High taxes— most of which went to pay off money grants to the railroad barons— and high mortgage and interest rates made the load even heavier. It no longer took so much courage, strength, ability to start a farm—it took $1000—

Only a little while ago the people owned this princely domain. Now
they are STARVING FOR LAND—starving for the right to create
from the soil a subsistence for their wives and little children. . . .
They want FREE LAND—the land that Congress squandered . . .
the land that should have formed the patrimony of unborn generations.

What had been done to the Indians, in terms of land titles,
was now being passed on to the farmers. "It is no longer a poor
man's country," complained one farmer. "There is no land for the
free. America is not American."

By the 1890s there were 9 million farm mortgages, a ransom
on the land of nearly $4 billion. In 1890, 53 percent of the farms
in Iowa were mortgaged, 49 percent in New Jersey, 30 percent in
Massachusetts, and there were more mortgages than familes
in Minnesota, the Dakotas, Kansas, and Nebraska.

Families poured their lives into the land for years only to have
it taken away after one bad season. After the drought of 1887
at least 11,000 Kansas families were evicted. Twenty towns in
the western part of the state were left to the ghosts.

Because of the constant demand for cash many westerners put
all their land into corn or wheat or oats, whichever could be
counted on to bring in the most money. As a result they fell into
the kind of one-crop farming that had already devastated the soil
of the South and that would eventually help turn large parts of
the West into a dustbowl.

The farms were too large for one man to handle, too poor to
give the soil the care it needed. "To talk of manuring all our farms
while they are so large is simply ridiculous," said one farmer.
"With the present scarcity and high price of labor, how is the
farmer to find time and money or labor to manure his farm of
from one hundred and sixty to fifteen thousand acres?"

Nevertheless, except for the railroads the westerners probably
could have made it. Having stolen half the West and levied
immense taxation to build the roads, the barons proceeded to

extort as much in freight rates as the traffic would bear. Farmers throughout the West were charged a bushel of corn or wheat just to ship a second bushel East. On the wheat crop of 1869 the Erie Ring got $12 million; the Minnesota farmers got $8 million.

Other middlemen—merchants, elevator operators, and politicians—took still more tribute. In wildly fluctuating markets, dairy, cattle, and corn farmers were lucky to get half the market value of their produce; wheat farmers generally got less than one-fifth. In the depression of the nineties, while the crowded cities starved, westerners burned corn for fuel because it was worth less than coal.

The farmers, in turn, got angry. They were tired, said William Peffer of Kansas, of being leached by "an army of middlemen, loan agents, bankers, and others who are absolutely worthless for all good purposes in the community, whose services ought to be and very easily could be dispensed with."

THE GRANGERS AND THE GREENBACKERS

Soon after the Civil War the National Grange of the Patrons of Husbandry sprang out of the soil of the midwest. Centered in Iowa and Illinois, the Grange was originally organized to bring farmers together socially and to exchange tips on farming. A secret organization, the Grange soon began working for cooperative purchasing and marketing, and in the early seventies ran more than 250 cooperative grain elevators in Illinois alone. By 1875 it claimed a million and a half members in 20,000 chapters throughout the country.

The national organization aided flood victims in the South and helped western farmers fight the grasshopper plague. In the face of a common danger, the Grange was bringing the isolated farmers together. "Human happiness," said the Grange constitution, "is the acme of earthly ambition. Individual happiness depends upon general prosperity. . . . The soil is the source from

OPPRESSION
USURPATION
BRIBERY.
EXTORTION
CONSOLIDATION TRAIN.
THE PARTISAN

The Grange Awakening the Sleepers, 1873

Source: Culver Pictures, Inc.

whence we derive all that constitutes wealth." "The Grange is the foe to selfishness," wrote Edward Martin.

It is too much the habit of the farmer to regard himself and his own family only, and to be careless of the welfare or interests of others. The Grange teaches him that he is only a single member of the vast community of men who till the ground, and that his interests are identical with theirs, and that he must consider others as well as himself.

As times got worse the Grangers drifted into politics. Although they claimed not to be "enemies" of capital, resolutions on the railroads were direct and bitter. "We hold, declare, and resolve," said the Illinois Grange in 1873, "that this despotism, which defies our laws, plunders our shippers, impoverishes our people, and corrupts our government, shall be subdued and made to subserve the public interest at whatever cost."

By 1876, in the midst of national depression, the Grange completely dominated the Illinois legislature and was a powerful political bloc in Iowa, Minnesota, and Wisconsin. The Illinois Grangers won a series of laws regulating freight rates, and the laws were eventually upheld by the Supreme Court in *Munn* v. *Illinois*.

But enforcement proved impossible. Railroads intimidated individuals who asked for legal rates, and the state machinery was unwilling or unable to enforce them. The political thrust of the Grange became an adventure in frustration.

By the mid-seventies the organization was also in serious financial trouble. The barons attacked the cooperative stores in court and with price wars, railroad boycotts, and by withholding credit. When the machinery trust refused to sell wholesale to the cooperatives, the National Grange tried to open a factory to manufacture its own harvesters. But the Crash of 1873 caught the organization short of money, and in a wave of lawsuits and bankruptcies the organization sank deep into debt. Local chapters disbanded for fear of being dragged into court.

Meanwhile, more and more farmers joined third party movements. In 1873 and 1874 new parties sprang up in eleven western states. Known variously as Farmers, Anti-Monopoly, Independent, and Reform parties, most of them merged in 1876 into the National Greenback Party.

The economic system, said the Greenbackers, had divided the American people into two classes—"Tramps and Millionaires." The currency would have to be inflated to make fixed debts, primarily mortgages, easier to pay. The government should issue Greenbacks to make the dollar cheaper and money easier for the general population to come by. "The adoration of gold and silver" wrote Ignatius Donnelly of Minnesota, "is a superstition of which the bankers are the high priests and mankind the victims. Those metals are of themselves of little value. What should make them so?"

The party nominated Peter Cooper, a New York industrialist and philanthropist, for president. But Cooper didn't campaign and received only 81,000 votes.

In 1878 the farmers allied with the Knights of Labor and the platform was expanded to include the demands of the factory workers. In the off-year elections the Greenback-Labor Party carried over a million votes and elected fourteen congressmen.

In 1880 the party nominated ex-General James B. Weaver of Iowa. He waged a vigorous campaign for popular control of the money system and against the "monopoly power," but only 300,-000 votes were recorded for him.

Four years later, with depression somewhat subsided, Ben Butler of Massachusetts made a weaker showing. The Grange and Greenbacker movements faded away.

The People's Party

But as the strength of the Grange waned, western farmers laid the groundwork for a larger, more powerful movement. In 1874 and 1875 the farmers of Lampasas County, Texas, formed a

Farmers' Alliance to protect themselves from horse thieves, land sharks, and cattle barons. The organization also sponsored a debating society and a cemetery association.

Soon after its formation the Alliance was drawn into the Greenbacker movement and was shattered by internal dissension. But the charter survived, and by 1885 the Grand State Alliance of Texas claimed 50,000 members in 1200 local chapters.

As low prices and hard times returned, the Alliance spread from Texas over the South and West and into the old Grange territory. By 1890 the Northern Alliance, centered in the West, had over a million members, the Southern Alliance as many as three million, and the Colored Farmers' Alliance, also centered in the South, another million and a quarter. "The people are aroused at last," proclaimed the *Western Rural* of Chicago. "Never in our history has there been such a union of action among farmers as now."

Like the Grange, the Alliance started into cooperative marketing and purchasing, and, like the Grange, it ran head-on into the money system. The first big cooperative was the Texas Farmers' Exchange in Dallas, which in 1887 began marketing cotton and grain on a commission basis and buying machinery at a discount which was passed on to the farmer. Soon the Exchange added dry goods and groceries in an effort to break the crop-lien system. In 1888 it claimed a volume of $1 million.

But the farmers had no cash and the Exchange couldn't get credit with local banks. Texas Alliancemen claimed that in fact the banks did their best to squeeze the Exchange out of business—

Those who controlled the moneyed institutions of the State either did not choose to do business with us or they feared the ill will of a certain class of businessmen who consider their interests antagonistic to those of our order and corporation.

Finally, amidst charges of corruption, the Dallas Exchange went under. Cooperatives were set up on the Texas model in eighteen other states but they all ran into similar problems and they all failed.

By the early nineties farmers everywhere were losing their land. Tenancy—families working land that now belonged to merchants, bankers, and speculators—involved fully one-fourth of all the farms in Kansas, Nebraska, Iowa, Missouri, Illinois, Indiana, Ohio, Pennsylvania, and New Jersey. In the South the figure was closer to half. It was a pill too bitter to swallow. The farmers, yelled Mary Lease of Kansas, were going to "raise less corn and more hell"—

Wall Street owns the country. It is no longer a government of the people, by the people, and for the people, but a government of Wall Street, by Wall Street, and for Wall Street. The great common people of this country are slaves, and monopoly is the master.

The West and South are bound and prostrate before the manufacturing East. Money rules, and our Vice-President is a London banker. Our laws are the output of a system which clothes rascals in robes and honesty in rags. The parties lie to us and the political speakers mislead us. . . .

There are thirty men in the United States whose aggregate wealth is over one and one-half billion dollars. There are half a million looking for work. . . .

We want money, land and transportation. . . . We will stand by our homes and stay by our firesides by force if necessary, and we will not pay our debts to the loan-shark companies until the government pays its debt to us.

The people are at bay, let the blood-hounds of money who have dogged us thus far beware!

Politicians commonly explained the low prices for farm produce in terms of "overproduction"—too much food on the market was driving the price down. Somehow, wrote W. Scott Morgan of the Arkansas Alliance, saying there was "too much food" was a little ridiculous when people were hungry. "To say that over-production is the cause of 'hard times,'" he wrote, "is to say that the people are too industrious; that they could make a better living if they did not work so hard; that they have raised so much they are starving to death, and manufacturing so many clothes they are compelled to go naked. . . . Over-production is impossible so long as the wants of the human family are unsupplied."

The problem wasn't overproduction, he said, it was "excessive rates of transportation and want of a sufficient medium of exchange." The solution was simple enough: "laws that will properly distribute that which has been produced."

As hard times persisted, the farmers challenged the parties that ruled them and the structure of the economic system. The *Farmers' Alliance* of Lincoln, Nebraska, shouted the cry of an angry movement—

What is life and so called liberty if the means of subsistence are monopolized? . . . Deny it if you can, competition is only another name for war. . . .

The corporation has absorbed the community. The community must now absorb the corporation. . . . A stage must be reached in which each will be for all and all for each. The welfare of the individual must be the object and end of all effort. . . .

Has there been a better system in the world? Does not the problem of humanity demand that there shall be a better system? . . . There MUST be a better one.

In 1890 (*the year of Wounded Knee*) Alliancemen poured into the elections—Weaver in Iowa, Ignatius Donnelly in Minnesota, Jerry Simpson, Mary Lease, William Peffer in Kansas, Tom Watson in Georgia, Reuben Kolb in Alabama, Leonidas Polk in North Carolina. Where Alliancemen themselves did not run, major party candidates sought the organization's endorsement.

The election revealed an astounding, unexpected strength. Alliancemen or Alliance-supported candidates won the governorships of Georgia, Tennessee, South Carolina, and Texas and took control of the legislatures of Florida, Georgia, the Carolinas, Tennessee, Missouri, and Mississippi. The Kansas People's party elected ninety-one state representatives and thus the new U.S. senator. Independents in Nebraska took both houses of the state legislature and elected a congressman. Third-party men held the balance of power in the legislatures of South Dakota, where they elected a senator, and Minnesota. In Michigan, Indiana, Illinois, Iowa, North Dakota, and Colorado, Independents ran strong enough to upset the electoral balance and elect many Democrats in traditionally Republican states.

In all the Alliance elected outright forty-four representatives and three senators. Tom Watson, the young newly-elected congressman from Augusta, Georgia, joyfully hailed the triumph. "Like the thunder that shakes yon sky," he shouted, "the voice of the people has shaken the power from the hands of the political bosses and placed it in the hands of the masses where it belongs!"

But electing men to office and bringing about real change were two entirely different things. Nebraska Independents won an Australian (secret) ballot, voted money for victims of the drought, and put grain elevators and warehouses under state regulation. But their crucial railroad bill was killed by the Republican governor. North Carolina passed a railroad bill, but nowhere were the farmers able to make a dent in freight or interest charges.

In Washington, Watson presented the Alliance subtreasury plan to Congress. Under the plan the farmers would deposit their produce at nearby government warehouses and automatically receive 80 percent of the market value, payment to be made in newly printed paper money based on the crops themselves rather than gold. The plan would put over $500 million in new currency into circulation. At the same time the income of the farmer would be based directly on how much he raised, free of taxation by middlemen. In effect the farmers were demanding a currency based on food rather than gold, and a stable, direct agricultural marketing system.

Baronial Washington greeted the plan with scorn. The Alliance was a bunch of "hayseed socialists" who were demanding "potato banks." The men who had looted the treasury and stolen the West now, through the *New York Times,* demanded to know if "the government will collect money from the great body of the people for the purpose of lending it to a favored class among them?" After all, the subtreasury was not in keeping with the free enterprise system. "It will be an unfortunate day," reported the House Ways and Means Committee, "when, in a simple republic, government takes charge of all farm products, stores them in granaries, and becomes the main agent for the transaction of the business of the citizen." It was, said the *Times,* "one of the wildest and most fantastic projects ever seriously proposed by sober man."

Meanwhile, hard times got harder. Alliancemen found that local Democrats and Republicans they had supported professed their sympathy but refused to support the actual Alliance programs. The farmers, in turn, began to think in terms of their own national party. "We must have relief," wrote the president of the Southern Alliance, "if we have to wipe the two old parties from the face of the earth."

In February 1892, thousands of militant farmers and workers flocked to Omaha to launch a new national party. Many couldn't afford train fare and walked or rode horses and wagons hundreds of miles to get there; they slept in parks and cheap hotels and packed the city's nickel lunch counters to overflowing.

The Knights of Labor and a few smaller workingman's organizations were represented on the convention floor, but the bulk of the delegates belonged to the Farmers' Alliance. On a hot July 4, after months of meetings, the People's party issued its program for a massive overhaul of the American economic and political system—

The conditions which surround us best justify our cooperation; we meet in the midst of a nation brought to the verge of moral, political, and material ruin. Corruption dominates the ballot-box, the legisla-

tures, the Congress, and touches even the ermine of the bench. The
people are demoralized. . . .

We have witnessed for more than a quarter of a century the
struggles of the two great political parties for power and plunder,
while grievous wrongs have been inflicted upon the suffering people. . . .

They propose to sacrifice our homes, lives, and children on the altar
of mammon; to destroy the multitude in order to secure corruption
funds from the millionaires. . . .

We demand a national currency, safe, sound, and flexible issued by
the general government only, a full legal tender for all debts, public
and private, and that without the use of banking corporations; a just,
equitable, and efficient means of distribution direct to the people,
at a tax not to exceed 2 percent, per annum, to be provided as set
forth in the subtreasury plan of the Farmers' Alliance, or a better
system. . . .

We demand free and unlimited coinage of silver and gold at the
present legal ratio of 16 to 1. . . .

We demand that the amount of circulating medium be speedily
increased to not less than $50 per capita. . . .

We demand a graduated income tax. . . .

Transportation being a means of exchange and a public necessity,
the government should own and operate the railroads in the interest
of the people.

The telegraph and telephone, like the post-office system, being a
necessity for the transmission of news, should be owned and operated
by the government in the interest of the people.

The land, including all the natural sources of wealth, is the heritage
of the people, and should not be monopolized for speculative purposes,
and alien ownership of land should be prohibited.

All land now held by railroads and other corporations in excess of
their actual needs, and all lands now owned by aliens should be
reclaimed by the government and held for actual settlers only.

The basic demands were thus public ownership of the railroad
and communications systems, abolition of the private banking
system, public control of money, and the return of corporate
land to the people.

In addition, the convention resolved in favor of the secret ballot, the limitation of the presidency to one term, direct election of senators, and the adoption of the initiative, referendum, and recall. The convention branded Pinkerton detectives as "a large standing army of mercenaries" who are "a menace to our liberties" and declared a boycott on the clothing trust of Rochester, against whom the Knights of Labor were conducting a strike. The party also renounced "any subsidy or national aid to any private corporation for any purpose."

The throng at Omaha greeted the reading of the preamble and platform with a gigantic burst of energy. The Civil War was over! The farmers of the North and South had joined! The agrarian community was coming together to save its way of life.

At the conclusion, as if by magic, everyone was upon his feet in an instant and thundering cheers from 10,000 throats greeted those demands as the road to liberty. Hats, papers, handkerchiefs, etc., were thrown into the air; wraps, umbrellas and parasols waved; cheer after cheer thundered and reverberated through the vast hall, reaching the outside of the building where thousands [who] had been awaiting the outcome, joined in the applause till for blocks in every direction the exultation made the din indescribable.

For fully ten minutes the cheering continued, reminding one of the lashing of the ocean against a rocky beach during a hurricane.

The party took Populist—from the Latin derivative for "people" —as its nickname and nominated Weaver of Iowa for President. The former Greenback-Labor nominee was old enough to reassure the more conservative of the farm community but was a consistent radical, a good speaker, and a trusted campaigner.

The vice-presidential nominee was James G. Field of Virginia, an ex-general of the Confederacy who had lost a leg in the Civil War.

With $50 in the treasury Weaver called the People's party to action—

The American people have entered upon the mightiest civic struggle known to their history. Many of the giant wrongs which they are seeking to overthrow are as old as the race of man and are rock-rooted in the ignorant prejudices and controlling customs of every nation in christendom.

We must expect to be confronted by a vast and splendidly equipped army of extortionists, usurers, and oppressors marshalled from every nation under heaven.

Every instrumentality known to man—the state with its civic authority, learning with its lighted torch, armies with their commissions to take life, instruments of commerce essential to commercial intercourse, and the very soil upon which we live, move and have our being—all these things and more, are being perverted and used to enslave and impoverish the people.

The Golden Rule is rejected by the heads of all the great departments of trade, and the law of Cain, which repudiates the obligations that we are mutually under to one another, is fostered and made the rule of action throughout the world.

Corporate feudality has taken the place of chattel slavery and vaunts its power in every state. . . .

But thanks to the all-conquering strength of Christian enlightenment we are at the dawn of the golden age of popular power.

We have unshaken faith in the integrity and final triumph of the people. . . .

We have challenged the adversary to battle and our bugles have sounded the march. . . .

Problems in the South

The nomination of two Civil War generals—one from the Union and one from the Confederacy—was more than a symbolic gesture. The People's party had to unite the farmers of the North and South, and not only the bitterness of the war but the foul legacy of two centuries of slavery were still very much to be overcome.

The slaveocracy of the South had been built on the plantation system, a network of large cotton, tobacco, and sugar estates. The wealth of the slaveowners came from the cash value of their crops. The land was cheap, and as long as there was a frontier, it was plentiful. A southern editor complained in 1860 that "The system is such that the planter scarcely considers his land as a part of his permanent investment. It is rather a part of his current expenses. . . . He buys land, uses it until it is exhausted, and then sells it, as he sells scrap iron, for whatever it will bring. It is with him a perishable or moveable commodity. It is something to be worn out, not improved."

The ruling caste of the South took on the life style of a pre-capitalist aristocracy, but the economy still ran on cash, cash earned by slave labor and wrung out of the earth. "Let the soil be worn out," wrote a southern historian, "let the people move to Texas . . . let everything happen provided all possible cotton is produced each year."

Single-crop farming rapidly destroyed the soil, and the southerners were in constant need of new lands. It was this, in large part, that made conflict with the farmers and industrialists of the North "irrepressible."

But entwined in the clash of economics was the clash of cultures. The South was a feudal empire, built on slave labor, ruled by a tiny group of agrarian lords. Of the 9 million southerners in 1860, half were black, nearly all of them slaves. Only a quarter of the white families owned any slaves at all. The rest, the "poor whites," were pushed out of the rich bottom lands into the hills of the back country, where, according to historian Philip Bruce, they lived like black slaves—

The narrowness of their fortunes was disclosed in many ways—in the sallowness of their complexions, resulting chiefly from insufficient and unwholesome food—in the raggedness of their clothing, in the bareness and discomfort of their cabins, which were mere hovels with the most slovenly surroundings, and in the thinness and weakness of the few cattle they possessed.

Nowhere could there be found a population more wretched in some respects than this section of southern whites, the inhabitants of the ridge and pine barren, men and women who had no interest in the slave system whatsoever.

Poor whites counted for nothing in southern life. Ten thousand families owned more than fifty slaves each, and it was to this caste that the South belonged. A rigid, violent, chivalric code defined the style of upper-caste life.

Many of the aristocrats took rank in the militia, and one could hardly enter a mansion without meeting at least one "colonel," "captain," or "major." Dueling was common, and politicians like Andrew Jackson, Henry Clay, Sam Houston, and John Randolph all fought on the "field of honor."

Despite the games of chivalry and "civilization" played by the slaveowners, the frontier was very much a part of southern life well into the nineteenth century. There were vicious Indian battles east of the Mississippi as late as the forties, and Texas joined the slave empire that same decade in a war on Mexico that killed more than 10,000 people.

But neither the frontier nor the medieval lifestyle explain the predominance of violence and the military in southern life—the explanation lies with slavery. Though a large, well-established school of southern writers "proved" time and again that the 4 million slaves were a docile, happy lot, the lives of the slaveowners said exactly the opposite. Every slaveowner was of necessity "a born petty tyrant." "The power of the master," wrote a North Carolina judge, "must be absolute, to render the submission of the slave perfect."

Accordingly, a slaveowner could legally do anything he wanted to a slave except kill him. All slave states had rigid codes on the behavior of blacks—regulating travel and personal habits, even making it illegal for them to learn to read or write. Legal and military systems of tracking runaways and preventing rebellion were elaborate and fierce. Slaveowners lived in constant fear of their "property," and the rebellions of Gabriel, Denmark Vesey, and Nat Turner sent waves of paranoia through the southern plantations. Governor Robert Hayne of South Carolina warned in 1833 that "a state of military preparation must always be with us as a state of perfect domestic security. A period of profound peace and consequent apathy may expose us to the danger of domestic insurrection."

The subsurface war erupted in the Texas insurrection of 1860. On July 8 most of the business section of Dallas burned to the ground and fires were reported in seven other Texas towns. Slaves were tortured and "confessed" to complicity in a slave-abolitionist conspiracy for revolution. In August most of the town of Henderson burned. Vigilantes swarmed across the state conducting "trials" and executions. From seventy-five to one hundred blacks and northern whites were killed.

At no time did southern martial law end with the slaves. White men caught fraternizing with blacks were often in legal trouble and physical danger. It was a felony in all slave states to "say or write anything that might lead, directly or indirectly, to discontent or rebellion."

When civil war came it took 500,000 deaths and four years of total war to uproot southern feudalism. The South was ripped to pieces. Sherman tore a seventy-mile-wide stretch of absolute desolation through the state of Georgia, and another Union general bragged that a crow flying over the Shenandoah Valley would have to bring its own food. Georgia was hit the worst, but all over the South there were areas that "looked for many miles like a broad black streak of ruin and desolation—the fences all gone; lonesome smoke stacks, surrounded by dark heaps of ashes and cinders, marking the spot where human habitations had stood; the fields along the road wildly overgrown by weeds, with here and there a sickly looking patch of cotton or corn cultivated by negro squatters."

The victorious North imposed a "Reconstruction" program on its new colony, ostensibly for the purpose of guaranteeing full citizenship to the blacks. The South was divided into five military districts and put under martial law to guarantee the voting rights of the ex-slaves and the disfranchisement of former Confederates.

In some cases Reconstruction brought to power blacks and poor whites who had been completely colonized by the slave-owners. At the same time northern radicals fought to break up the old plantations and redistribute them to the blacks. Thaddeus Stevens, leader of the Radical Republican Congress, fought hard on the principle that "forty acres of land and a hut would be more valuable than the immediate right to vote." With their own land, he argued, real freedom would come to the ex-slaves naturally.

But mainstream Republicans balked at redistributing land, even that of the caste that had brought on the Civil War. "A division of rich men's lands," warned the *Nation*, "would give a shock to our whole social-political system from which it would hardly recover without the loss of liberty."

In the South, the Reconstruction governments met armed resistance. There were major riots in 1866 in New Orleans, where forty-eight people died, and two years later in Memphis, where whites burned schools, churches, and homes and "shot, beat, robbed, and raped" blacks. In 1868 Arkansas whites assassinated government officials, shut down the courts, and shot hundreds of people. In October 1870, thirteen people were killed in a riot at Laurens, South Carolina. A U.S. attorney estimated that 1000 blacks a year were killed in Texas from 1868 to 1870. General Philip Sheridan guessed that 3500 people, mostly black, were killed or wounded in Louisiana in the ten years after the war. Mass murders in rural areas were common.

The Reconstruction governments organized black militias, and armed blacks often marched independently to meet the white terrorists. But the power of the whites was overwhelming. In the January following the election of 1872, armed bands of blacks and whites paraded the streets of New Orleans and rival candidates for governor took oaths of office and set up legislatures. The New Orleans police broke up the Democratic legislature, but the following year the White League, the armed wing of the Democratic party, attacked and captured the New Orleans City Hall, police station, and telegraph office. At Liberty Square they routed police and militia and took control of the state capital in a battle that left twenty-seven people dead and over a hundred wounded.

The Republican governor fled to the customs house and called President Grant for additional federal troops, which eventually reinstated him.

Two years later in 1876 (*the year of Little Big Horn*), the national Republican party used the troops remaining in Louisiana, South Carolina, and Florida to steal the presidential election for its candidate Rutherford B. Hayes. Hayes got 250,000 fewer votes than the Democrat Samuel Tilden, but the fraudulent electoral votes of the three southern states gave the Republicans the election.

The "victory" almost brought on a shooting war between the two party organizations, and one of the concessions the Republicans had to make was the removal of the last troops from the South.

Thus ended the "Second American Revolution." War and Reconstruction had left the South a ruin. The blacks were no longer chattel slaves, but they were also landless and destitute. The poor whites were as poor and more bitter than ever.

THE "NEW SOUTH"

What the destruction of the slave system did do, however, was pave the way for an industrial revolution—of sorts.

Soon after the war northern industrialists began incorporating the South into their mushrooming industrial machine. *How to Get Rich in the South* (1888) reported there was "no country that offers such tempting inducements to the capitalist for profitable investments." Chauncey Depew, president of the New York Central, told Yale alumni that "The South is the bonanza of the future. . . . We have developed all the great and sudden opportunities for wealth—or most of them—in the northwestern states and on the Pacific slope." The South, he said, had "vast forests untouched, with enormous veins of coal and iron."

By 1876 the Illinois Central was running special trains to carry land speculators to Louisiana and Mississippi. A Congressman and two Michigan companies got over 1.5 million acres of Louisiana. One English firm took 4.5 million acres of Texas and another got 1.5 million acres of Louisiana coastal land at 12½ to 75 cents per acre. Twelve railroad corporations took 32.4 million acres in grants from the state of Texas. Florida governor George "Millionaire" Drew and his successor William Bloxham helped grant over 22 million acres of public land to speculators even though the actual public domain never exceeded 15 million acres.

In 1876 a Richmond paper noted that "a new race of rich people have been gradually springing up among us, who owe their wealth to successful trade and especially to manufactures." Birmingham became the fiefdom of Henry F. DeBardeleban's Pratt Coal and Coke Company. "I was the eagle," he said, "and I wanted to eat up all the little crawfish I could, swallow up all the little fellows, and I did it." James B. Duke carved an empire of eastern tobacco fields. New England-based mills and factories relocated in the "new South" to profit from the low wages that would hire the southern landless and poor. A railroad boom began in the late seventies and the Louisville and Nashville Railroad took over the state of Kentucky and much of Alabama, where it owned 500,000 acres. Timber companies poured into the magnificent pine and cypress stands of Georgia, producing what one forestry expert termed "probably the most rapid and reckless destruction of forests known to history."

The "redemption" Democratic governments had little trouble matching their corrupt Republican counterparts in the North and

West. In 1883 Marshall Polk, nephew of the former President James K. Polk, disappeared from his post as treasurer of Tennessee with some $366,000 in state funds. Three weeks later Isaac Vincent, treasurer of Alabama, got $232,980.79, and a month after that it was discovered that Thomas J. Churchill of Arkansas had defaulted with $138,789 in state money. James "Uncle Dick" Tate, treasurer of Kentucky, got $229,009, and William L. Hemingway of Mississippi got a five-year sentence for an unexplained shortage of $215,612.

Top prize went to Major E. A. Burke of Louisiana, who disappeared in 1889 with $793,600 in state funds. The major surfaced a year later in Tegucigalpa, capital of Honduras, where a New Orleans reporter found that he had "the government at his beck and call" and was "virtually the controlling force in Honduras."

The redeemer governor of Florida was a timber speculator, and the two redemption governors of Mississippi were corporate lawyers. Tom Scott of Pennsylvania had little trouble extracting a $6 million "subsidy" from the Texas legislature, and the state of Louisiana was ruled by the administrators of the state lottery, whose yearly income was well over $20 million.

Where there had been three castes in the South—slaveowners, poor whites, and black slaves—there were now, according to historian Fred Shannon, "essentially two classes: on the one hand, the landlord-merchant-banker-capitalist group, numbering approximately a sixth of the total population and having all the political power; on the other, the great bulk of field workers, living from enfeebled hand to empty mouth."

Corporate power was maintained through the Democratic party, which after 1877 ruled as a virtual dictatorship from state to state. The machine assumed the mantle of "white supremacy," labeling the Republicans "the party of War and the negro." At the same time Democratic managers courted black leaders who, with the death of the southern Republican party, had nowhere else to turn. Landowning Democrats counted on—and enforced—voting support from the black tenants and sharecroppers on their plantations. Thus the traditional hostility of hillbilly whites against the low-country rich was played off on black votes by the party of "white supremacy" until poor white and black alike throw up their hands in despair.

In undisputed control of the electoral machinery, the Democrats stole at the ballot box those elections they could not win by persuasion. The Ku Klux Klan, knights of the White Camelia, Red Shirts, and White League policed the countryside, terrorizing blacks and poor whites who dared challenge Democratic rule.

The foundation of the party's power rested on the prison system, whose equal one historian found in "the persecutions of the Middle Ages or in the prison camps of Nazi Germany." Prisoners were kept in packed, closed cabins and shuttled around in box cars. One year's death rate in the Arkansas penitentiaries was estimated at 25 percent. A Mississippi grand jury reported that most of the prisoners it saw had "their backs cut in great wales, scars and blisters, some with the skin peeling off in pieces as the result of severe beatings. . . . They were lying there dying, some of them on bare boards, so emaciated that their bones almost came through their skin, many complaining for want of food. . . . We actually saw live vermin crawling over their faces, and the little bedding they have is in tatters and stiff with filth."

Convict and chain-gang labor was commonly used by southern politicians and factory owners as a source of cheap manpower for private business. Senator Joseph Brown of Georgia paid the state seven cents a day per man to use convicts in his Dade Coal Mines, and prisoners were often used to break labor strikes, most notably in the mines of Tennessee.

But despite the influx of industry, the South remained essentially agrarian. The southern industrial cities were relatively small and the vast majority of southerners, black and white, still lived on and farmed the land.

And the basic nature of southern agriculture remained the same. The slave plantations were not only not broken up, they expanded and multiplied. Louisiana, which counted more farms than plantations before the Civil War, was a tight plantation and corporate monopoly by 1900. Title to the plantations now belonged to "a new, capitalistic sugar aristocracy, organized in corporations and financed by banks," wrote southern historian C. Vann Woodward. "At least half the planters after 1870 were either northern men or were supported by northern money."

Throughout the South the plantations were still the cornerstone of the agricultural economy; now they were owned by money men instead of slaveowners.

And instead of slaves the land was worked by tenants, sharecroppers, and victims of the crop-lien system. The crop-lien system was a very short step away from tenantry. Lacking cash, the farmer would sign over part of his coming year's crop in exchange for supplies from a local merchant or banker. Once in debt, few farmers ever escaped—

When one of these mortgages has been recorded against the southern farmer, he has usually passed into a state of helpless peonage. . . .

From this time until he has paid the last dollar of indebtedness, he is subject to the constant oversight and direction of the merchant. Every mouthful of food he purchases, every implement that he requires on the farm, his mules, cattle, the clothing for himself and family, the fertilizers for his land, must all be bought of the merchant who holds the crop lien, and in such amounts as the latter is willing to allow.

Deep in debt, working land they didn't own, the southern farmers were completely flattened by the postwar agricultural depression. Prices plunged across the board; the price of cotton dropped in half from 1873 to 1877, until in some instances it sold for less than it cost to raise. In 1880 one estimate of the national per capita wealth put it at $870; the figure in the state of Mississippi was $286. Kentucky, the best-off of the southern states, was still $44 below Kansas, the poorest of the states outside the South.

For southern farmers this meant nothing less than absolute

destitution and starvation. After suffering through slavery, war, and Reconstruction, the southerners found themselves more colonized, landless, and destitute than ever. The spirit of the South could hardly have been lower. "These faces, these faces," wrote an observer, "One sees them everywhere; on the street, at the theatre, in the salon, in the cars; and pauses for a moment, struck with the expression of entire despair." The farmers of Georgia, said Tom Watson, were "like victims of some horrid nightmare. . . . powerless—oppressed—shackled."

THE BIRTH OF A NATION

In the midst of the Depression of 1873 the Grange and Greenbacker movements began to gather southern strength. In 1878, Virginia was captured by an agrarian third party that abolished the poll tax and the whipping post. Repudiationists demanding the cancellation of state debts alarmed the money men, and as Readjuster, Independent, and Greenback-Labor partisans gained strength, the Democrats retaliated—

Independent candidates were run out of their counties, beaten, or murdered. . . . Ballot boxes were stuffed, fraudulent returns were made, and thousands of opposition votes were thrown out on technicalities. With mock solemnity, newspapers reported that boxes containing anti-Democratic majorities had been eaten by horses or mules.

Many of the back-country rebels were ready to fight fire with fire—

Greenback men, you must learn to shoot. You must make up your mind to kill. Nothing will check this hellish spirit of intolerance but lead.

But it was not until the late eighties that the lower-class whites could mount a serious challenge to the Democratic machine. Then, as depression racked the national farm community, the Farmers' Alliance swept through the South like wildfire. Organizers were amazed by how fast sub-Alliances were springing up and by the fervor of the backwoods farmers.

In 1888 the Alliance ran a successful boycott against a price hike from the jute-bagging trust. By the early nineties Alliance exchanges were going all over the South. The Southern Alliance claimed over 3 million members, the Colored Farmers' Alliance another million and a quarter. At last there seemed a chance to break through. "A new era had dawned in Georgia politics," wrote Watson. "The old order of things is passing away. The masses are beginning to arouse themselves, reading for themselves, thinking for themselves. The great currents of thought quicken new impulses. At the bar of public opinion the people are pressing their demands and insisting they be heard."

Generally, the rise of the Alliance meant stiffer fighting between poor whites and blacks. Many of the militant white farmers demanded disfranchisement of the blacks, leaving them to take on the machine alone, without having to deal with "white supremacy" or the forced black vote.

But as the Alliance and third-party movements gained power, the gigantic leap to a black-white alliance became a reality, a reality that meant revolution. United, no one could stop the black and white farmers, not even the Democratic machine. Watson laid the foundation of the new coalition—

The Negro Question in the South has been for nearly thirty years a source of danger, discord, and bloodshed. It is an ·ever-present irritant and menace. . . .

Never before did two distinct races dwell together under such conditions.

And the problem is, can these two races, distinct in color, distinct in social life, and distinct as political powers, dwell together in peace and prosperity? . . .

The white tenant lives adjoining the colored tenant. Their houses are almost equally destitute of comforts. Their living is confined to bare necessities. They are equally burdened with heavy taxes. They pay the same high rent for gullied and impoverished land.

They pay the same enormous prices for farm supplies. Christmas finds them both without any satisfactory return for a year's toil. Dull and heavy and unhappy, they both start the plows again when "New Year's" passes.

Now the People's Party says to these two men, "You are kept apart that you may be separately fleeced of your earnings. You are made to hate each other because upon that hatred is rested the keystone of the arch of financial despotism that enslaves you both.

You are deceived and blinded that you may not see how this race antagonism perpetuates a monetary system which beggars both.

While the westerners spoke of reform, the southern Populists talked freely of revolution. "While this system lasts," said Watson, "there are no pure politics, no free men, in Georgia. . . . It is rotten to the core, and there is no remedy for it but destruction."

The Southern Alliance drew up its 1890 platform with the Knights of Labor, and radical Populists called for a revolutionary alliance with urban workers. The *Southern Mercury* of Dallas announced "a bitter and irrepressible conflict between the capitalist and the laborer. . . . Every wage earner [must] combine and march shoulder to shoulder to the ballot box and by their suffrage over-throw the capitalistic class." "Men of the country!" yelled Watson "Let the fires of . . . this revolution grow brighter and brighter! Pile on the fuel till the forked flames shall leap in wrath around the foul structure of government wrong, shall sweep it from basement to turret, and shall sweep it from the face of the earth!"

In the elections of 1890 the Alliance established itself as a major power in southern politics. But the step to an independent third party was tricky. Tied as it was to the Civil War, loyalty to the Democrats was the lifeblood of southern politics. Breaking with the party of the Confederacy was, said one Virginian, "like cutting off the right hand or putting out the right eye."

The new party also faced a maze of confusing alliances. In Georgia and Alabama the Populists, led by Watson and Reuben Kolb, stayed independent of both the Republicans and Democrats.

But in North Carolina the Populists allied with the Republicans. In South Carolina and Texas, Ben Tillman and James Hogg capitalized on the uprising by using it to take over the Democratic machinery, preempting the Populists entirely. Both won governorships in 1890. Both combined radical rhetoric with reactionary politics, and Tillman in particular was a violent racist. Neither was a Populist; both fought hard against the People's party.

The confusion of the party system was nothing compared to the waves of terrorism and electoral fraud brought down by the Democratic machine. In 1892 Watson was thrown out of his Congressional seat in an election that counted twice as many votes as registered voters in the Augusta district. Fifteen people were killed in the course of the election. "Watson ought to be killed," said the governor of Georgia, "and it ought to have been done a long time ago."

In 1894 Kolb was beaten a second time for the governorship of Alabama in an election so dominated by fraud and violence that he staged his own "inauguration" while the Democratic governor surrounded the state capitol with troops. A Democratic paper summarized the "election"—

It is needless to attempt to disguise the facts of the Alabama election. The truth is that Kolb carried the state, but was swindled out of his victory by the Jones faction, which had control of the election machinery and used it with unblushing trickery and corruption.

The Virginia *Sun* described the election of 1892 in that state as a "bacchanalia of corruption and terrorism." The Populist problem, said Weaver, was not building a popular following, but "the securing of an honest vote and a fair count of the ballots."

Democratic manipulation of the vote-count was backed by an unending stream of intimidation and violence. People who worked against the machine were foreclosed, denied supplies and loans, and terrorized. Frank Burkitt, a Populist leader in Mississippi, was knocked unconscious from a speaker's platform, and Joseph Manning of Alabama was attacked and run out of the town of Florence. Populist farmers spent the days before the 1892 Georgia election armed and on horseback trying to protect black allies from lynch mobs. Six men died in party warfare in San Augustine County, Texas, including a Populist sheriff. Violence became a constant in the life of the Populist farmers. "The feeling of the Democracy against us is one of murderous hate," explained a southerner. "I have been shot at many times. Grand juries will not indict our assailants. Courts give us no protection."

Even so the strength of the People's party continued to soar. In 1893 the national economy fell apart and the depression in the West, South, and among urban workers reached unbearable depths. In 1894 Grover Cleveland, the first Democratic President since the Civil War, used federal troops to destroy a national rail strike—a bitterly resented intervention that resulted in a week of violence and at least twenty-five deaths.

Seven years earlier Cleveland had vetoed a minimal farm aid bill. "Though the people support the government," he explained, "the government should not support the people."

Now, in the depths of the nineties, Cleveland and Congress refused to end the gold standard or extend aid. The temper of the farmers and workers reached fever-pitch. Rock-bottom prices, unrelenting freight and interest charges, and a series of crushing natural disasters in the West and South put the struggle in life-or-death terms. Ms. Susan Orcutt wrote the new Populist governor of Kansas,

I take my pen in hand to let you know that we are starving to death. . . . My husband went away to find work and came home last night and told me that we would have to starve. He has been in 10 counties and did not get no work. . . . I haven't had nothing to eat today and it is 3 o'clock.

"We have reached the stage," said a Kentuckian, "where slow, reasoned arguments cannot any longer affect us, neither the ties of partisanship or political loyalty. It is a question of bread and meat and we are ready to fight."

Cleveland became a symbol of class hatred, both within and without his own party. With the eastern conservatives in control, the national Democrats seemed "buried under a drift a thousand feet deep" while the People's party gained strength every day. Should the Democrats collapse the Populists would hold the same position the Republicans had before the war, with a good chance to become the second major party and then to take the White House.

In 1894 the Populist vote increased to almost 1.5 million, a jump of 42 percent over 1892. The party elected radical governors in Kansas and Colorado. The Populist vote doubled in California, tripled in Minnesota.

As the campaign of 1896 drew closer, the American people braced for a second civil war. "This country," reported the *Weekly Progress* of Charlottesville, Virginia, "is upon the edge of a great revolution . . . a test of strength is to be made in blood between labor and capital."

The Catastrophe of 1896

Facing the collapse of their party, reform Democrats searched desperately for an issue to oust the Cleveland machine. They found it in free silver.

Shortly after the Civil War the Republicans had enacted "the crime of 1873," legislation restricting the coinage of silver and contracting the currency. Money and gold were driven up which benefited the rich at the expense of the poor. The dollar tripled in value in the thirty years after the war, which made mortgages even harder to pay.

Populist speakers in the South and West found that the

silver issue was extremely popular; the farmers wanted cheaper money, and expanding the currency by coining all the silver that was mined seemed the simplest way to get it. Free coinage of silver also had obvious appeal in the western mining states and could be counted on to bring financial backing from mine owners.

By the elections of 1894 both reform Democrats and western Republicans were preparing to break from their parties. A movement spread through the South and West to win Democrats to silver and to draw Populists away from the radical demands of the 1892 Omaha platform.

The strategy succeeded. In the summer of 1896 silverites flooded the Democratic convention at Chicago. They overpowered Cleveland and the eastern machine and took control of the party.

The silverite leader was William Jennings Bryan, a young (36) Congressman who had made his political fortunes in Nebraska by fusing Democratic and Populist support. A hypnotizing speaker and a boisterous, energetic campaigner, Bryan vowed to crusade for "the masses against the classes." He had been practicing variations of his "cross of gold" acceptance speech for at least two years, and when he finally delivered it, it electrified the nation—

We do not come as aggressors. Our war is not a war of conquest. We are fighting in the defense of our homes, our families, and posterity. We have petitioned, and our petitions have been scorned; we have entreated, and our entreaties have been disregarded; we have begged, and they have mocked when our calamity came.

We beg no longer; we entreat no more; we petition no more. We defy them! . . .

There are two ideas of government. There are those who believe that if you will only legislate to make the well-to-do prosperous, their prosperity will leak through on those below.

The Democratic idea, however, has been that if you make the masses prosperous, their prosperity will find its way up through every class which rests upon them.

You come to us and tell us that the great cities are in favor of the gold standard; we reply that the great cities rest upon our broad and fertile prairies.

Burn down your cities and leave our farms, and your cities will spring up again as if by magic; but destroy our farms and the grass will grow in the streets of every city in the country. . . .

Having behind us the producing masses of this nation and the world, supported by the commercial interests, and the toilers everywhere, we will answer their demand for a gold standard by saying to them: You shall not press down upon the brow of labor this crown of thorns, you shall not crucify mankind upon a cross of gold.

The St. Louis Confusion

The silverite triumph threw the Populists into hopeless confusion. Though Bryan's speeches read and sounded like Populist attacks, the Democratic platform contained nothing of substance beyond free silver. Bryan refused to advocate government ownership of the railroads, choosing instead to doubletalk the issue. The Democrats, he said, "will prefer government ownership of railroads to railroad ownership of government if they have to choose between the two. It will be easy, therefore, to agree upon strict regulation and control of the railroads and other corporations by both federal and state governments within their respective spheres."

The subtreasury plan, the return of corporate land to the people, the democratic control of the money system—all were conspicuously absent from the Democratic platform and from Bryan's speeches. For vice-president the party nominated Arthur Sewall of Maine, a conservative millionaire banker and railroad owner.

The People's party convention had been scheduled for St. Louis to follow the major nominations. The plan was to gather up disgusted Democrats and Republicans and forge an alliance strong enough to push the Democratic party out of existence.

But the unexpected nomination of Bryan split the Populists down the middle.

Opposition to fusion was fierce. Free silver was all right, but it wouldn't save the farmer. "Not a Populist in the land is hostile to free silver," wrote G. C. Clemens of Kansas, but "in the world of to-day, with its gigantic trusts and combinations—none of which will our proposed allies permit us to touch—would free silver restore the conditions of twenty-three years ago? What folly to even dream!" The Topeka *Advocate* agreed. Expanding the money supply would be a welcome reform, but

There must be a complete revolution in our social system to make it conform to the new conditions resulting from the adoption of labor-saving machinery and modern methods of production and distribution. It is folly . . . to think that a simple change in our money system will remedy the evils from which we are suffering. . . . Every monopoly must be operated by the public and for the public good.

"For God's sake don't endorse Bryan," a Texan wrote to his state delegation. "Our people are firm, confident, and enthusiastic; don't betray their trust. Don't try to force us back into the Democratic party; we won't go." The farmers, warned the *Southern Mercury*, had better "fear the Greeks, even when bearing gifts."

Furthermore, said Cyclone Davis, another Texan, electing Bryan was like signing his death warrant. "Elect Bryan and Sewall" he said, "and before March is over Sewall will be made president through the assassination of Bryan accomplished by the money power, and thus you will have a national banker for president."

But if the substance of Populism was missing from the Democratic platform, the rhetoric, the appeal, and the nearness to power were there. The Populists were trapped. To support Bryan might mean the end of the party; to oppose him would guarantee the election of William McKinley and bring down unforgiveable hardship on the farm community.

Democratic managers swarmed to St. Louis to get the nomination for Bryan. The convention refused to alter the basic 1892 platform, but then elected a Bryan man permanent chairman.

Radicals then won the procedural change of nominating the vice-presidential candidate first to guarantee at least one pure Populist on the ticket.

On that basis, Watson was nominated for vice-president. A fiery speaker and voluminous writer, the redheaded Georgia lawyer was the most revolutionary of the southern Populist leadership. Through the early days of the convention he maintained, by correspondence from his home, a bitter opposition to fusion. "Free silver," he said, "is right and we ought to have it, but it is a mere drop in the bucket to what we must have if we are ever to save our people from financial ruin."

As for cooperation between the People's and the Democratic organizations, it was easy enough for the westerners, where Democrats and Populists had already joined to fight the ruling Republicans. But in the South it was the Democrats who ruled, and the line between them and populism was "a line of bloody graves." To ask southern Populists to join with the Democrats was to ask suicide.

But the convention was in chaos. Deluged with desperate pleas from his supporters, Watson wired that he would accept the nomination. He opposed Bryan but would campaign on the same ticket if the convention chose him. He did this on the assumption the Bryan would drop Sewall and accept an explicit alliance with the People's party.

William V. Allen, chairman of the convention, and James K. Jones, the Democratic national chairman who was in St. Louis working to get the Populist nomination for Bryan, each received telegrams from Bryan rejecting a Populist runningmate. The telegrams were suppressed, and even after they became public the Populists were misled and confused as to Bryan's "real" intention.

Radical opposition to Bryan continued, most of it centered

on nominating Eugene V. Debs, president of the American Railway Union and leader of the 1894 Pullman strike. Support for Debs was as high as one-third of the convention.

But when he withdrew the movement caved in. Bryan was nominated in a shroud of in-fighting, and the Populists went home confused and bitter.

MONEY-MEN OF THE WORLD UNITE!

The silverite conquest of the Democratic party and Bryan's approval by the People's party sent a wave of paranoid hysteria through the baronial east. The southern and western hordes were about to storm Wall Street! "Probably no man in civil life had succeeded in inspiring so much terror, without taking life, as Bryan," wrote the *Nation*. "At no time since 1860 have the issues of a presidential campaign been so distinctively moral," screamed the *New York Times*. "If there were ever a crisis in the history of this country when the teachings of the Gospel of peace and justice were involved in the duty of the citizen it is the present crisis."

Newspapers and right-wing politicians spewed reams of hate and fear. J. Sterling Morton, Cleveland's secretary of agriculture, screamed that

Mules, swine, and dogs could be taught the automatic vote, furnished with tickets and determine an election with just as much sense as many of those who wield the ballot power at the elections in the United States.

"Populists, Anarchists and Communists must not be permitted to destroy the financial credit of our country," vowed the Catholic bishop of Omaha. Adolph Ochs of the *New York Times* charged that Bryan was trying to "stir up hatred, envy, and malice between Americans and foreigners, between classes and between sections." He preached the "beliefs of an ignorant fanatic," said the *Times,* and he was a "demagogue and a revolutionist by nature without an anchorage of knowledge, experience, or sober purpose to steady him."

Half the Democratic press and much of the regular machine fled the party, leaving Bryan with a small organization and almost no money. The Cleveland wing held its own "Gold Democrat" convention and nominated a candidate who urged supporters to vote for McKinley. Convention delegates referred to Bryan as "an ugly little anarchist."

Nonetheless Bryan staged an amazing campaign. He barnstormed the West and South by train, covering 18,000 miles and making as many as thirty-six speeches a day.

He spoke to 5 million people—people whose enthusiasm often bordered on frenzy. The campaign was a crusade to save the farm community. Free silver meant "food and clothes for the thousands of hungry and ill-clad women and children . . . the reopening of closed factories, the relighting of fires in darkened furnaces . . . hope instead of despair; comfort in place of suffering; life instead of death." Women brought their children to the whistle-stops to be blessed, and sons were "named William, Jennings, or William Jennings, or William Jennings Bryan, triplets named, William, Jennings, and Bryan"—

> No crown of thorns to its brow shall press,
> Never again, say we,
> No cross of gold mankind distress;
> Never again, say we,
> We'll loosen all the cords that bind;
> Give equal chances to all mankind,
> And here a new Redeemer find,
> Leading to victory.

McKinley, meanwhile, campaigned from his front porch in Canton. Lifeless and colorless, the Ohio senator was "destined for a statue in a park and was practicing the pose for it." Railroads brought well-dressed, well-behaved crowds to his door, to whom he read prepared speeches, of which everyone in the audience had a copy.

Behind McKinley, Mark Hanna was driving a new order of political steamroller. Corporations paid an informal tax of 5 percent to the campaign, putting as much as $15 million at Hanna's disposal. Standard Oil in nearby Cleveland contributed $250,000, and the Chicago beef trust put in another $400,000. E. H. Harriman gave Hanna $35,000, and Marshall Field threw in another $10,000. The Mutual, Equitable, and New York Life Insurance companies poured policy-holders' funds into the Republican machine, which in turn churned out speakers, literature, and coercion on a scale never before seen in the United States. While Bryan distributed 10 million pieces of literature, Hanna sent out at least 120 million—nearly ten pieces per voter—in addition to a steady stream of articles and cartoons which no less than 13,000 newspapers could be counted on to carry. Every major newspaper in Chicago backed McKinley, and Jim Hill bought the only silver paper in Minneapolis, shutting out Bryan there too.

Everywhere Bryan spoke one or more of Hanna's stable of 18,000 speakers followed. Letters were mailed to every church in the country charging that free silver would hinder their religious work, and Bryan was falsely branded an anti-Semite. Universities forced professors to speak for McKinley, and one newspaper urged readers to vote for him because a poll showed the inmates at Sing Sing favored Bryan.

The verbal attack found its most telling mark in Bryan's single issue—silver. McKinley had conspicuously voted for coining silver in Congress, and the Republicans took great pains to endorse "international bimetallism." It was a sham—McKinley and the Republicans would coin silver only when the nations of Europe agreed to, an agreement they knew was not forthcoming. But McKinley straddled the fence. "With me," he said, "political

Milking the Farmer

Conceived by Ben Tillman, this was the most popular Democratic cartoon of the 1896 campaign.

and economic questions are a conviction. . . . I have always been in favor of the free and unlimited coinage of the silver product of the United States, and have so voted on at least two occasions. . . ."

At the same time, the silver issue had little appeal to urban workers who sympathized with Bryan but those wages would be shrunk by inflation. The increasingly militant unions were, in fact, far readier to accept the radical demands of the Populist program than they were the single Democratic issue of silver.

Far more importantly, though, factory owners all over the country told workers that if silver won the election on Tuesday there would be no jobs on Wednesday. Industrial orders were placed subject to cancellation if Bryan won. Factories were flooded with pamphlets and speakers, all with the same message —if Bryan wins, the factory shuts down. Workers known to support Bryan were fired and blacklisted, and railroads hired detectives to find out who planned to vote for him. Some of the coercion was organized by the Republican party, but in general

There was no employers' conspiracy. Mark Hanna did not exercise vast and mysterious power to control factory owners scattered across the nation. Such measures were not necessary.

Insurance companies holding mortgages in crucial midwestern farm states sent agents to offer low-interest mortgage extensions on the condition that McKinley won.

In October, McKinley supporters in Chicago organized an anti-Bryan rally of 100,000 marchers wearing gold badges, hats, and shoes. On the Saturday before elections in New York, 110,-000 marchers tramped the streets of the city chanting "We'll hang Billy Bryan from a sour apple tree."

But the Bryan campaign continued to hold up. "The last week of the campaign is getting on everybody's nerves," wrote John Hay. "Most of my friends think Bryan will be elected and we shall all be hanged to the lampions of Euclid Avenue."

For the most part it had been a contest between men and money. Money won—

> Election night at midnight:
> Boy Bryan's defeat.
> Defeat of western silver.
> Defeat of the wheat.
> Victory of Letterfiles
> And plutocrats in miles
> With dollar signs upon their coats,
> Diamond watchchains on their vests
> And spats on their feet.
> Victory of custodians,
> Plymouth Rock,
> And all that inbred landlord stock.
> Victory of the neat.
> Defeat of the aspen groves of Colorado Valleys,
> The blue bells of the Rockies,
> And blue bonnets of old Texas,
> By the Pittsburg alleys.
> Defeat of alfalfa and the Mariposa lily.
> Defeat of the Pacific and the long Mississippi.
> Defeat of the young by the old and silly.
> Defeat of tornadoes by the poison vats supreme.
> Defeat of my boyhood, defeat of my dream.
>   Vachel Lindsay

McKinley was declared the winner with 50.8 percent of the popular vote, carrying the cities and the Midwest. "We have escaped the calamity of the commune," sighed the secretary of agriculture. The Republicans had handled the country, said Brooks Adams, "like a squad of police against a mob."

Kentucky, West Virginia, Ohio, Michigan, Indiana, and Illinois all had areas where there were more ballots counted than there were people. Weaver claimed the count in Iowa was "absurd and dishonest," and similar cries came from virtually everywhere. Edward Rosewater, a Republican national committeeman, later told Roosevelt how a large number of ballots had been printed to look like votes for Bryan but were in fact votes for McKinley. The price of votes in New York, Philadelphia, Baltimore, Louisville, and Chicago was quoted at $5 each for up to sixteen repeats. Both Bryan and John Altgeld, governor of Illinois, claimed that a fair count would have given Bryan the presidency.

The count, however, was final, as was the inauguration of McKinley. "Do you think," Hanna asked Horace Keefer of Kansas, "that we'd let that damned lunatic get into the White House? Never! You know you can hire half of the people of the United States to shoot the other half if necessary, and we've got the money to hire them!"

What the Republicans did to the Democrats hardly compared to what the Republicans and Democrats did to the Populists. In "What's the Matter with Kansas?" which Hanna reprinted and spread all over the country, the young journalist William Allen White shouted the alarm—

We all know; yet here we are at it again. We have an old mossback Jacksonian who snorts and howls because there is a bath-tub in the State House. We are running that old jay for Governor.

We have another shabby, wild-eyed, rattle brained fanatic who has said openly in a dozen speeches that "the rights of the user are paramount to the rights of the owner." We are running him for Chief Justice. . . .

Then for fear some hint that the State had become respectable might percolate through the civilized portions of the nation, we have decided to send three of four harpies out lecturing, telling the people that Kansas is raising hell and letting corn go to weeds.

Bryan, said Theodore Roosevelt, was "a sham and a compromise." But the People's party was "plotting a social revolution and the subversion of the American Republic." It "could only be suppressed, as the Commune in Paris was suppressed, by taking ten or a dozen of their leaders out, standing . . . them against a wall, and shooting them dead." Should the revolt continue to gain strength, he pledged, "I shall be found at the head of my regiment."

Bryan, meanwhile, didn't formally accept the Populist nomination until October. He never dropped Sewall as his running mate and never acknowledged either Watson's candidacy or the Populist platform.

Fusion between Populists and Democrats in the West worked to some degree, but open warfare for control of the South raged on. In Louisiana, Arkansas, Missouri, Kentucky, and North Carolina, the Bryan-Watson ticket appeared on the ballot. But in the rest of the South, including Georgia, the Democratic machine blocked it off. Senator James K. Jones of Arkansas, the Democratic national chairman who had played a key role in getting the Populist nomination for Bryan, told newspapers that the western Populists were all right, but "the southern delegates were not a creditable class. . . . They will go back with the negroes, where they belong."

In some southern states Populists found themselves working in local alliances with Republicans while supporting a Democratic candidate for President. Confusion and bitterness were everywhere. The Populist chairman in Florida told farmers to vote for McKinley. "I confess that I myself am 'befogged' at present," wrote William Guthries, the Populist candidate for governor of North Carolina. "[I] hardly know where to go, what to say, when I speak, or 'where I am at.'"

Watson campaigned for Bryan and populism, but it was with deep bitterness and apprehension. "We have conceded everything short of extinction of our party," he said. "It is not so much free silver they want as the death of the People's Party. . . . It appears the Democratic managers would be willing to make a sacrifice of both Bryan and silver, if they can but destroy Populism."

Watson got twenty-seven electoral votes for the vice-presidency, but local Populist strength was shattered. Bands of armed Democratic "regulators" roamed the northern parishes of Louisiana and the hill country of other southern states, terrorizing the Populist strongholds. Vote counts in Louisiana were "two, three,

and four times as great as the number of males of voting age."
William Oates, Democratic governor of Alabama, summarized the
election—

I told them to go to it, boys, count them out. We had to do it. Unfortunately I say, it was a necessity. We could not help ourselves.

Having gambled everything on a losing candidate, the People's
party fell apart. The West-South alliance was broken, the party
membership bitterly divided, and the organization in ruins.

Senator Marion Butler of North Carolina vowed that the
party would remain "the nucleus around which the patriotic
host must and will gather to redeem a betrayed republic and
to restore prosperity to an oppressed and outraged people."

But the general mood was undeniably grim. "Go behind the
barn and kick yourself into Missouri," chided a Kansas paper,
"for not having intelligence enough to know the legitimate and
inevitable consequences of political prostitution."

Watson bore personally the brunt of the defeat. Blocked off the
ballot in his own state, he appeared and felt ridiculous campaign-
ing for a candidate who recognized neither him nor his party's
platform. "Our party, as a party, does not exist anymore," he
wrote. "The sentiment is still there, the votes are still there, but
confidence is gone, and the party organization is almost gone.
. . . The work of many years is washed away and the hopes of
many thousands of good people are gone with it."

"All our high-blown hopes have burst under us," wrote Ignatius
Donnelly. "It seems useless to contest against the money power.
. . . I tremble for the future."

I Ain't Got No Home

Shortly after the election new mining techniques and the
discovery of gold in South Africa, Australia, and Alaska led to an
expansion of currency, which partly satisfied the demand for free

silver. A European crop failure and the imperial expansion of American markets brought a semblance of prosperity to large parts of the farm community.

In 1898 the American military conquered Cuba, Puerto Rico, and the Philippines in a "crusade" that further divided the farmers and turned their attention from domestic to foreign affairs.

In the ensuing years many western Populists became Progressives, and many others became Debsian socialists, loyal supporters of the *Appeal to Reason* of Girard, Kansas. But the heart of the movement was gone and the Republican machine rapidly retook control of the West.

The Democrats, meanwhile, proceeded to wipe southern populism off the face of the map. Disheartened and bitter, Tom Watson personified the state of the southern People's party after 1896—

Politically I was ruined. Financially I was flat on my back. How near I came to loss of mind only God who made me knows—but I was as near distraction, perhaps, as any mortal could safely be.

The chief victory in 1896 had been in North Carolina, where a Populist-Republican, black-white coalition swept into control of the state government. The Democrats publicized the "return of nigger domination" throughout the South and vowed to retake North Carolina for the white race. The party organized a series of "white supremacy jubilees," and in the midst of the 1898 elections a Democratic mob attacked and burned a black newspaper office in Wilmington, then charged the black section of town, killing at least twenty people and possibly as many as one hundred. Democratic boss Furnifold Simmons sent "some of our boys" to terrorize Populist Senator Marion Butler, who was, bragged Simmons, scared "almost to death." The Republican governor "was so badly frightened that he slipped away from Raleigh immediately after the election."

Twelve blacks were killed near the South Carolina home of Ben Tillman, and the "jubilee" in Atlanta consisted of four days of looting, burning, and lynching. The *Southern Mercury* was forced to concede that "the Democratic party can declare for anything it likes and win."

Now in full control, the Democrats shut the black community entirely out of southern life. In 1890, Mississippi had approved an extensive program of voting qualifications designed to prevent blacks from voting. In 1895, Tillman made a variation of the "Mississippi Plan" law in South Carolina.

With the collapse of populism the rest of the South fell into line. By means of the "grandfather" clause, poll taxes, literacy tests, and property qualifications, the blacks were virtually excluded from all voting rights.

The Mississippi Plan also disfranchised poor whites and put control of elections more firmly in the hands of the Democratic machine than ever. The laws, said Oates of Alabama, barred "all those who are unfit and unqualified, and if the rule strikes a white man as well as a negro, let him go. There are some white men who have no more right and no more business to vote than a negro and not as much as some of them." A Vicksburg paper pointed out that "the poll tax gets rid of the negro votes (in Mississippi), but it gets rids of a great many whites at the same time—in fact a majority of them."

But poor whites still supported the Mississippi Plan in the name of "white supremacy." The black-white alliances had smashed into a brick wall; the only visible way up seemed to be to write the black man out of politics and take on the machine alone.

But exclusion of the blacks went way beyond electoral politics. Jim Crow laws—of which there had been few until the nineties—formally separated the races in residential areas, on trains and streetcars, and in public parks and hospitals. Courtrooms provided separate Bibles and schools stored texts separately on the basis of which race used them. It was illegal in some states for blacks and whites to fight, fish, boat, or play dominoes or checkers together. Where there had been two classes in the South—owners above poor whites and blacks, now there were again three —owners above poor whites above blacks. If the whites couldn't crack the social tyranny of the South, they could at least feel someone else was on the very bottom.

By 1900 Bryan and the southern Democrats were formally reallied with the eastern Democratic machine. The Nebraska "revolutionary" stunned his agrarian supporters in midcampaign by making an open alliance with Tammany Hall.

For the Republicans had retaken the West and the base of the Democratic party, the South, had become the undisputed colony of eastern finance. In 1894, J. P. Morgan tied some thirty companies around the bankrupt Richmond Terminal System to create the Southern Railway Company, involving some 7500 miles of road. In 1902 he added the Louisville and Nashville and soon controlled 20,000 miles of track in the South, which was now, with its vast natural wealth, the base of his empire. In the panic of 1907 he picked up the Tennessee Coal and Iron Company, adding to the House of Morgan the ore and coal fields of Tennessee and Alabama and the steel mills of Birmingham.

Texas was rapidly divided between Standard Oil, the Texas Company of speculator John W. Gates, and Gulf Oil, property of the Mellon banking family of Pittsburgh, who also owned the Aluminum Corporation of America and with it the bauxite fields of Georgia, Arkansas, Alabama, and Tennessee.

Florida became the province of Henry Flagler, a Rockefeller partner who pushed rail lines to his hotel empire in the baronial playgrounds of St. Augustine, West Palm Beach, Miami, and the Florida Keys. James Duke continued to command his tobacco empire from a mansion in New Jersey that now featured, at its front, a bronze statute of William McKinley, three times as large as life.

Despite the radical rhetoric of the Progressives who rode the wake of the People's party, the key programs of the Populist movement never materialized. Public ownership of the money, banking, transportation, and communications systems, the subtreasury plan, the return of homestead land to the farmers—all fell by the wayside. The farmers were left prey to devastating freight rates and taxes, bloated land prices and interest charges, and an irrational and unstable marketing system.

As early as 1900 three of every four southern farmers was a sharecropper, a tenant, or a prisoner of the crop-lien system. By 1910 the majority of farms in eight southern states were run by tenants.

After World War I the general agricultural market fell apart again, this time for good. The agrarian depression of the twenties and the Great Depression of the thirties, which the Populist program would have prevented, wiped out the American family farm in the West. The small, independent farmers were shoved off their land and forced to become tenants or to wander to the overcrowded and hungry cities, leaving the land in the hands of bankers, merchants, insurance and loan companies, railroads.

In 1900 there were 40 million Americans living on some 6 million farms; in the late 1980s, in a nation three times as large, there were less than 6 million Americans living on just over two million farms.

The prairie schooners riding east from Kansas, the Depression jalopies trekking west from Oklahoma, carried refugee families whose land had been stolen, whose way of life had been killed.

> My brothers and my sisters
> They are stranded on this road
> A hot and dusty road
> That a million feet have trod
> Rich man took my home
> And he drove me from my door
> And I ain't got no home in this world anymore

Farmin' on the shares
And always I was poor
My crops I laid
Unto the banker's store
My wife took up and died
Upon the cabin floor
And I ain't got no home in this world anymore

Now as I look around me
It's mighty plain to see
The world is such a great
And a funny place to be
The gamblin man is rich
And the working man is poor
And I ain't got no home in this world anymore

—Woody Guthrie

D. R. Fitzpatrick, *St. Louis Post-Dispatch*, 1923

The Revolt of the Workers

Years ago I recognized my kinship with all living things, and I made up my mind that I was not one bit better than the meanest of the earth. I said then, I say now, that while there is a lower class, I am in it; while there is a criminal element, I am of it; while there is a soul in prison, I am not free.

Eugene V. Debs

Where warehouses are full of food, go in and take it; where machinery is lying idle, use it for your purposes; where houses are unoccupied, enter them and sleep.

Big Bill Haywood

On the first day of summer 1877, in the depths of the worst depression America had ever seen, ten gallows were set up in the Schuylkill Valley. In Pottsville and Wilkes-Barre, in the heart of the Pennsylvania coal regions, local police were preparing to hang ten Molly Maguires.

Long years of bitter struggle to organize the miners of the Schuylkill brought violence and espionage from mine owners and police. In response, the mine workers formed the Molly Maguires, named for an Irish revolutionary hero, a secret, underground cadre of organizers and guerrilla terrorists. By 1875 the workers were able to wage their "long strike," a bitter, bloody attempt to raise wages and to establish their right to a union.

In the middle of the strike the Maguires were broken by a Pinkerton detective named James McParlan who had infiltrated the organization as a double agent. On June 21, ten Maguires

were hung—ten more would follow. The *Irish World*, voice of
the miners' Ancient Order of the Hibernians, spat its fury—

Drive a rat into a corner and he will fight. Drive your serfs to desperation, you grinding monopolists, chain them in enforced idleness half
the year and lash them with the whip of hunger to work at semi-
starvation wages—semi-starvation for themselves and their little ones
—the other half, and in their desperation they will some day pounce
upon you and destroy you!

Revenge for the Mollies came soon. The biggest strike in
American history was already in the making, and by mid-July
Pittsburgh was in flames.

The Earthquake

On the eve of the Civil War, America was still at least two-
thirds rural. In a country with about 30 million residents, some 25
million lived on the land.

In the next sixty years, the rural population doubled, but the
urban population multiplied by a factor of ten.

The new city dwellers were in large part the displaced
peasantry of Europe. There the industrial revolution tore up the
last roots of the feudal agrarian culture and made millions of
families landless and homeless. In the 1840s the potato famine in
Ireland and unsuccessful revolution in Germany sent waves of
peasant families across the Atlantic to start new lives. From
1840 to 1890 some 4 million Germans and 3 million Irish made
the voyage to America.

Then the tide shifted to southern and eastern Europe, and from
1880 to 1920 some 4 million Italians, 4 million Austro-Hungarians,
and 3 million Russians came to the United States. In all, well
over 30 million immigrants landed on the East Coast from the
Civil War to World War I, a wave that of itself nearly doubled
the country's population.

As the corporations swallowed up the land, millions of the immigrants were trapped in the cities. The urban tenement became the core of American life. Jacob Riis saw,

[A] man, his wife, and three small children shivering in one room through the roof of which the pitiless winds of winter whistled. The room was almost barren of furniture; the parents slept on the floor, the older children in boxes, and the baby was swung in an old shawl attached to the rafters by cords by way of a hammock. . . .

Perhaps this may be put down as an exceptional case, but one that came to my notice some months ago in a seventh ward tenement was typical enough to escape that reproach. There were nine in the family; husband, wife, an aged grandmother, and six children; honest, hard-working Germans, scrupulously neat, but poor.

All nine lived in two rooms, one about ten feet square that served as parlor, bedroom and eating room, the other a small hall-room made into a kitchen. The rent was seven dollars and a half a month, more than a week's wages for the husband and father.

A 1903 New York City report described a common tenement as consisting of "vile privies and vile sinks; foul cellars full of rubbish; . . . dilapidated and dangerous stairs; plumbing pipes containing large holes emitting sewer gas throughout the houses; rooms so dark that one cannot see the people in them; cellars occupied as sleeping places; . . . pigs, goats, horses, and other animals kept in cellars; dangerous old firetraps without fire escapes; . . . buildings without adequate water supply—the list might go on indefinitely."

Caked with filth, festering with disease, the working-class tenements killed hundreds of thousands of babies and made bleak homes for men, women, and children who trudged through garbage-filled streets to deathly jobs.

The cities themselves had become virtual Towers of Babel. The slow-moving peasant families spoke all the tongues and practiced all the religions of Europe. Huddled together in national or religious ghettoes, they faced an industrial world that was completely alien. Rootless, confused, unable to communicate with each other, grasping desperately at whatever Old World traditions could be saved, the new American working class lay at the disposal of the corporations and the mercy of the barons.

Many of the immigrants were brought over as contract labor, an arrangement that meant virtual slavery. Those lucky enough to find jobs on their own were also lucky to earn a subsistence wage. Children began work before they were ten. There were always men looking for jobs; those that had them were at the mercy of their employers.

When the national economy crashed in 1873, things actually got worse. As many as 3 million people lost their jobs. Ninety thousand worker families in New York were evicted and wandered the streets of the city.

Many of the railroads responded to the depression by cutting wages 10 percent. In early 1877, Tom Scott of the Pennsylvania cut still another 10 percent to help in his war with Rockefeller.

A delegation of workers protested. Scott explained that wages were only down 20 percent, while dividends had been cut twice that.

Somehow, the argument was unconvicing.

On July 17, at Martinsburg, West Virginia, workers on the Baltimore and Ohio met with most of the people of the town to block freight trains trying to move out of the rail yards. The local militia boarded a train and, with the help of two strikebreakers, started to take it out on the main line.

William Vandegriff, a striker, stood at a switch that would have thrown the train onto a sidetrack. As the locomotive approached he fired his pistol at a soldier. The soldier fired his rifle point-blank; Vandegriff was fatally wounded.

The sight of blood was enough for Martinsburg. The scab engineer and fireman jumped down and the train went back to the yards.

But the strike was on. In New York, the *Times* screamed for "complete and absolute supremacy of law"; the Martinsburg blockade was "a rash and spiteful demonstration of resentment by men too ignorant or too reckless to understand their own interests."

While the governor of West Virginia called for federal troops, the strike spread to Cumberland, Maryland, where eleven people were killed, and then to Baltimore. Depression had hit Baltimore extremely hard. In addition to the general unemployment, local canmakers, box-workers and garment-workers were on strike. The crowds that joined the rail-workers were immense and angry.

When the militia tried to keep townspeople from stopping trains, the people responded by stoning them. Fifteen thousand people surrounded the railway station and burned it. The militia opened fire, killing at least eleven—

When soldiers did fire directly on the mob, they did so in deadly earnest, as the vast preponderance of the dead over the wounded testifies. Almost every man shot was hit in either the chest or head, and nearly all wounds were fatal.

In Pittsburgh the local militia refused to fight the townspeople. Tom Scott's monopoly ruled the city, and the people, including the militia and the police, were united in their hatred of the Pennsylvania.

When the militia refused to fight, railroad vice-president Alexander Cassatt, ignoring the impassioned pleas of local businessmen, called for troops from Philadelphia. "We must have our property," he explained.

As the Philadelphia militia crossed the state their train was stoned by mobs at Harrisburg, Johnstown, and Altoona. There had been no violence in Pittsburgh until they arrived.

On July 21, a month after the Molly Maguire hangings, the Philadelphia militia established Gatling gun positions at the 28th Street rail crossing, where townspeople were blocking trains. Under a hail of rocks the troops opened fire, killing as many as twenty-five people.

The town went crazy. Mobs were everywhere. The militia fled to the central railyards, later charging that the Pittsburgh police had fired on them. Townspeople ignited freight cars and pushed them toward the depot, until finally it caught fire. The troops shot their way out, killing at least ten more people, and then escaped across the Monongahela River.

The townspeople proceeded to loot and burn all the railroad property they could lay their hands on, then all the monopoly-owned property in town, including an express company and a giant grain elevator. Mobs fought off firemen until the buildings were gutted. A reporter found "but one spirit and one purpose among them: That they were justified in resorting to any means to break down the power of corporations."

By the time things quieted down as many as fifty people were dead. It was, according to the Pittsburgh papers, the "Lexington of the Labor Conflict"—

There is tyranny in this country worse than anything ever known in Russia. . . . The principle that freed our nation from tyranny will free labor from domestic aggression. . . . The cowardice and imbecility of the railroad sharks, who sought to overawe all this community by imported bummers, met its proper rebuke.

Governor Hartranft raced back from his vacation in the West to enter the city with four federal troop trains and a Gatling gun mounted on the lead locomotive.

But the fighting in Pittsburgh was over. Now it exploded in the mines around Pittsburgh and Scranton, and among rail workers in Harrisburg, Allentown, and Philadelphia, in Columbus, Cleveland, Cincinnati, Toledo, and Newark, Ohio, and as far west as San Francisco. In St. Louis the well-organized Workingman's Party virtually controlled the city with a week-long general strike of black and white workers. In Chicago police systematically scattered worker rallies and fired on an unarmed crowd, killing eighteen people.

The size of the uprising and the speed with which it spread stunned the upper class. The baronial press rang the alarm—

[They have] declared war against society. . . . They have practically raised the standard of the Commune in free America. . . . Men who love order or have property to lose cannot afford to see with indifference the steady advances of communism in this country.

Baronial attempts to strengthen the federal Army were resisted by the public, but throughout the country state and local militias were expanded and given more guns and new armories, while the barons began building their private armies in earnest.

The Knights and the Trades

Organization within the working class dates back to the colonial era. It became a major force in the days of Jackson, when workingman's unions and political parties joined radical Democrats to fight the monopolies and national bank and to press for free land in the West.

After the Civil War, as the industrial revolution accelerated and the numbers of immigrants swelled, the American union movement felt the influences of revolutionary Marxism and European socialism.

As had the earlier depressions, the Crash of 1873 wiped out most of the previous gains in unionization. Millions of people looking for work allowed employers to hire and fire as they chose and to break strikes and unions almost at will.

But with the explosion of 1877 and the subsequent let-up in unemployment, the union movement grew radically.

The first strong national organization to emerge was the Holy Order of the Knights of Labor, which held its first national convention in 1878. The Knights met in secret with elaborate customs and rituals. Their slogan was "An injury to one is the concern of all!" and their program was the early urban counterpart of populism—government ownership of the rail, telephone, and telegraph systems, abolition of the militia and the use of Pinkertons, initiative and referendum, and a postal savings bank to replace the private banking system—

> Toiling millions now are working—
> See them marching on;
> All the tyrants now are shaking,
> Ere their power's gone.
> Storm the fort, ye Knights of Labor,
> Battle for your cause
> Equal rights for every neighbor—
> Down with tyrant laws!

Like most of the early unions, the Knights demanded an end to the wage system and the beginning of a cooperative society. Instead of employers hiring employees, industry would be owned and run by those who actually worked. "There is no good reason," wrote Knight president Terence V. Powderly, "why labor cannot, through cooperation, own and operate mines, factories, and railroads. . . . We are the willing victims of an outrageous system. . . . We should not war with men for being what we make them, but strike a powerful, telling blow at the base of the system which makes the laborer the slave of his master."

The Knight leadership opposed strikes as "private warfare," but by the mid-eighties the locals had left them behind. In 1885 Knight railworkers won a wage increase from Jay Gould by threatening to shut down his entire western system. The victory brought workers from all over the country into the organization, which jumped from 100,000 to 700,000 members from July 1885 to July 1886.

As the membership mushroomed, the union structure crumbled under the strain. The leadership remained moderate and abandoned the unskilled workers in preference for the trade unions.

Soon they were involved in a death-struggle with the young

American Federation of Labor for the loyalty of the skilled workers. The AF of L won. In the nineties the Knights' strength shifted to the West and became increasingly agrarian-oriented. By 1893 its membership had slipped to 75,000.

The AF of L

As the Knights faded away, a basic division within the labor movement took on critical importance. The division often expressed itself in conflict between Socialists and non-Socialists, and the critical question was whether to organize all workers together or to organize separately by crafts.

The schism had a definite economic basis. Although the vast majority of American workers were unskilled, a significant number were trade workers and, relative to the unskilled, were fairly well paid. They were identifiable as "a small but significant elite of laboring families who had gained a foothold in the lower fringes of the middle-class occupational world."

There was no significant mobility out of the working class— only a tiny number of workers ever escaped to become businessmen or professionals.

But those who were able to establish themselves at a trade were often able to get out of the ghetto and accumulate some property. Historian Stephan Thernstrom wrote:

Substantial saving by a working class family thus tended to be confined to the years when the children were old enough to bring in a supplementary income but too young to have married and established households of their own.

The tiny lots, the humble homes, and the painfully accumulated savings accounts were the fruits of those years. They gave a man dignity, and a slender margin of security against unpredictable, uncontrollable economic forces which could deprive him of his job at any time. . . .

Families belonging to the propertied stratum of the working class . . . had climbed a rung higher on the social ladder and had established themselves as decent, respectable, hard-working, church-going members of the community.

Through the trade unions the skilled elite began to separate themselves from the rest of the working class. Their leader was Samuel Gompers.

Gompers was born in England, then lived in the Jewish ghetto of New York. He supported his family first as a cigar maker, then as an organizer.

In the early days the lot of even the skilled worker and trade organizer was pretty rough. Gompers once had to physically force a doctor to aid in the difficult birth of one of his six children because he could not pay the fee—

Sometimes black despair almost daunted us. We struggled on in our efforts at organization, but we saw little encouragement in the future. Our thoughts were hard for anyone to understand who has not been caught in a situation that holds one powerless, tormented by unsatisfied desires, longings, ambitions.

Gompers' chief associate, Adolph Strasser, had been a Socialist, and throughout his career Gompers made sweeping attacks on the American ruling establishment.

But very early in his career Gompers rejected both radicalism and formal socialism. His mind was made up in 1874. Mid-depression worker demonstrations had led to a mass rally at Tompkins Square Park on January 13. The rally was peaceful until

Without a word of warning they [the police] swept down the defenseless workers, striking down the standard-bearer and using their clubs right and left indiscriminately on the heads of all they could reach.

Shortly afterwards the mounted police charged the crowd on Eighth Street riding them down and attacking men, women and children without discrimination. It was an orgy of brutality. I was caught in the crowd on the street and barely saved my head from being cracked by jumping down a cellarway.

The attacks of the police kept up all day long—wherever the police saw a group of poorly dressed persons standing or moving together.

The police attack had a profound affect on Gompers. While radicals saw it as an illustration of the need to break with the system, Gompers interpreted it the other way around. "I was in no way connected with the arrangement of this demonstration," he said. "I saw how professions of radicalism and sensationalism concentrated all the forces of organized society against the labor movement and nullified in advance normal, necessity activity."

Gompers' stiffest fight for control of the AF of L were with the Socialist faction. Federation membership jumped from 150,000 in 1886 to over a million after 1900, and as the organization grew more powerful, it and Gompers grew more conservative, endorsing the basic structure of the capitalist and wage system—

We are living under the wage system, and so long as that lasts, it is our purpose to secure a continually larger share for labor. . . .

It is our duty to live our lives as workers in the society in which we live, and not to work for the downfall or the destruction or the overthrow of that society, but for its fuller development and evolution.

Within the short terms of the struggle the men of the trade unions saw the road to a better society through improved working conditions, shorter hours, and better pay. Through them, society itself would be gradually uplifted.

But Gompers' "pure and simple" trade unionism was rough on the unskilled workers. The AF of L time and again refused to support the strikes of unaffiliated unions, often, in fact, helping to break them. The "privilege" of skilled labor was jealously guarded. Union dues were set high, and blacks, women, and new immigrants were barred, which often kept them from getting jobs.

Gompers was the only major labor leader who didn't endorse Bryan in 1896. By 1904 he was serving as temporary president of the National Civic Federation, the powerful, conservative organization of major barons and professionals whose first president had been Mark Hanna. As the "business organization of the wage-

The Endless Chain

Source: One Big Union Monthy

earner" the AF of L began to develop Tammany-like locals that followed the standard procedures of American economic life.

Labor leaders in San Francisco, as elsewhere, were go-getters of the first order, motivated by the same psychology as the directors of great trusts and corporations. They demanded high wages for labor and graft for themselves, and, holding an advantageous position, managed to get both.

The membership of the trade unions was limited and corresponded to the body of stockholders in a capitalist "racket." . . . They laughed at naive Socialists who were conducting class in economics, educating labor groups. . . .

They had small concern for the "laboring stiffs" outside the unions; there were thousands of workmen in San Francisco who could not join unions, and therefore could get no work, because of prohibitive intiation fees.

The left wing, in turn, fought Gompers and the conservative faction in the AF of L with a bitterness that intensified each year. Radicals like Joe Ettor accused the trade unions of dividing the working class and undercutting its strength by destroying its unity and selling-out to the bosses—

The most unscrupulous labor fakers now betraying the workers were once our "industrialist," "anarchist," and "socialist" comrades, who grew weary of the slow progress we were making on the outside, went over, and were not only lost, but . . . became the greatest supporters of the old and [the] most serious enemies of the new.

The Birth of Ideology

In 1886 the call went out for a nationwide general strike to win the eight-hour day. On May Day some 200,000 workers across the country walked off their jobs.

Two days later police killed as many as four strikers at the

McCormick Reaper factory in Chicago. The strike at McCormick had been going on since February, when the company locked out its 1,400 employees in a struggle over the right of the workers to a union.

The killing fit the standard pattern of political violence at the factories. Union men confronted strikebreakers. Police appeared on behalf of the factory owners, after which serious violence erupted.

More often than not violence to human life arrived with the police. The overwhelming majority of casualties in the battles of American labor have been workers killed or wounded by police or soldiers.

The Chicago working community in 1886 was in large part made up of German immigrants and led by revolutionary anarchists. On May Day some 60,000 Chicago workers had walked off their jobs for the eight-hour day. The McCormick killing infuriated the labor movement. August Spies, editor of the anarchist *Die Arbeiter Zeitung*, issued a call to arms. On May 4 he and other labor leaders addressed a public meeting at Haymarket Square on the west side of town. About 1200 people showed up, including Mayor Carter H. Harrison.

After a few hours a light rain began to fall, and most of the crowd, including the mayor, left. The mayor walked to a nearby police station and told the captains there would be no trouble and that the special force held in the station could be dismissed. Then he went home.

The meeting at Haymarket had dwindled to about a third its original size as the last speaker was finishing up. Suddenly the two captains arrived with 180 policemen and ordered the crowd to disperse, which it started to do.

Then, without warning, a bomb flew through the air and exploded in front of the police ranks. One policeman was killed, seventy injured, of whom six more would die.

The police immediately regrouped and opened fire on the

fleeing crowd, killing at least one and wounding at least twelve. The newspapers screamed murder—someone had killed a police-man—"NOW IT IS BLOOD!"

Wild stories of the number of bombs thrown and who threw them splattered the front pages of the national media. It was the work of "long-haired, wild-eyed, bad-smelling, atheistic, reckless foreign wretches," and they would have to pay.

Eight anarchists were rounded up and charged with murder while the Chicago police engineered the nation's first modern red scare. Captain Michael J. Schaack was in charge. Homes were ransacked; suspected radicals arrested; meetings broken up; con-spiracies bared. Chicago was in a state of official terror. Police Chief John Ebersold was amazed.

I have often wondered whether [Schaack's] delusions resulted from a kind of self-hypnotism or from mere mania; but certainly he saw more anarchists than vast hell could hold. Bombs, dynamite, daggers, and pistols seemed ever before him.

Finally, Chief Ebersold tried to stop it—

He wanted bombs to be found here, there, all around, everywhere. I thought people would lie down to sleep better if they were not afraid their homes would be blown to pieces any minute. . . . After we got the anarchist societies broken up, Schaack wanted to send out men to organize new societies right away. You see what this would do. He wanted to keep the pot boiling, keep himself prominent before the public.

The Haymarket affair shattered the general strike. Gompers and Powderly fell over each other denouncing radicalism. "I hate Anarchy and I hate Anarchists," said Powderly.

All eight men picked up on the murder charges were convicted —one for throwing the bomb, the other seven as "accessories" to the "conspiracy." "Even if they had not opened their lips on Tuesday night," charged a Chicago paper, "their very presence, with all their well-known and destructive views, would have been an invitation to the mob . . . to commit acts of lawlessness."

Seven of the eight men were sentenced to death. Four were hung, and another committed suicide in prison. The trial had been such a mockery that a movement to free the men grew up as soon as they were convicted. The Chicago Knights of Labor, who originally denounced the anarchists, proposed a plaque at Haymarket condemning the police for "brutality and unheard-of infamy." "Human beings," they said, "have been imprisoned and hanged on evidence furnished by a police system which is the most corrupt and vicious the country has ever known." In 1893 a Populist-labor alliance elected John Altgeld governor of Illinois. In the face of a storm of right-wing protest Altgeld freed the remaining three prisoners.

THE BLOODY NINETIES

By the late eighties and early nineties political violence at the mines, factories, and on the railroads had become a daily occurrence.

In 1887 blacks in Louisiana sugar fields formed a Knights of Labor local which was soon joined by many whites. In October they demanded a standard wage of $1 cash a day (their average pay was $13 a month, in scrip), and early in the month 10,000 workers walked out on strike. The plantation owners brought in the militia who joined vigilante groups in the general slaughter. By the end of the year forty men were dead and the strike was broken.

Sporadic fighting raged through the eighties in the coal mines of Tennessee, where mine owners used convicts leased from the state to break the strikes. In 1891 miners at Briceville burned the prison stockades that had been built at the mines and set the convicts free. Open war spread to coal regions throughout the state, culminating in a major battle at Tracy City in 1892. The following year a Populist-labor legislative alliance abolished the convict-lease system.

While fighting went on in Tennessee, the Amalgamated Association of Iron & Steel workers, an AF of L affiliate, struck Andrew Carnegie's plant at Homestead, near Pittsburgh. Carnegie prided himself on his relations with the workers in his factories, claiming "the reward that comes from feeling that you and your employees are friends. . . . I believe that higher wages to men who respect their employers and are happy and content is a good investment, yielding, indeed, big dividends."

When a struggle developed over wages and union recognition, Carnegie promptly sailed to his castle in Scotland, leaving Henry Frick, the plant manager, in charge of crushing the strike.

Frick prepared to bring in scabs. He ordered a three-mile-long wooden wall topped with barbed wire built around the factory. The wall had shoulder-level holes "for observation purposes." The union claimed the holes were for rifles.

At 4:00 A.M. on July 6, two barges carrying 300 Pinkerton gunmen were towed up the Monongahela River toward the Homestead plant. As the barges approached, the company beach strikers tore a hole in the wall and met the Pinkertons as they attempted to land.

A twelve-hour gun battle ensued. The strikers poured oil into the river and set it afire, threw dynamite, and pushed a rail car into the water in a vain attempt to sink the barges. Three Pinkertons and at least ten workers were killed.

Finally, late in the afternoon, the Pinkertons raised a white flag and surrendered. Only the impassioned speeches of a few strikers saved them from being massacred, and many were beaten by strikers' families as they were marched out of the barges.

Frick then called in 8000 state militiamen, had Homestead put under martial law, and evicted many of the striking families from their homes. Strike leaders were indicted for murder and conspiracy and thirty-three of them were charged with treason against the commonwealth of Pennsylvania. The plant was opened with scabs, and the strike and the union fell apart. Only 800 of the original 4000 strikers were able to get their jobs back.

In the course of the strike an anarchist named Alexander Berkman shot Frick, but he survived. "We had to teach our employees a lesson," said Frick, "and we have taught them one that they will never forget." Carnegie, now touring the Continent, wired "Congratulations all around—life worth living again—how pretty Italia."

Shortly after the Homestead strike, forty-two New Orleans locals joined in a general strike for a ten-hour day, overtime pay, and the preferential closed shop. Coordinated by the democratically elected, black-white Workingmen's Amalgamated Council, the strike involved 20,000 workers and their families and brought the economic life of the city to a virtual standstill.

There was no violence, but on the third day of the strike the governor declared martial law and implied that he would call in the militia unless the workers called it off. The Council then accepted a compromise decision that raised wages and shortened hours but did not include collective bargaining or the closed shop.

Meanwhile, another strike was being broken at the silver mines of Coeur d'Alene, Idaho. Aside from miserable pay and long hours, the miners there were forced to work extensively with arsenic which, said organizer "Mother" Mary Jones, "paralyzes arms and legs"—

It causes the teeth to fall out, the hair to fall off. Weird-looking men worked in the mines: gaunt, their faces sunken in, their eyelashes and eyebrows off, a green aspect to their skin.

Striking miners blew up a quartz mill, drove out strikebreakers and took possession of the mines. The governor then declared martial law and brought in federal troops. Through the weeks of violence some twenty-five people were killed. All the union men in the area were arrested and several hundred were held in a barbed-wire concentration camp for months.

PULLMAN

The following year, 1893, the national economy fell apart. Joblessness and abject poverty among the farming and working classes reached catastrophic proportions.

In early summer 1894, workers at the Pullman Palace Car Company touched off the Second Great Railway Strike.

The' Pullman factory-model city complex had been built by the company in the early eighties as an experiment in labor relations. George Pullman explained the arrangement as "simplicity itself—we are landlord and employers."

Located on Lake Calumet, nine miles south of Chicago, Pullman was billed as "the first all-brick city," a place where "everything fits." The stores, churches, houses, and public library (which charged $3 a year) were all owned by the company. "With such surroundings and such human regard for the needs of the body as well as the soul," explained Pullman, "the disturbing conditions of strikes and other troubles that periodically convulse the world of labor would not be found here." "The building of Pullman," said a company official, "is very likely to be the beginning of a new era for labor."

By 1893 the town had over 12,000 residents. Pullman ran the government, collected the rents and utilities payments, and employed "spotters" to check on the employees. "The company owns everything," wrote a reporter from the Cleveland *Post*, "and it exercises a surveillance over the movements and habits of the people in a way to lead one to suppose that it has a proprietary interest in [their] soul and bodies."

With the Crash of 1893, Pullman began lowering wages and laying off workers. Rents stayed the same. In May 1894 a committee of workers asked Pullman to discuss their grievances; he refused to consider wage increases or rent reductions and then fired three members of the grievance committee.

Pullman workers affiliated with the American Railway Union

(ARU) took their grievances to the union convention in Chicago the next month. The ARU sent a delegation to Pullman, who told them "there is nothing to arbitrate." One June 27 the union, 150,000 strong, declared a boycott on all Pullman cars. The strike was on.

Rail workers began detaching Pullmans and stopping trains that still included them. The owners agreed to fire all workers who participated in the boycott and brought scabs down from Canada.

But the strike spread out of control. Led by ARU President Eugene Debs, the boycott was effective throughout the country and the Chicago railway system was paralyzed.

The owners were stunned. "We can handle the railway brotherhoods," said the chairman of the Chicago Managers' Association, "but we cannot handle the ARU. We cannot handle Debs. We have got to wipe him out."

On July 2 the managers got an omnibus injunction against Debs and the rest of the strike leadership for conspiring to violate the Sherman Anti-Trust Act, the first time the act had been enforced. Judge Peter Grosscup ruled that the union was acting "in restraint of trade." His injunction made it illegal for the strike leaders to telegraph, write, or speak any support for the Pullman boycott.

Attorney General Richard Olney justified the injunction on the grounds that the union was stopping mail delivery. He argued that although they were not publicly owned, the railroads were public highways; the strike, therefore, was a "public nuisance." "I feel," he said, "that the true way of dealing with the matter is by force which is overwhelming and prevents any attempt at resistance."

The union offered to furnish men to run mail trains. They were not stopping mail cars, they argued, only Pullmans—it was the managers who were stopping the mail by refusing to allow Pullmans to be detached from the trains.

President Cleveland decided the owners were right. "If it

SOLDIERS FIRING INTO THE MOB AT FOR Y-NINTH STREET.

takes every dollar in the treasury and every soldier in the United States Army to deliver a postal card to Chicago," he vowed, "that postal card shall be delivered."

On July 4, Cleveland ordered General Nelson Miles (*the butcher of Wounded Knee*) and four companies of federal infantry into Chicago. As the soldiers arrived, sporadic violence turned into general warfare. Strikers burned hundreds of freight cars, destroyed railyards, and burned to the ground much of the 1893 World Exposition.

By July 6, Chicago was an armed camp ruled by 14,000 local, state, and federal troops. Some 2600 of the troops were special "marshals," local labor spies, and gangsters described by the Chicago police as "thugs, thieves and exconvicts." One of them, who was identified but not prosecuted, wounded a bystander and then walked to where he was lying on the ground and shot him dead. The police chief of Chicago charged that "innocent men and women were killed" by the marshals. "Several of these officials were arrested during the strike for stealing property from railroad cars," he said. "In one instance, two of them were found under suspicious circumstances near a freight car which had just been set on fire."

On July 7 a crowd stoned a national guard contingent which was protecting a wrecking car. An officer ordered the troops to open fire—

There seemed to be no alternative left to the commanding officer except to order his men to fire at will and to make every shot count.

The strike was now in chaos and near collapse. The governor of Michigan called out the militia; killing spread to the areas around Chicago, to Hammond, Indiana, and Spring Valley, Illinois—

Men have been arrested in Chicago because they refused to turn switches when told to; they were arrested when they refused to get on an engine and fire an engine; . . . in Albuquerque, New Mexico, they arrested a man and he was sentenced to fifteen days in jail because he refused to get on an engine and fire it when told; the fact that he did not get on the engine was considered contempt of court.

Debs, who had urged nonviolence throughout the strike, defied the omnibus injunction and called for a nationwide general strike. But it was a move of desperation. The AF of L refused to support the ARU, and Gompers later turned down Debs' request to intercede with the managers.

On July 10, Debs was arrested for contempt of court and his books, personal papers, and unopened mail were confiscated. By July 19, twenty-five people had been killed and the strike starved out. Federal troops left Chicago. The government, said Olney, had "done its best to hold an entirely even hand as between the strikers on one hand and capital on the other."

Farmers and workers across the country let out a cry of outrage against "government by injunction." Tom Watson charged that "if Grover Cleveland possesses lawfully the power he has exercised, then the only difference between our president and a European emperor, king, or czar consists merely in the name." Before being taken to jail, Debs, who had campaigned three times for Cleveland, told a crowd that "I am a Populist and I favor wiping out both old parties as they will never come into power again. I have been a Democrat all my life and I am ashamed to admit it."

Debs was defended on the conspiracy charge by Clarence Darrow, a young Chicago lawyer. "Conspiracy," Darrow told the court, "from the days of tyranny in England down to the day the General Managers' Association used it as a club, has been the favorite weapon of every tyrant. It is an effort to punish the crime of thought."

The government couldn't prove conspiracy but stuck Debs with six months anyway—for contempt. He was jailed at Woodstock, Illinois, where he underwent some basic changes.

AMERICAN SOCIALISM

Debs was born in Terre Haute to French immigrant parents. His mother and father were followers of the French romantic tradition, and from his childhood Debs was influenced by the revolutionary school of Hugo, Voltaire, and Rousseau.

Debs' roots, however, were deep in the Midwest where he grew up and lived all his life. He went to work on the railroads at fourteen. At nineteen he started supporting himself with various jobs around Terre Haute while working for the local chapter of the Brotherhood of Locomotive Fireman.

In 1877 he denounced the Great Railway Strike in terms that brought warm praise from a local railroad president. The Brotherhood policy was one of "ignoring strikes," and Debs attacked those who believed in "a necessary conflict between labor and capital" as either "very shallow thinkers, or else very great demagogues."

But the repression that followed 1877—the use of labor spies, blacklisting and the ever-present Pinkertons—weighed heavily on the labor movement. In 1885 the Brotherhood renounced its no-strike policy. Through the late eighties, while Gompers was tying craft unions into loose confederation, Debs was organizing the railroad trades into an industry-wide union that would admit all rail workers and bargain with the owners as a unit.

In 1893 the American Railway Union was born. Early the following year Debs led a successful action against James J. Hill and the Great Northern. ARU membership soared to 150,000.

But the Pullman massacre destroyed the union in a stroke: the treasury was cleaned out, the leadership jailed, and the membership blacklisted. In 1895 Debs found himself spending long hours in the Woodstock jail reading and discussing economic and political theory. Correspondence and visitors poured in from all sects of the left wing.

During the months at Woodstock, Debs had his first important contact with formal socialism, most notably through a visit from Victor Berger of Milwaukee. Slowly he crept toward a renunciation of the ruling American ethic.

Now the best-known radical labor leader in the country, Debs might have carried the Populist nomination in 1896 had he been willing to campaign for it. Instead, he backed Bryan,

not because I regarded the free coinage of silver as a panacea for our national ills; for I neither affirmed nor advocated such a principle, but because I believed that the triumph of Mr. Bryan and free silver would blunt the fangs of the money power. . . . The free silver issue gave us, not only a rallying cry, but afforded common ground upon which the common people could unite against the trusts, syndicates, corporations, monopolies—in a word, the money power.

But the money power proved unbeatable. The victory of the Republican machine and the ensuing destruction of populism forced Debs over the line. The reform issues had been transcended; it would have to be revolution. On January 1, 1897, he published a personal manifesto in the *Railway Times*—

The issue is Socialism versus Capitalism. I am for Socialism because I am for humanity. We have been cursed with the reign of gold long enough. Money constitutes no proper basis of civilization. The time has come to regenerate society—we are on the eve of a universal change.

The first solid bridge between European socialism and the mainstream of the American working class had been formed. The socialism of the early unions had been real enough, but its roots were still very definitely in Europe and its chief proponents were intellectuals. Innumerable factions and splinter groups bickered endlessly over the "proper line," looking down their noses at the Populist farmers and other heretics as if somehow "revolutionary activity consisted in enunciating formulas."

For Debs, socialism was a simple reality. "Our conduct is largely determined by our economic relations," he said. "If you and I must fight each other to exist, we will not love each other very hard."

There could be no compromise with reform. The basic premises were wrong, the system was rotten at its core, and it would have to be done away with whole—

Every hint at public ownership is now called Socialism, without reference to the fact that there can be no Socialism, and that public ownership means practically nothing, so long as the capitalist class is in control of the national government. Government ownership of public utilities means nothing for labor under capitalist ownership of government.

Debs' ideology and his conduct through the next three decades as leader of the American Socialist movement reflected a deep distrust of centralized power in any form. He and the libertarian Socialists that followed him rejected the traditional Marxist call for a dictatorship of the proletariat. Debs was "opposed and strongly opposed to dictatorship, regardless of the class by which it is produced."

Common ownership of the economy and popular control of the government would result in social democracy. The competitive system would give way to the cooperative commonwealth. Social classes would be abolished and a new culture, a new way of life, "the earth for all the people, . . . the beginning of MAN would come at last."

If I rise, it will be WITH the ranks, not FROM them. I do this because it pleases me. . . . When I see suffering about me, I myself suffer, and so when I put forth my efforts to relieve others I am simply working for myself. . . . When the bread and butter problem is solved and all men and women and children the world around are rendered secure from the dread of war and fear of want, then the mind and soul will be free to develop as they never were before.

We shall have a literature and an art such as the troubled heart and brain of man never before conceived. . . .

We shall have beautiful thoughts and sentiments, and a divinity in religion, such as man weighted down by the machine could never have imagined.

In 1898 the Socialist Labor party had amassed 82,000 votes in various local elections. But the party was prone to verbosity and in-fighting, and in 1900 a dissident faction joined with Debs' Social Democratic party. Debs and Job Harriman drew 96,000 votes, and in 1901 most of the major Socialist factions united behind Debs to form the Socialist Party of America. "Socialism is coming," wrote Julius Wayland in the *Appeal to Reason*. "It's coming like a prairie fire and nothing can stop it. . . . You can feel it in the air. You can see it in the papers. You can taste it in the price of beef. . . . The next few years will give this nation to the Socialist party."

By 1912 Debs' electoral strength had multiplied ten times, to 960,000 in the midst of a movement deeply divided over the validity of voting at all. The platforms of those years spelled out the basic tenets of American socialism—

Human life depends upon food, clothing, and shelter. Only with these assured are freedom, culture, and higher human development possible.

To produce food, clothing, or shelter, land and machinery are needed. Land alone does not satisfy human needs. Human labor creates machinery and applies it to the land for the production of raw materials and food.

Whoever has control of land and machinery controls human labor, and with it human life and liberty.

Today the machinery and the land used for industrial purposes are owned by a rapidly decreasing minority. . . .

In spite of the organization of trusts, pools, and combinations, the capitalists are powerless to regulate production for social ends. Industries are largely conducted in a planless manner. Through periods of feverish activity the strength and health of the workers are mercilessly used up, and during the periods of enforced idleness the workers are frequently reduced to starvation.

The climaxes of this system of production are the regularly recurring industrial depressions and crises which paralyze the nation every fifteen or twenty years. . . .

To maintain their rule over their fellow men the capitalists must keep in their pay all organs of the public powers, public mind, and public conscience. They control the dominant parties and, through them, the elected public officials. They select the executives, bribe legislatures, and corrupt the courts of justice. They own and censor the press. They dominate the educational institutions. They own the nation politically and intellectually just as they own it industrially.

(1908)

Our political institutions are also being used as the destroyers of that individual property upon which all liberty and opportunity depend.

The promise of economic independence to each man was one of the faiths upon which our institutions were founded. But, under the guise of defending private property, capitalism is using our political institutions to make it impossible for the vast majority of human beings ever to become possessors of private property in the means of life.

Capitalism is the enemy and destroyer of essential private property. Its development is through the legalized confiscation of all that the labor of the working class produces, above its subsistence wage.

The private ownership of the means of employment grounds society in an economic slavery which renders intellectual and political tyranny inevitable.

Socialism comes so to organize industry and society that every individual shall be secure in that private property in the means of life upon which his liberty of being, thought and action depend. . . .

(1904)

The Socialist Party . . . proposes that, since all social necessities today are socially produced, the means of their production and distribution shall be socially owned and democratically controlled. . . . We advocate . . . the collective ownership and democratic management of railroads, wire and wireless telegraphs and telephones, express service, steamboat lines, and all other social means of transportation and communication and of all large-scale industries.

The immediate acquirement by the municipalities, the states or the federal government of all grain elevators, stock yards, storage warehouses, and other distributing agencies, in order to reduce the present extortionate cost of living.

The extension of the public domain to include mines, quarries, oil wells, forests, and the water power.

The further conservation and development of natural resources for the use and benefit of all the people. . . .

The collective ownership of land wherever practicable, and in cases where such ownership is impracticable, the appropriation by taxation of the annual rental value of all land held for speculation or exploitation.

The collective ownership and democratic management of the banking and currency system.

Political Demands:

The absolute freedom of press, speech, and assemblage.

The adoption of a graduated income tax, the increase of the rates of the present corporation tax, and the extension of inheritance taxes. . . .

The abolition of the monopoly ownership of patents and the substitution of collective ownership, with direct rewards to inventors by premiums or royalties.

Unrestricted and equal suffrage for men and women.

The adoption of the initiative, referendum, and recall and of proportional representation, nationally as well as locally.

The abolition of the Senate and of the veto power of the president.

The election of the president and vice-president by direct vote of the people.

The abolition of the power usurped by the Supreme Court of the United States to pass upon the constitutionality of the legislation enacted by Congress. National laws to be repealed only by act of Congress or by a referendum vote of the whole people.

Abolition of the present restrictions upon the amendment of the constitution, so that instrument may be made amendable by a majority of the voters in a majority of the States. . . .

The extension of democratic government to all United States territory. . . .

The immediate curbing of the power of the courts to issue injunctions.

The free administration of the law.

The calling of a convention for the revision of the constitution of the United States.   (1912)

Equal civic and political rights for men and women, and the abolition of all laws discriminating against women. . . .

Abolition of war and the introduction of international arbitration.
(1900)

Debs ran vigorously on the Socialist platform in four consecutive campaigns. "He never felt fear," said Clarence Darrow. "He had the courage of the babe who has no conception of the word or its meaning."

With his roots deep in the soul of the country, Debs became to the working class what Watson and Bryan had been to the farmers, and perhaps more—

The picture of Gene was on their walls alongside those of Sir Moses Montefiore, the Rabbi of Libawich, "Goan of Vilna" and other heroes of these immigrants. For them Debs was the liberator, the first who had come to them from the ranks of American workers, holding out his hands and saying "I am your brother." They had respect and admiration for radicals of their own race. But they worshipped Debs.

Touring the country in the "Red Special" campaign train, the "American saint" was greeted by packed houses and enthusiastic crowds wherever he spoke. When he visited the big cities the streets were lined with red flags—

> I'll vote for Debs, for the Faith I have
> That we'll reach the promised land;
> A joyous vote and a splendid vote,
> And a clasp of a comrade's hand
> I'll vote for Debs for the Hope I have
> That shall flood the world with its light!
> And I must answer the call I hear
> That the working class unite!

By 1912 the Socialist party had more than 100,000 dues-paying members and had elected the mayor in Milwaukee and in some

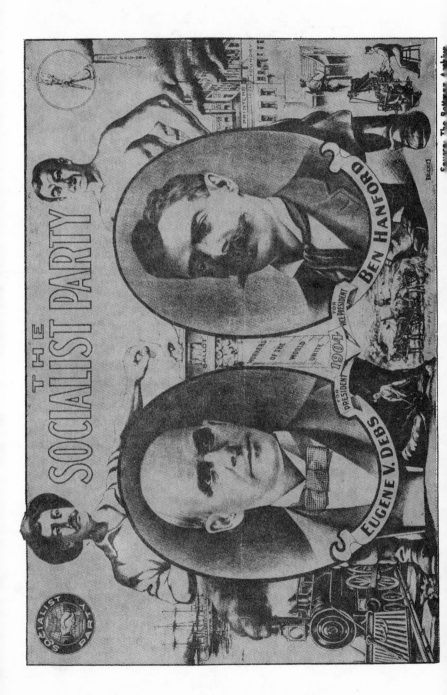

THE SOCIALIST PARTY

EUGENE V. DEBS
FOR PRESIDENT

BEN HANFORD
FOR VICE PRESIDENT

WORKINGMEN OF THE WORLD UNITE

BALLOT 1904

eighty other cities and towns, plus 1,200 local officials and state representatives throughout the country. In 1916 the first Socialist congressman was sent to Washington. There were eight Socialist daily newspapers and more than 300 smaller periodicals. The three biggest—the *Appeal to Reason, National Rip Saw,* and *Jewish Daily Forward*—accounted for a circulation of over a million.

Socialist campaigns in many localities had forced the Democratic and Republican machines to merge. "The growth of the socialistic party," wrote Roosevelt, "[is] far more ominous than any populist or similar movement in times past." A Harvard historian warned in 1912 that "a large minority of the American people, which is likely soon to be a majority, feels dissatisfied and resentful and is bound to make things different. Unless that movement is checked, within sixteen years there will be a Socialist president of the United States."

Class War

In 1897, 100,000 miners in Pennsylvania, Ohio, Indiana, Illinois, Kentucky, and Tennessee responded to a strike call from the United Mine Workers, an AF of L affiliate. The response startled both owners and union leaders and completely paralyzed mining operations in those states. In 1898 the UMW led 100,000 Pennsylvania anthracite miners on strike. It was the beginning of a long struggle for higher wages and union recognition.

Over the next few years John Mitchell, the young president of the UMW and a close associate of Gompers,' negotiated with J. P. Morgan through President Theodore Roosevelt. Morgan was ready to grant higher wages but not union recognition. Radicals urged rejection of the compromise: "Tell Roosevelt to go to hell," yelled organizer "Mother" Mary Jones.

Mitchell replied that "It would not do to tell the President that," and accepted the wage increase while agreeing to label the union negotiator "an eminent sociologist" because the mine owners refused to deal directly with a "union man."

In 1899 the long struggle in the Idaho mines erupted again at Coeur d'Alene when the mill of the Bunker Hill Company was blown up. Governor Frank Steunenberg, who had been elected with Populist-labor support, called McKinley for federal troops to beat back the "insurrection and rebellion."

McKinley ordered up several companies of black militia from Brownsville, Texas, even though regiments of white soldiers were stationed closer by. Bill Haywood of the Western Federation of Miners (WFM) accused McKinley of calling in black troops specifically to create racial tension—

We always believed that the government officials thought it would further incite the miners if black soldiers were placed as guards over white prisoners.

Miners and their families were herded into "bullpens," after which the officers in charge continued to play black against white in "a deliberate attempt to add race prejudice to the situation."

Coeur d'Alene threw into tragic relief the plague of racism in the working class. Time and again the wage system played black, Oriental, and white (as well as native and immigrant) off one against the other.

In the West, Chinese coolies were paid slave wages to build the railroads, driving down the pay of native whites and bringing on intense, violent anti-Oriental riots all over California and the West.

Throughout the rest of the country the barons time and again shuttled trainloads of blacks from destitute rural areas into mines and factories for use as strikebreakers. When blacks abandoned the South and began arriving in northern cities at the turn of the century, the conflict worsened. To white workers the blacks were competition that would drive down wages. "The Caucasians," vowed Gompers in 1905, "are not going to let their standard of living be destroyed by negroes, Chinese, Japs, or any others."

In turn the blacks saw the white workers as violent antagonists who shut the doors to the unions. As at Coeur d'Alene, the barons and the government often took full advantage of the conflict. The result was a vicious circle of violent mistrust that has thoroughly crippled American society.

In May 1901 a local of the WFM struck the gold and silver mines at Telluride, Colorado. After a month the Smuggler-Union management brought in armed and deputized strikebreakers.

On July 3 the strikers ambushed the "deputies" and after a few hours battle took the upper hand. In return for safe exit the workers took control of the mines. A commission reported to the governor a few days later that "everything is quiet in Telluride; the mines are in peaceful possession of the miners."

By this time unions throughout the country had been infiltrated with company-paid labor spies. A reporter interviewing striking steelworkers in 1901 complained that friendly workers clammed up as soon as talk turned to the unions. A Vandergrift man wrote anonymously in the *National Labor Tribune* of Pittsburgh that "a man must not think loud here, as even the trees have ears. When any two or more men get together, since the sheet workers went on strike, there is sure to be some Judas . . . not far off. . . . The men dare not trust one another."

"If you want to talk in Homestead," the saying went, "talk to yourself."

In 1902 a UMW strike of 16,000 West Virginia miners was broken by state militia. The following year a local of the WFM struck the mines at Cripple Creek, Colorado. Governor James Peabody, a banker, ordered up the Denver militia, which took over the city hall of Victor, enforced military censorship on the local newspaper, and arrested its editor and most of the staff in addition to a few local elected officials. Union men were picked off the streets for "vagrancy," held incommunicado in bullpens, and forced onto chain gangs. Meanwhile the Citizens' Alliance, a vigilante group organized by the mine owners, terrorized the strikers' families.

When some union men were brought to trial, the militia surrounded the courthouse and established a Gatling gun emplacement in the street. Businesses that sold provisions to the strikers were blown away—

Shop keepers were forbidden to sell to miners. Priests and ministers were intimidated, fearing to give them consolation. The miners opened their own stores to feed the women and children. The soldiers and hoodlums broke into the stores, looted them, broke open the safes, destroyed the scales, ripped open the sacks of flour and sugar, dumped them on the floor, and poured kerosene oil over everything. The beef and meat was poisoned by the militia. Goods were stolen. The miners were without redress, for the militia was immune.

In the midst of the fighting the Vindicator mine was blown up and two men were killed. The WFM, now 250,000 strong, called for support. The strike spread over the state. The governor extended martial law, and a general vagrancy order was issued subjecting strikers to forcible deportation.

In June 1904 a train bringing in strikebreakers was blown up. Two hundred twenty-five miners were deported to Kansas and New Mexico. Relief supplies were seized by the militia. By July the strike was broken.

At about the same time a year-long UMW strike against Rockefeller's Colorado Fuel and Iron Company was broken by similar methods.

THE WOBBLIES

In the face of class war many radicals and Socialists demanded a revolutionary union.

The votes cast for Debs and local Socialist candidates only loosely reflected the strength of the movement for social democracy. On the one hand, many of the men who ran on the Socialist ticket, particularly in the East, were both wealthy and conservative. They often became more so after they were elected.

But on the other hand were the millions of farmers and workers who may or may not have subscribed to socialism, but who at any rate never considered voting worth the bother and never would. Even in 1912, one of the most hard-fought elections in American history, a nation of around 100 million cast only 14 million votes (including graveyards, repeats, and other ballot-stuffs).

Furthermore, many Socialists felt that when they did elect a president, that would be the exact moment of a military-capitalist *coup d'état* abolishing the electoral process. There was deep scorn for the "visionary politician" who imagined that "through some mystic alchemy the ballot will terminate capitalism and the socialist commonwealth will rise like a fairy out of the ballot box."

The revolution, even if it could be won with the ballot, would have to be backed up by an industrial army. A unified industrial union would offer a solid alternative to the AF of L and would provide the muscle of the revolution.

In 1905 some 200 Socialist and radical labor leaders met in Chicago. The conference was attended by Debs, Daniel DeLeon of the Socialist Labor party, Charles Sherman of the United Metal Workers, Mother Jones, William Trautmann of the United Brewery Workers, Bill Haywood, and Charles Moyer of the WFM.

Haywood, a massive ex-homesteader and cowboy who had lost an eye in a mining accident, rapped a loose board on a table. "Fellow workers," he said, "this is the Continental Congress of the Working Class." The Industrial Workers of the World was born. "The working class and the employing class," declared the Preamble, "have nothing in common"—

There can be no peace so long as hunger and want are found among millions of working people and the few, who make up the employing class, have all the good things of life.

Between these two classes a struggle must go on until all the toilers come together on the political, as well as on the industrial field, and take and hold that which they produce by their labor, through an economic organization of the working class without affiliation with any political party.

The rapid gathering of wealth and the centering of the management of industries into fewer and fewer hands make the trades unions unable to cope with the ever-growing power of the employing class, because the trades unions foster a state of things which allows one set of workers to be pitted against another set of workers in the same industry, thereby helping defeat one another in wage wars.

The trades unions aid the employing class to mislead the workers into the belief that the working class have interests in common with their employers. These sad conditions can be changed and the interests of working class upheld only by an organization formed in such a way that all its members in any one industry, or in all industries, if necessary, cease work whenever a strike or lockout is on in any department thereof, thus making an injury to one an injury to all.

Six months after the first IWW convention a booby-trap bomb killed Frank Steunenberg, ex-governor of Idaho who had called the troops down on Coeur d'Alene. Early the next year a drifter and sometime union man named Harry Orchard was arrested in Denver. Orchard "confessed" to assorted murders and bombings and accused Haywood, Moyer, and George Pettibone, a Colorado businessman, of plotting the murder of Steunenberg.

Orchard's confession came after long sessions in prison with James McParlan, the Pinkerton detective who had informed on the Molly Maguires in Pennsylvania. A second witness named Steve Adams produced a confession that confirmed Orchard's story.

Haywood, Moyer, and Pettibone were taken from Denver to stand trial in Boisie City. Just before the trial Adams repudiated his story and claimed that Idaho Governor Frank Gooding had threatened to hang him unless he backed up Orchard's testimony. Adams was promptly charged with the murder of a claim jumper.

On the witness stand Orchard claimed to have been the hired assassin of the WFM and confessed to twenty-six murders and bombings.

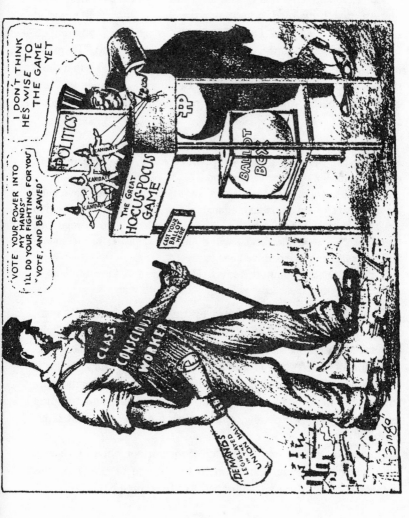

Now He Understands the Game

Source: Solidarity, November 11, 1916

The trial and Orchard's testimony enraged the working community, which claimed it was all a frame-up. Roosevelt branded Haywood, Moyer, and Debs "undesirable citizens," whereupon people across the country donned badges that read "I am an undesirable citizen." On May 4 more than 100,000 marchers staged processions down Fifth and Lexington Avenues in New York in sympathy with the accused men. Debs called for a general strike—

AROUSE YE SLAVES!
Nearly twenty years ago the capitalist tyrants put some innocent men to death for standing up for labor. . . .
They are now going to try it again. Let them dare! There have been twenty years of revolutionary education, agitation, and organization since the Haymarket tragedy, and if an attempt is made to repeat it, there will be a revolution and I will do all in my power to precipitate it. The crisis has come and we have to meet it. . . .
If they attempt to murder Moyer, Haywood, and their brothers, a million revolutionists at least will meet them with guns.

Clarence Darrow, the defense attorney, tore Orchard's testimony apart as the fabrication of Pinkerton McParlan, a man "who never did anything in his life but lie and cheat and scheme." "The life of a detective is a living lie," he told the jury. "That is his business; he lives one from the time he gets up in the morning to the time he goes to bed; he is deceiving people, and trapping people, and lying to people, and imposing on people; that is his trade."

Haywood, Moyer, and Pettibone were not convicted. Orchard, who became a devout Christian in the course of the trial, was convicted of murder and sentenced to life in prison.

Direct Action

Through the time of the trial the issues of elections, sabotage, and violence split the IWW. In 1907 Haywood and the western left wing took control. The "Wobblies" now denounced "political action" altogether. The new society would be created not by voting but by "direct action"—organization, strikes, sabotage, all leading to the physical takeover of industry. The wage-earners would battle the owners "until the workers of the world organize as a class, take possession of the earth and the machinery of production, and abolish the wage system—

> Arise!!! Slaves of the World!!!
> No God! No Master!
> One for all and all for one!!!

Known academically as "syndicalist-anarchism," the Wobbly plan of revolution was based on the general strike. When conditions were ripe, when all the workers belonged to the "One Big Union," everyone would lay down their tools at once—

With passive resistance, with the workers absolutely refusing to move, lying absolutely silent, they are more powerful than all the weapons and instruments that the other side has for attack.

On that day, the capitalist system would die, the workers would own the factories, wage slavery would cease, the collective society would begin—

> In the gloom of mighty cities,
>   Mid the roar of whirling wheels,
> We are toiling on like chattel slaves of old;
>   And our masters hope to keep us,
> Ever thus beneath their heels,
>   And to coin our very life blood into gold.
>
> But we have a glowing dream,
>   Of how fair the world will seem,
> When each man can live his life secure and free;
>   When the earth is owned by Labor,
> And there's joy and peace for all,
>   In the Commonwealth of toil that is to be.

The Wobbly organizational scheme was dubbed "Father Hagerty's Wheel of Fortune." It classified workers by industry

in readiness for the day the "One Big Union" woud take charge
of the economy—

The army of production [is] organized, not only for the everyday
struggle with the capitalists, but to carry on production when capitalism shall have been overthrown. . . .
By organizing industrially we are forming the structure of the new
society within the shell of the old.

Government ownership was not part of the Wobbly program.
The government, said Vince St. John, was "a committee to look
after the interests of the employers."
The land and the machinery were the common property of all
the people. The factories and farms would be collectively owned,
cooperatively run for the good of the whole community—

> Then up with the masses and down with the classes,
>   Death to the traitor who money can buy.
> Cooperation's the hope of the nation,
>   Strike for it now or your liberties die.

The Wobbly creed spread like wildfire in the eastern immigrant
ghettoes and across the Mississippi among the workers of the
West, in the mines, timber forests, port towns, and among the
migrant workers and hoboes who rode the boxcars and populated
the hobo "jungles" along the railroads. Dues were low and membership was wide open to all: blacks, women, immigrants of all
varieties. Scores of Wobbly papers in ten and more languages
carried songs, stories, and cartoons that were mailed in or picked
up along the rails and signed by "Red," "a Wob" or nobody. They
were spontaneous chords of bitterness and of poverty-stricken
freedom—

> O! I like my boss,
>   He's a good friend of mine,
> And that's why I'm starving
>   Out on the picket line!

> Hallelujah! I'm a bum!
> Hallelujah! Bum again!
> Hallelujah! Give us a hand-out
> To revive us again!

Wobbly organizers like James Walsh traveled by hopping freights and supported themselves by selling the IWW paper and song sheets—

Well, we're in the yards, gathered together at the water tank. In order to know if all are present we have numbered ourselves. The numbers run from one to nineteen, Mrs. Walsh making twenty.

A switchman is seen and he informs us where our "Special Car" will be found. The train is late, however, and we are delayed a few hours. "Fly Cops" are pretty busy in the yards. They are watching their master's property, that some hobo may not break a sacred seal and pile into a car where valuable merchandise is stored.

Two blasts of the locomotive whistle are heard, and the train is starting on its journey, and simultaneously nineteen men, all dressed in black overalls and jumpers, black shirts and red ties, with an IWW book in his pocket and an IWW button on his coat are in a "cattle car" and on our way.

In a short time a glim appears and the brakeman jumps into the car. His unionism is skin-deep. He belongs to the B of RT but never heard of the class struggle. He is unsuccessful, however, in the collecting of fares, and we continue on our journey. . . .

It is time for another street meeting, and so I must close to join the revolutionary forces on the street, who are now congregating after a big feed in the jungles.

Strikes could be for higher wages and better working conditions, but they were only a small part of the larger war. "A strike," said Haywood, "is an incipient revolution. Many large revolutions have grown out of a small strike."

The Wobbly unions refused to sign contracts with the employers. Returning to work after a strike was merely an interlude in the class war, and "all peace as long as the wage system lasts is but an armed truce."

> Whose the sweat, his the land!
> Whose the sweat, theirs the machines!

The Wobblies advocated and used sabotage, a practice that helped bring an open break with the Socialist party. Sabotage essentially meant "striking on the job"—demonstrating inside the factories, subverting production, withholding labor. The tactic, wrote Frank Bohn in *Solidarity*, "does not necessarily mean destruction of machinery or other property, although that method has always been indulged in and will continue to be used as long as there is a class struggle."

Ancient Hebrews in Egypt practiced sabotage when they spoiled the bricks. Slaves in the South practiced it regularly by putting stones and dirt in their bags of cotton to make them weigh heavier. An old cotton mill weaver in Massachusetts once told me that when baseball was first played, the boys in his mill struck a bobbin in the running gear of the water wheel and so tied up the shop on Saturday afternoon that they could go and see the ball game. . . .

When the workers face a specific situation, they will likely continue to do as their interests and intelligence dictate.

In 1906 Wobblies organized the nation's first sitdown strike at the Schenectady General Electric plant. In 1909, 600 clothing workers striking Lamm and Company in Chicago were replaced by scabs. Workers in firms supplying Lamm and Company " 'sabotaged' their work to such perfection" that the company caved in almost immediately. In the wheatfields of Kansas signs announced "$3.00 a day, shocks right side up; $2.00 a day, shocks upside down." A favorite tactic in the factories was to follow the rules of the shop to absolute perfection, thus ruining production. The symbols of sabotage were the wooden shoe and the black cat, bad luck for the boss—

> Lawyers have no bunk to fill me,
>   Cops and soldiers cannot kill me.
> Hurry now! Wonder how? MEOW—
>   SABOTAGE!

Perch I will on the System's coffin,
    On the hearse they take it off in,
Hurry now! Wonder how? MEOW—
    SABOTAGE!

Some Wobbly-led strikes involved defensive violence against police, mostly in the West, where nearly all strikes were violent anyway, but also at McKees Rocks, where in 1909 strikers carried out their vow to kill one Pennsylvania "Black Cossack" for every striker that was killed. Organizer Elizabeth Flynn outlined the general Wobbly attitude toward violence—

Physical violence is dramatic. It is especially dramatic when you talk about it and don't resort to it.

But actual violence is an old-fashioned method of conducting a strike. And mass action, paralyzing all industry, is a new fashioned and a much more feared method of conducting a strike.

That does not mean that violence shouldn't be used in self-defense. . . . In the Paterson strike police persecution did drop off considerably after the open declaration of self-defense was made by strikers. . . .

Everybody believes in violence for self-defense. Strikers don't need to be told that.

The strength of the IWW was impossible to measure. Membership could not be counted, numbers didn't matter. In 1918 the government estimated membership at 200,000. The central organization was constantly torn by faction fighting, which made little difference. Distrustful of any sort of authority, the Wobbly locals continually ignored and fought to do away with the national office.

Early Wobbly struggles centered on "free speech fights," mostly fought out in western towns. The basic IWW media were soapbox speeches on street corners. When the Wobblies came, local officials would find a law to ban public speakers and then throw the organizers in jail.

In San Diego, San Pedro and Fresno, California, Spokane, Washington, and Missoula, Montana, speeches were stopped. Organizers sent out the word for support. Hundreds of Wobblies then poured into town in boxcars and gathered on the street corners. They mounted the soapboxes in rapid procession, usually yelling "Fellow Workers!" and then being carried off to jail, to be followed by another "speaker" and another and another and another. Small towns like Missoula cracked early. But in Spokane, where two men died in jail, at least 600 Wobblies and sympathizers were arrested, the overflow from the jails being imprisoned in a nearby schoolhouse.

Wobblies organized strikes in the mining towns of the West, the timber forests of the Northwest and the South, among rubber workers in northern Ohio, dock workers on the Great Lakes and both coasts, field hands on the ranches of the Great Plains and California, construction workers on the West Coast and in Canada, steel and textile workers in the East, window washers, shoe workers, streetcar workers, and cannery workers—

It is we who plowed the prairies; built the cities where they trade;
    Dug the mines and built the workshops; Endless miles of railroad laid.
Now we stand outcast and starving, mid the wonders we have made;
    But the Union makes us strong.

They have taken untold millions that they never toiled to earn;
    But without our brain and muscle not a single wheel can turn.
We can break their haughty power; gain our freedom when we learn;
    That the Union makes us strong.

Solidarity Forever!
Solidarity Forever!
Solidarity Forever!
The Union makes us strong!

In 1909 the International Ladies Garment Workers Union struck the Triangle Shirt-Waist Company. Company guards assaulted and beat picketing strikers. Twenty thousand garment workers then joined the "girls' strike," which the union won in 1910. That year an unsuccessful garment-workers' strike in Chicago brought 850 arrests and 10 deaths.

In Los Angeles a fierce struggle to unionize the building trades led to more than forty bombings in the period from 1908 to 1911. The unionization struggle was led by the Iron Workers Union, an AF of L affiliate. The "open shop" movement was led by General Harrison Otis of the *Los Angeles Times*.

On October 1, 1910, while Otis was in Mexico negotiating a land deal with dictator Porfirio Diaz, an explosion leveled the *Times* building, killing twenty-one people. On Christmas Day the Llewellyn Iron Works, which was being struck at the time, was also blown up.

The following spring John J. McNamara, Secretary-Treasurer of the union, was arrested in Detroit. His brother James was arrested in Indianapolis.

Darrow was the defense attorney, and Debs and Gompers issued long, vitriolic denunciations of the trial. A parade of 20,000 in Los Angeles protested the actions of Otis and the government. As election day drew closer it seemed certain that Socialist Job Harriman would be elected mayor of Los Angeles.

But shortly before the election James McNamara confessed to dynamiting the *Times* building, and his brother admitted blowing up the Llewellyn plant. James said he hadn't meant to kill anyone, that the bomb had struck a gas main and taken down the entire building by accident. The people had been killed because the company had locked them into the building, a standard corporate procedure.

He refused, however, to renounce the act. "I'll swing for a principle," he said. "Poor Darrow, he's all in. If I swing, it'll be for a principle—a principle."

Although detective William J. Burns said Gompers knew the men were guilty, the AF of L chief issued a tearful statement claiming he had been betrayed and renouncing violence. Debs continued to defend the two brothers—

If you want to judge John McNamara you must first serve a month as a structural iron worker on a skyscraper, risking your life every minute to feed your wife and babies, then be discharged and blacklisted for joining a union.

Every floor in every skyscraper represents a workingman killed in its construction.

It is easy enough for a gentleman of education and refinement to sit at his typewriter and point out the crimes of the workers. But let him be one of them himself, thrown into the brute struggle for existence from his childhood, oppressed, exploited, forced to strike, clubbed by the police, jailed while his family is evicted and his wife and children are hungry, and he will hesitate to condemn those as criminals who fight against the crimes of which they are the victims of such savage methods as have been forced upon them by their masters.

In January 1912, 14,000 textile workers walked out of the mills of Lawrence, Massachusetts. Within weeks the number of striking workers had jumped to 23,000.

The mill workers of Lawrence were almost all newcomer immigrants—Poles, Italians, Syrians, French, and Belgians. In the spirit of Progressive reform the state of Massachusetts had ordered the work week for women and children cut from 56 to 54 hours. The mill owners responded by shortening the work week for all workers; then they cut wages 32 cents—the cost of three loaves of bread.

Bread, molasses, and beans were the staples of the Lawrence diet, and three loaves of bread meant a considerable loss.

When the pay cut came on January 11, strike leaflets circulated through town. The mayor ordered the local militia to patrol the streets. In zero-degree weather picketing workers were drenched with fire hoses. When they retaliated by throwing chunks of ice, thirty-six were arrested. Most were sentenced to a year in prison.

The governor then sent in the state militia. "Most of them had to leave Harvard to do it," reported one officer, "but they rather enjoyed going down there to have a fling at those people."

To sustain the strike the IWW organized a vast relief system. Soup kitchens and food distribution centers worked well enough to keep more than half the working population of Lawrence going for ten weeks. Volunteer doctors provided medical care, and contributions poured into the strike fund from around the country—

> Long haired preachers come out every night,
>   Try to tell you what's wrong and what's right;
> But when asked how bout something to eat,
>   They will answer with voices so sweet:
>
> You will work, bye and bye,
>   In that glorious land above the sky;
> Work and pray, live on hay,
>   You'll get pie in the sky when you die.

A week after the strike began, police "discovered" twenty-eight sticks of dynamite in three different places around Lawrence. The *New York Times* screamed that "the strikers display a fiendish lack of humanity which ought to place them beyond the comfort of religion until they have repented." Later a local undertaker admitted planting the dynamite and was fined $500.

Soon after finding the dynamite, police broke up a picket line and killed Anna LoPizzo, a striker. Joe Ettor and Arturo Giovannitti, who were three miles away addressing a meeting of German workers, were arrested and charged as accessories; Joseph Caruso, a striker who was home eating dinner at the time, was charged with the actual killing.

The arrests brought Haywood, Elizabeth Flynn, and other Wobbly organizers to Lawrence. The cry went out for a boycott.

Boycott Lawrence—Railroad men: Lose their cars for them!
Telegraphers: Lose their messages for them!
Expressmen: Lose their packages for them!
Boycott Lawrence! Boycott it to the Limit!

Because of the extent of child labor in the Lawrence mills, the strike centered strongly on its children. The spirit was unearthly—

It is the first strike I ever saw which sang. . . . And not only at the meetings did they sing, but in the soup houses and in the streets . . .

It was the spirit of the workers that was dangerous. They were always marching and singing. The tired gray crowds ebbing and flowing perpetually into the mills had waked and opened their mouths to sing.

Martial law was declared. A fifteen-year-old Syrian boy was killed by a trooper's bayonet.

The strikers then sent their children to New York City. First 120, then 92 more went to stay with sympathetic families. They were met with mass rallies and a parade down Fifth Avenue in support of the strike—

As we come marching, marching, we bring the greater days,
   The rising of the women means the rising of the race,
No more the drudge and idler—ten that toil where one reposes,
   But a sharing of life's glories: Bread and Roses! Bread and Roses!

As we come marching, marching in the beauty of the day,
   A million darkened kitchens, a thousand mill lofts gray,
Are touched with all the radiance that a sudden sun discloses,
   For the people hear us singing: "Bread and Roses!" "Bread and Roses!"

After the second group left, city officials issued an edict forbidding any more children from leaving town. On February 24, 150 more prepared to go to Philadelphia. Two companies of militia and fifty policemen surrounded the station. As the children boarded the train the police attacked.

Children were clubbed and torn away from their parents and a wild scene of brutal disorder took place. Thirty-five frantic women and children were arrested, thrown screaming and fighting into patrol wagons. They were beaten into submission and taken to the police station. There the women were charged with "neglect" and improper guardianship and ten frightened children taken to the Lawrence Poor Farm.

Strikers formed endless locked-arm chains around the mills wearing white armbands that read: "DON'T BE A SCAB!"

They locked arms in the downtown districts and when the police attacked they ran in and out of the stores in large groups: "They had our shopkeepers in terror!"

On March 12 the American Woolen Company gave in. The workers got higher wages and better working conditions. By the end of the month the rest of the Lawrence mills also settled, and as a rash of strikes broke out in the rest of New England wages went up throughout the industry.

In August, Ernest Pitman, a Lawrence contractor, admitted that the dynamite plot had been planned in the Boston offices of millowner William Wood. Pitman then committed suicide. Wood was never indicted.

At the end of September mill workers staged a twenty-four-hour walkout in support of the Wobbly prisoners still in jail. The mayor organized a counterdemonstration—

> For God and Country!
> The Stars and Stripes forever!
> The red flag never!

Opponents of the workers were urged to wear little American flags in their lapels.

Ettor, Giovannitti, and Caruso were tried in Salem. Ettor, who was kept in a steel cage throughout the two-month trial, summarized his own defense—

An idea consisting of a social crime in one age becomes the very religion of humanity in the next. . . . Whatever my social views are, they are what they are. They cannot be tried in this courtroom.

Since there was no evidence against them, all three men were found innocent and freed after eight months in prison.

A few months after the Lawrence strike began, the UMW led 70,000 miners on strike in the Cabin Creek coal region of West Virginia. Over the next year bloody fighting resulted in two declarations of martial law. Each time the troops were withdrawn, the strikers shut down the mines.

In February 1913, mine guards machine-gunned a strikers' camp at Holly Grove from a Chesapeake & Ohio train. The miners retaliated with an attack on the guards' camp at Mucklow. After the second battle mine owners granted a nine-hour day and the right to a union.

In March, Mother Jones and forty-nine miners were tried in a military court at Paint Creek Junction on murder charges. The defense attorney demanded they be tried as members of an opposing army, not under civil law. "The miners accept it as war," he argued. "If they will resort to violence, their acts will be acts of war, which society should not judge by ordinary rules of law and morality."

In the fall 11,000 miners at Rockefeller's Colorado Fuel and Iron Company marched out of the company camps and established their own in the countryside surrounding the mines.

Rockefeller had already called in Baldwin-Felts gunmen who toured the area in, among other things, an armored car known as "The Death Special." In October the detectives killed a man at the Forbes tent colony and pumped nine bullets into the leg of a ten-year-old boy.

Later that month miners attacked a trainload of guards which was moving with machine guns toward the Ludlow colony. By late October at least nine men were dead.

At the end of the month the governor declared martial law and ordered in the Colorado national guard. A Rockefeller vice-president wrote New York that "we have been able to secure the cooperation of all the bankers of the city [Denver], who have had three or four interviews with our little cowboy governor, agreeing to back the state and lend it all funds necessary to maintain the militia."

As winter set in, the tent colonies suffered from lack of food and bitter cold. Violence continued. The national guard began escorting in strikebreakers from other states.

In the spring much of the regular guard was replaced by company gunmen who wore guard uniforms but who drew their salary directly from the company. On the morning of April 20, 1914, the troops opened fire on the colony from the surrounding hills.

There were very few guns in the tent colony. Not over fifty, including shotguns. Women and children were afraid to crawl out of the shallow pits under the tents. Several men were killed trying to get to them. The soldiers and mine guards tried to kill everybody; anything they saw move, even a dog, they shot at.

The Guard then poured oil onto the tents and set them afire, trapping whole families in the holes they had dug to avoid the machine-gun bullets. After nearly twelve hours the camp was a smouldering coffin. Twenty-six bodies, including those of eleven children, were recovered from the wreckage.

The following day, as American marines stormed the Mexican port of Veracruz, armed strikers swarmed the area of the Rockefeller mines. The Denver militia was ordered in, but eighty-two of them mutinied, refusing to "engage in the shooting of women and children."

Three guards were killed at the Empire mine near Aguilar, and its mouth dynamited. Militia and company guards met "armed bands of strikers whose ranks are swelled constantly by men who swarm over the hills from all directions," and within days twenty more people had died.

At the end of April, Wilson sent in federal troops, and for the next six months miners peacefully awaited the outcome of negotiations. By December nothing had happened and, facing another winter, the strike died. The union didn't win recognition; over sixty people had died.

In January 1915, strikers at two fertilizer factories near Elizabeth, New Jersey, were attacked by deputies. "If those deputies say they fired in the air and that the strikers fired first, they lie," reported the *New York World*. "The strikers did not fire. They had nothing with which to fire. They were simply butchered." Twenty-eight strikers were wounded, of whom six died. Twenty-

"The Judge" in a Hell of a Fix

Source: Solidarity, October 31, 1914, from the Archives of Labor History and Urban Affairs, Wayne State University

two deputies were indicted for manslaughter, but none was prosecuted.

That summer eight men were killed and seventeen wounded by hired gunmen at the Standard Oil plant in Bayonne, New Jersey. The *New York Call* complained that "murder by deputy sheriffs is getting monotonous."

On November 19, a five-man firing squad killed Joe Hill at the Utah State Penitentiary. A Swedish immigrant, Hill was the best-known of the Wobbly bards. His songs, poems, cartoons, and stories filled the pages of the Wobbly magazines. He had been an organizer in California and part of an abortive scheme, based in Tiajuana, that would have turned Baja California into a giant commune. He was "the man who never died."

Tomorrow I expect to take a trip to the planet Mars and, if so, will immediately· commence to organize the Mars canal workers into the IWW and we will sing the good old songs so loud that the learned star-gazers on earth will once and for all get positive proof that the planet Mars really is inhabited. . . .

I have nothing to say for myself only that I have always tried to make this earth a little better for the great producing class, and I can pass off into the great unknown with the pleasure of knowing that I never in my life double-crossed a man, woman, or child.

> My will is easy to decide,
> For there is nothing to divide.
> My kin don't need to fuss and moan—
> "Moss does not cling to rolling stone"
>
> My body?—Oh!—If I could choose,
> I would to ashes it reduce,
> And let the merry breezes blow
> My dust to where some flowers grow
>
> Perhaps some fading flower then
> Would come to life and bloom again.
> This is my last and final will.
> Good luck to all of you,

Joe Hill

As Wilson dragged the country into World War I, vigilanteeism against Socialists, Wobblies, and other union organizers reached the level of total suppression. Known radicals, especially in the West, were in constant danger of arrest and physical violence. It was a foregone conclusion that virtually any strike for any reason would be met with violence. Espionage, mass arrests and deportations, the bombing of union headquarters and lynchings of organizers became standard antilabor tools of the "win the war" movement.

The AF of L made its final, definitive split with the radical labor movement by supporting the war. Gompers joined the war government and used his position to help crush the Socialist opposition.

The vast majority of workers opposed the war bitterly. As "preparedness" turned into conscription and military rule, the Socialist party made huge gains at the polls and the Wobblies and other labor radicals struck harder and harder in the face of the entire weight of the federal government. In 1917, Wobbly lumberjacks shut down the timber industry of western Washington. "You cannot get at the organization!" cried a frustrated senator. "It is something you cannot get at. You cannot reach it. You do not know where it is. It is not in writing. It is not in anything else. It is a simple understanding between men, and they act upon it without any evidence of existence whatever."

Days of Magic

Poor human nature, what horrible crimes have been committed in thy name!

Every fool, from king to policeman, from the flathead parson to the visionless dabbler in science, presumes to speak authoritatively of human nature. The greater the mental charlatan, the more definite his insistence on the wickedness and weaknesses of human nature.

Yet, how can any one speak of it today, with every soul in a prison, with every heart fettered, wounded, and maimed?

Emma Goldman

That we have a separate personal consciousness is not denied, but it is not humanity.

The human consciousness is collective. . . . We are not separate creatures at all.

Charlotte Gilman

Social, political, industrial, and scientific revolution brought on a cultural explosion that, at some point in the new century, would bury the Victorian way of life and obliterate the Puritan mind.

Mark Twain gave a preview. From his Missouri childhood young Sam Clemens wandered into typesetting. Then he was a riverboat pilot, journalist, adventurer, and wandering humorist. In the seventies he married and settled comfortably in Hartford. There he wrote *Tom Sawyer*, *Huckleberry Finn*, and *Life on the Mississippi*.

But the world was changing, and Twain's writing turned from simple humor to biting satire. With his friend Charles Dudley Warner he produced *The Gilded Age*, a scathing caricature of upper-class life that gave the post-Civil War period its name. "It could probably be shown by facts and figures," he said elsewhere, "that there is no distinctly native American criminal class except Congress."

Twain hated war, and as the American armies plunged into the business of conquering an empire, he became sick to his soul. The war in the Philippines dragged on endlessly—

We have pacified some thousands of the islanders and buried them; destroyed their fields; burned their villages, and turned their widows and orphans out-of-doors; furnished heartbreak by exile to some dozens of disagreeable patriots; subjugated the remaining ten millions by Benevolent Assimilation, which is the pious new name of the musket; we have acquired property in the three hundred concubines and other slaves of our business partner, the Sultan of Sulu, and hoisted our protecting flag over that swag.

And so, by these Providences of God—the phrase is the government's, not mine—we are a World Power.

In Twain's "War Prayer" a man in a white robe interrupts the sermon of a prewar preacher. The man asks the congregation to pray for a patriotic victory, for the murder of the young men in the other army, for the burning of their homes, the desolation of their land and crops, the widowhood of their wives, and the orphaning of their children. The congregation dismisses the man as a lunatic. Twain kept the poem to himself.

Twain thought Victorian sex was ridiculous, and his *Letters from the Earth* couldn't be published until long after his death "because it would be a felony."

During twenty-three days in every month (in the absence of pregnancy) from the time a woman is seven years old till she dies of old age, she is ready for action, and COMPETENT. Competent every day, competent every night. Also, she WANTS that candle—yearns for it, longs for it, hankers after it, as commanded by the law of God in her heart.

But man is only briefly competent. . . . After fifty his performance is of poor quality, the intervals between are wide, and its satisfactions of no great value to either party; whereas his great-grandmother is as good as new. . . .

Now if you or any other really intelligent person were arranging the fairnesses and justices between man and woman, you would give the man a one-fiftieth interest in one woman, and the woman a harem. Now wouldn't you?

As for the church, there was no institution on earth that deserved more scorn, except maybe God Himself—

In man's heaven EVERYBODY SINGS! . . . The words are always the same, in number they are only about a dozen, there is no rhyme, there is no poetry: hosannah, hosannah, hosannah, Lord God of Sabaoth, 'rah! 'rah! rah! siss!—boom! . . . a-a-ah! . . .

In time, the Deity perceived that death was a mistake, a mistake in that it was insufficient; insufficient; for the reason that while it was an admirable agent for the inflicting of misery upon the survivor, it allowed the dead person himself to escape from all further persecution. . . .

The Deity pondered this matter during four thousand years unsuccessfully, but as soon as he came down to earth and became a Christian his mind cleared and he knew what to do. He invented Hell, and proclaimed it. . . .

> Constipation, O constipation,
>   The joyful sound proclaim
> Till man's remotest entrail
>   Shall praise its Maker's name.

Jack London followed Mark Twain as the country's most popular writer. London was the illegitimate son of a wandering astrologer named William Henry Chaney. He was raised in Oakland, California, by his mother and her husband, John London, in the dire poverty typical of the time.

London had a wild, strung-out youth. Before the age of twenty he had supported himself as an oyster pirate in the San Francisco Bay and, as a factory worker, had crossed the Pacific as a working seaman and was already fighting a long, futile battle to kick his addiction to alcohol.

In the late nineties he went to the Klondike in search of gold. He didn't find it, but on returning to California found he could earn a living by writing stories of the northland. At twenty-seven he wrote *The Call of the Wild*, which almost instantly became the best-selling book in the United States.

London was a Socialist and considered himself a revolutionary. In 1905 he became the first chairman of the Inter-Collegiate Socialist Society—founded by Upton Sinclair—a group of young writers dedicated to revolutionizing the nation's wealthy, conservative campuses. That year he spoke to some students at the University of California who had come to hear a lecture on *The Call of the Wild—*

As I look over the universities of my land today, I see the students asleep, asleep in the face of the awful facts of poverty I have given you, asleep in the greatest revolution that has come to this world.

Oh, it is sad! Not long ago revolutions began, grew, broke out in Oxford. Today Russian universities seethe with revolution.

I say to you, then: in the full glory of life, here's a cause that appeals to all the romance in you. Awake! awake to its call! . . . The revolution is here, now! Stop it who can!

"Fight for us or fight against us!" he yelled at the students of Yale. "Raise your voices one way or the other; be alive!"

Although he produced some revolutionary theory, London's most important political book was *The Iron Heel*, published in 1907. The story centers on Ernest Everhard, model revolutionary, hero of the Chicago commune.

Amid massive social upheaval, Everhard travels the middle-class circuit, preaching the cause of revolution. Soon war breaks out between the United States and Germany. The industrial oligarchy—the Iron Heel—begins to stamp out all political opposition. "Watch out for the suppression of the socialist press and socialist publishing houses," warns the hero. "I'm afraid it's coming. We are going to be throttled."

The Iron Heel establishes a fascist dictatorship. Everhard and his lover are forced underground. The raw class struggle reaches apocalyptic proportions. Everhard is killed. Revolution rises up again and again only to be suppressed and to rise up yet again. After a battle of centuries, it wins.

The Iron Heel's prediction of war with Germany, dictatorship in the United States, and suppression of the revolutionary movement aroused the ire of many Socialists, who found it depressing and overly pessimistic. But the book's wild excitement and realism made it an underground classic throughout the United States and Europe; "a whole generation of revolutionaries was brought up on it."

Of greater immediate impact than *The Iron Heel* was *The Jungle* by Upton Sinclair, published a year earlier. Sinclair came from an old but poor Baltimore family. He worked his way through City College of New York as a hack writer, producing jokes for *Argosy* and other pulp magazines.

Then he churned out the weekly "Mark Mallory Series" of West Point adventures and another bogus series about life at the Naval Academy. Working with two stenographers he produced a million words a year, and when he quit at the age of twenty-one he estimated that he "had published an output equal in volume to the works of Walter Scott."

Revolted by hack writing and by the publishing industry in general, Sinclair became an active Socialist. In 1905 he got a $500 advance from the *Appeal to Reason* and went to live in the Chicago stockyards, where he wandered for seven weeks "white-faced and thin, partly from undernourishment, partly from horror."

He then returned to his wife and infant in their cabin in rural New Jersey, where they were just recovering from the effects of a disease-plagued winter spent in dire poverty. He wrote a gruesome account of the destruction of an immigrant family in the stockyards. At the end, the father becomes a revolutionary. "We shall have the sham reformers self-stultified and self-convicted," he proclaims. "Then will begin the rush that will never be checked, the tide that will never turn till it has reached its flood —that it will be irresistible and overwhelming—the rallying of the outraged workingmen of Chicago to our standard! And we shall organize them, we shall drill them, we shall bear down the opposition, we shall sweep it before us—and

> Chicago will be ours!
> *Chicago will be ours!*
> CHICAGO WILL BE OURS!

"Externally," said Sinclair, "the story had to do with a family of stockyard workers, but internally it was the story of my own family."

Jack London wrote the announcement for the book, proclaiming that "what *Uncle Tom's Cabin* did for the black slaves *The Jungle* has a large chance to do for the white slaves of today."

The book thoroughly shocked the American consciousness. But not exactly as London and Sinclair hoped. Sinclair wanted to show the sufferings of the workers and call them to revolution; the middle-class reading public reacted mainly to passing descriptions of the putrid meat sold by the beef trust—

> Mary had a little lamb,
> And when she saw it sicken,
> She shipped it off to Packingtown,
> And now it's labelled chicken.

Whatever its effect *The Jungle* marked a takeoff point in realist and naturalist literature. The stale parlor romance of the Gilded Age was shoved over for literature that dealt vividly and realistically with the lives of the mass of the American people.

Hamlin Garland pioneered the idiom with tales of the rural Midwest. Stephen Crane's *Red Badge of Courage*, which attained mass popularity in 1896, painted a devastating portrait of a boy's forced maturity on the battlefield. Frank Norris' *The Octopus* (1901) and *The Pit* (1902) followed the course of wheat from monopolized and oppressed California farmers to the vicious wheeling and dealing in the Chicago markets.

Theodore Dreiser's *Sister Carrie* told the story of a businessman's fall from the middle class on account of his love for a younger woman. The book was printed in 1901 by Frank Doubleday but was held in a warehouse because Doubleday's wife objected to a story that allowed a "woman of sin" to escape without proper punishment.

Meanwhile, a group of young East Coast painters rebelled against the "fig leaves and gauze draperies" of official Victorian art. Known as "the Eight," Robert Henri, John Sloan, and six other young artists opened an independent New York show in 1908 that marked the end of Victorian rule in the visual arts.

Like many of the realist writers, the Eight were strongly influenced by newspaper work. They merged the realist school of Thomas Eakins with the freedom and color of the French Impressionists to create vibrant, colorful portraits of the life around them. They were called "apostles of ugliness" by outraged critics, who also labeled them "the Ashcan School" and "the Revolutionary Black Gang." One of Maurice Prendergast's landscapes was described as "an explosion in a paint factory."

Meanwhile, Alfred Steiglitz and Edward Steichen led the "Mop and Pail Brigade" from the Gallery of Photo-Secession, founded at 291 Fifth Avenue in 1905. Aside from the founders' photographs and paintings, the gallery held the first show of children's art, the first major show of black sculpture, and the first American display of the cubist works of Pablo Picasso.

By the time *The Jungle* was published, mass-circulation newspapers and magazines were filled with muckraking journalism and cartoons and powerful, stunning photographs of working-class life, most notable those of Jacob Riis.

Stories, songs, cartoons, revolutionary politics, humor, and philosophy spread everywhere through the "underground" Wobbly papers. The *Appeal to Reason*'s "Little Blue Books"—the form in which *The Jungle* first appeared—sold for a nickel and could be found in the pockets of farmers, workers, and students throughout the country. The written word and visual arts were being wrenched from upper-class control and made to come alive.

Black Power

Alongside rebellion in the arts came the rising tide of black consciousness.

After Reconstruction the black community lay defenseless before the southern lynch mob. Black leadership, most notably that of Frederick Douglass, was articulate but powerless in the face of the white power structure.

Soon, however, the rise of populism and the revolutionary labor movement had its impact. T. Thomas Fortune, militant editor of the *New York Age*, raised the cry of revolution in 1884. Lynch law, he said, was a rational capitalist tool—

The white men of the South, the capitalists, the land-sharks, the poor-white trash, and the nondescripts . . . organized themselves into a band of outlaws, whose concatenative chain of auxiliaries ran through the entire South, and deliberately proceeded to murder innocent men and women for POLITICAL REASONS and to systematically rob them of their honest labor because they were too accursedly lazy to labor themselves. . . .

The future struggle in the South will be, not between white men and black men, but between capital and labor, landlord and tenant. . . . When the issue is properly joined, the rich, be they black or be they white, will be found upon the same side; and the poor, be they black or be they white, will be found on the same side.

In the early nineties the Colored Farmers' Alliance, the largest organization of blacks the nation had ever seen, joined with the white farmers of the West and South. Black Populists, like H. S. Doyle of Georgia, who campaigned for Tom Watson, risked their lives to preach the gospel of the People's party.

But the alliance was shaky and fell apart under the strain of party warfare. As populism collapsed the southern white farmer was once again at the throat of the black.

In 1895, Booker T. Washington asked for peace. Founder of Tuskegee Institute and an ex-slave, the quiet, conservative Washington made his name with a speech at the Cotton States International Exposition in Atlanta. Black participation in politics had been a mistake, he said. The black and white communities would remain "separate as the fingers, yet one as the hand in all things essential to mutual progress." The black man should forget about political and civil rights and "cast down your bucket where you are" to concentrate on business, industrial education, and agriculture. There was "but one hope of solution," he said elsewhere, and that was to "throw aside every nonessential and cling only to the essential . . . property, economy, education, and Christian character." As a means to self-respect and self-defense, the black community must "get some property" and get it as a community —"we must cooperate or we are lost."

Washington's influence mushroomed. To his base at Tuskegee he added control of the Afro-American League, begun in 1890 by Fortune to promote black banking and cooperative industry. In 1900 he founded the National Negro Business League, funded in large part by Andrew Carnegie. Contributions from Rockefeller, Huntington, and other barons poured into the Tuskegee treasury. Through his well-cultivated contacts with the regular political parties Washington also controlled patronage, and "few political appointments of Negroes were made anywhere in the United States without his consent." The hold of the conservative "Tuskegee Machine" on the emerging black middle class was virtually absolute; Washington had become "the political boss of his race."

Washington's hold began to crack in 1903 with the publication of *The Souls of Black Folk* by W. E. B. Du Bois. Du Bois grew up in Great Barrington in western Massachusetts. Steeped in abolitionist tradition, he attended Harvard and was the first black man to receive a Ph.D. His *Philadelphia Negro* was the pioneer work in Afro-American studies.

While lauding the Tuskegee president's contribution to the community, Du Bois asserted that he and other blacks "feel in conscience bound to ask of this nation three things: The right to vote, civic equality, the education of youth according to ability. . . . So far as Mr. Washington apologizes for injustice, North or South, does not rightly value the privilege and duty of voting, belittles the emasculating effects of caste distinctions, and opposes the higher training and ambition of our brighter minds—so far as he, the South, or the Nation does this—we must unceasingly and firmly oppose them."

Beyond the attack on Washington, *Souls* was a lyrical account of black history, folk traditions, music, and customs. It was a strong new assertion of black cultural identity.

In 1905, Du Bois and other black radicals met at Niagara Falls to pledge themselves to struggle for civil rights and political power. The "Niagara Movement" led in turn to an alliance with white liberals in the National Association for the Advancement of Colored People, founded in 1910. Washington founded a more conservative version a year later in the National Urban League.

Despite its intensity, the Du Bois-Washington conflict was a small reflection of the vast upheaval within the black community. At the turn of the century agricultural depression and white-Democratic terrorism swept the South. Cotton prices plunged, and tenantry and share-cropping strengthened their death grip on the southern economy.

And from 1885 to 1900, amidst massive political revolt, more than 2000 were lynched. The Afro-American community, nine-tenths of which lived in the South, began to think about leaving.

In the late seventies, thousands of blacks moved from the Deep

South to Kansas and Arkansas. In the early nineties a similar, larger movement grew to emigrate to Oklahoma and to turn it into an all-black state. By 1892 there were seven all-black towns in the territory, and twenty-five were eventually established. Their residents discovered "a type of Afro-American citizenship different from that found elsewhere. . . . the consciousness of the power that ensued from close communal life and cooperation."

But there were economic troubles in Oklahoma as well as conflict with whites and with Indians, whose Oklahoma reservations were a last, pitiful refuge.

There was some talk and some actual movement towards emigration to Africa, but when blacks did begin to move en masse they moved in one direction—to the cities, primarily those of the North, where there was hope of higher wages and freedom. By 1910, New York, Philadelphia, Baltimore, Washington, and New Orleans all had black populations of more than 80,000; Chicago's black population jumped from 4,000 in 1870 to 50,000 by 1910; Birmingham's black community more than doubled in size in one decade.

As blacks began to leave, many southern governments took legal steps to stop them from going; taxing northern labor recruiters and enforcing antimigratory laws that amounted to nothing more than peonage. Thus the South witnessed the weird spectacle of a power structure trying to keep its "cheap labor" from leaving in the daytime, while at night lynching those who dared to struggle for their rights.

But the North wasn't much better. Blacks who came to the big cities had to compete with the white working class for jobs and housing. Employers gleefully used black workers as strikebreakers while the bulging immigrant ghettoes and the bulging black ghettoes began to overlap, driving up rents and bringing on riots.

Meanwhile violently racist books like *Our Country* and *The Negro Beast* flooded a white community now deep in the business of holding down nonwhites in Latin America and Asia as well as at home.

In the late nineties two Supreme Court decisions—*Plessy* v. *Fergusen* and *Williams* v. *Mississippi*—affirmed segregation and disfranchisement as national policies. It was an "interesting coincidence," said the *Nation*, "that this important decision is rendered at a time when we are considering the idea of taking in a varied assortment of inferior races in different parts of the world . . . which, of course, could not be allowed to vote."

Progressive Presidents Roosevelt and Wilson referred to the people of Latin America as "dagoes" and "our little brown brothers." Roosevelt remembered his cowboy days thusly—

I don't go so far as to think that the only good Indians are dead Indians, but I believe nine out of every ten are, and I shouldn't like to inquire too closely into the case of the tenth. The most vicious cowboy has more moral principle than the average Indian.

In 1912, Roosevelt was instrumental in blocking southern blacks out of the Progressive party convention. The election was won by Woodrow Wilson, who supported segregation of federal employees (reversing a fifty-year policy) and approved the firing of black postal workers in the South on racial grounds. His campaign publicity director and later Secretary of the Navy was Joseph Daniels, a Raleigh newspaper owner and machine Democrat who had helped lead the 1898 anti-Populist "white supremacy jubilee" in North Carolina. The nation would not be secure, said Daniels, until the North adopted a "southern" race policy.

Meanwhile, despite the best efforts of southern governments to prevent it, the black literacy rate soared from under 20 percent in 1870 to well over 70 percent by 1915.

The ghettoes, particularly Harlem, became the scene of a "Black Renaissance" in music, literature, and the arts. Jack Johnson beat "Gentleman" Jim Corbett and became heavyweight champion of the world.

In 1912 James Weldon Johnson published *The Autobiography of an Ex-Colored Man*. The principal figure, a light-skinned mulatto, hides his true racial identity and becomes a successful "white" businessman.

As a youth he had "felt leap within me pride that I was colored; and I began to form wild dreams of bringing glory and honour to the Negro race." But the end of the book finds him "an ordinary successful white man who had made a little money. . . . I cannot repress the thought that, after all, I have sold my birthright for a mess of pottage."

In 1913 a forty-seven-year-old black man named Timothy Drew founded the Moorish Science Temple in Newark, New Jersey. The Temple was based on the faith of Islam, recognized "all the Divine Prophets, Jesus, Mohammed, Buddha, and Confucius," and proclaimed that the true roots of the black race were in Asia.

He became obsessed with the idea that salvation for the Negro people lay in the discovery by them of their national origin; i.e., they must know whence they came, and refuse longer to be called Negroes, black folk, colored people, or Ethiopians. They must henceforth call themselves Asiatics, to use the generic term, or, more specifically, Moors, or Moorish Americans.

In 1916, Marcus Garvey landed in New York to promote the black nationalist United Negro Improvement Association. Thousands of blacks across the country poured into the Garvey movement while members of the Moorish Temple "would accost white people on the streets, and showing their membership cards or the buttons they wore in their coat lapels, would sing the praises of their prophet, now known as Noble Drew Ali, because he had freed them from the curse of European (white) domination."

Sexual Liberation

The struggle of the blacks was entwined with that of women. Frederick Douglass played a key role in adding women's suffrage to the seminal "Declaration of Sentiments" drafted by militant women at Seneca Falls, New York, in 1848. At the same time radical women were a strong force in the abolitionist crusade.

In fact, the antislavery campaign boosted the women's movement—in a backhanded way. Abolitionist women were slighted and kept in lesser positions by the male leadership. When they spoke in public against slavery, they were heckled because they were women. The experience was infuriating and enlightening. "We have good cause to be grateful to the slaves," said Abby Kelley, "for the benefit we have received to *ourselves* in working for *him*. In striving to strike his irons off, we found most surely, that we were manacled ourselves."

Women also played a crucial role in the farm movement. The Grange ruled that "no chapter shall be organized, or exist, without women." Equal rights was a part of the Populist program, and Populist meetings were filled with "women with skins tanned to parchment by the hot winds, with bony hands of toil and clad in faded calico, [who] could talk in meeting, and could talk right straight to the point."

In the cities, there were 6 million women working outside the home by 1900. Thousands of working women joined the Knights of Labor, the Socialist party, and the IWW. A coal strike at Arno, Pennsylvania, in 1909 was won by the wives of the miners—

Up the mountain side, yelling and hollering she [an Irish woman with "wild red hair"] led the women, and when the mules came up with the scabs and the coal, she began beating on the dishpan and hollering and all the army joined in with her.

The sheriff tapped her on the shoulder. "My dear lady," said he, "remember the mules. Don't frighten them."

She took the old tin pan and she hit him with it and she hollered, "To hell with you and the mules!"

He fell over and dropped into the creek. Then the mules began to rebel against scabbing. They bucked and kicked the scab drivers and started off for the barn. The scabs started running down hill, followed by the army of women with their mops and pails and brooms.

Scabs were kept out as "every day women with brooms or mops in one hand and babies in the other arm wrapped in little blankets, went to the mines and watched that no one went in."

The very presence of revolutionary women bothered some policemen who still clung to notions of "chivalry." Almost against his will a Spokane official prosecuted a very pregnant Elizabeth Flynn, complaining he would have ignored her "if she had not formed a dangerous organization, had not sung the Red Flag song, had not called Justice Mann an illiterate old fool, had not preached the gospel of discord and discontent."

In 1900, 20,000 women textile workers began the "girls' strike" in the face of mass beatings by police. In strike meetings they discussed "violence and insults by police and of how the prostitutes in jail jeered at their low wages and told them they could do better at THEIR trade." The battle, however, laid the foundation for the International Ladies' Garment Workers Union. "When the strike started," wrote Elizabeth Flynn, "there were two union shops. When it ended, there were over 300 union shops, with shorter hours and more pay."

Meanwhile, middle-class women, many of whom were entering professional fields, took up the fight for suffrage. Four western states—Wyoming, Colorado, Utah, and Idaho—had the woman vote before 1900. Now women demanded national suffrage and full legal equality, demanding in particular the right to own property after marriage and the right to custody of their children.

The suffrage movement was, as the moderate *Woman's Journal* put it, "bourgeois, middle-class, a great middle-of-the-road movement; evidence of a slow-come mass conviction." It had "no official ideology" and, by and large, renounced radical politics.

But as the fight wore on the suffrage movement staged mass demonstrations and marches—more violent in England than here —bringing on the formation of the militant Woman's party in 1916. By 1920 women had won the vote.

But many women viewed suffrage as a minor reform. Emma Goldman felt the vote would only make the American woman "a better Christian and home-keeper, a staunch citizen of the State." Mother Jones told a mass-meeting in New York that "the women of Colorado have had the vote for two generations and the working men and women are in slavery. The state is in slavery, vassal to the Colorado Fuel and Iron Company and its subsidiary interests. . . . You don't need a vote to raise hell! You need convictions and a voice! . . . Whatever your fight, don't be ladylike. God Almighty made women and the Rockefeller gang of thieves made the ladies."

For Mother Jones the struggle was to free women from their "careers" in the factory so they could raise their children in peace. But Goldman and others launched a full-scale attack on the institution of marriage, the nuclear family, and the Victorian view of sex.

Goldman said women were being reared as a "sex commodity." America was "the stronghold of the Puritan eunuchs" and was keeping the image of the frail, innocent woman alive by isolating her from the real world, cutting her off from life itself, which "with its great clarifying sorrows and its deep, entrancing joys, rolls on without touching or gripping her soul."

Charlotte Gilman agreed that women had been crippled by their traditional role and, more particularly, by the economic system. A woman had to rely on her sex role because "she had no other hold, no other assurance of being fed." Marriage was just "legal prostitution." In fact, said Havelock Ellis, "the wife who married for money, compared with the prostitute, is the true scab. She is paid less, gives much more in return in labor and care, and is absolutely bound to her master. The prostitute never signs away the right over her own person, she retains her freedom and personal rights, nor is she always compelled to submit to man's embrace."

But the new century was bringing economic independence. "Women have ceased to exist as a subsidiary class in the community," wrote Rheta Dorr. "They are no longer wholly dependent, economically, intellectually, and spiritually on a ruling class of men."

The historic function of the Lutheran marriage, wrote Ellen Key, had been "to unite man and woman, with or without love, as a means to securing their mutual morality, to make them breeders of children for society, and in addition to retain the husband as a bread-winner."

A higher culture demanded a "true monogamy" based on love. And a relationship based on love didn't need the church or the state—"only cohabitation can decide the morality of a particular case—in other words, its power to enhance the life of the individuals who are living together and of the race. . . . This is the new morality."

Accordingly, Elizabeth Flynn explained her relationship with Carlo Tresca in terms of "the new sex code"—"not to remain with someone you did not love, but to honestly and openly avow a real attachment," regardless of marriage.

Ellen Key was a Swede whose books, translated into English, were widely read throughout the early years of the new century.

Charlotte Gilman, however, was recognized as "the most influential woman thinker in the pre-World War I generation in the United States." A member of the Inter-Collegiate Socialist Society, Gilman was a descendant of Lyman Beecher and Harriet Beecher Stowe.

The Protestant ethic, she said, had made man a wage slave and woman a house servant. In theory the nuclear home had provided what seemed to be an absolute necessity—a place of unquestioned refuge.

But in practice it failed. It offered only a false sense of security and promoted the illusion of isolation from the world as a whole. It provided no real privacy and managing it was "a source of constant friction and nervous as well as financial waste."

In its two basic functions—providing food and raising children

—there was enormous inefficiency and waste. "We pay rent for twenty kitchens where one kitchen would do," she wrote. "We have to pay severally for all these stoves and dishes, tools and utensils, which, if properly supplied in one proper place instead of twenty, would cost far less to begin with." The current situation amounted to one-half of humanity—the "beloved female domestics"—serving the other half, which was morally wrong and physically wasteful.

Furthermore, she said, it was too decentralized for the benefits of science to penetrate. With their "home-cooking" Americans would continue to "revel in fat-soaked steaks and griddle-cakes" and eat their meals "without ever giving one thought to the nutritive values of that food. . . . Until the food laboratory entirely supersedes the kitchen," she said, "there can be no growth."

Gilman attacked the Puritan home as a prison for both mother and child. Parents and children were creatures of separate worlds. Children were a separate class "with citizen's rights to be guaranteed only by the state." The private home treated them as private property and worked as "unchecked tyranny or as unchecked indulgence." As an alternative the state should provide nurseries with "elected mothers" where children would enjoy the company of their contemporaries and an atmosphere of "child-culture as an art and science," while the mothers would be free to do other things.

Ellen Key agreed that the family was repressive but attacked Gilman for wanting to break it up. She said that "almost every child is happier in an ordinary, average home than in an admirable institution, because every child needs—has needed, and will continue to need—a mother's care. . . . Until automatic nurses have been invented, or male volunteers have offered themselves, the burden must fall upon other women, who—whether themselves mothers or not—are thus obliged to bear a double one. Real liberation for women is thus impossible; the only thing possible is a new division of the burdens."

She argued that one way of sharing the work was a "collective motherliness" on the part of the community which would guarantee that all children had what they needed no matter what the mother's income.

Generally missed in the intellectual attack on the nuclear family was the fact that many Americans—perhaps even most—didn't live in them. The model unit of man, wife, and children had only passing relevance to the millions of immigrant, black, farm, and working-class families that were "extended" with grandparents, uncles, aunts, in-laws, cousins, and "cousins" who shared kitchens, living space, cooking, and care of the children among themselves.

And as the gray Victorian walls crumbled, people also began to deal openly with the problems of sexuality.

Emma Goldman, Margaret and William Sanger, and others lectured and distributed literature on birth control, for which they were frequently arrested. Goldman complained in *Mother Earth* that "The custom of procuring abortions has reached such vast proportions in America as to be almost beyond belief. According to recent investigations along this line, seventeen abortions are committed in every hundred pregnancies." But "prevention, even by scientifically determined safe methods, is absolutely prohibited; nay, the very mention of the subject is considered criminal."

Goldman also lectured on homosexuality, one of the very few who would even talk about it in the open—

The men and women who used to come to see me after my lectures on homosexuality, and who confided to me their anguish and their isolation, were often of a finer grain than those who had cast them out. Most of them had reached an adequate understanding of their differentiation only after years of struggle to stifle what they had considered a disease and a shameful affliction. One young woman confessed to me that in the twenty-five years of her life she had never known a day when the nearness of a man, her own father and brothers even, did not make her ill. The more she had tried to respond the sexual approach, the more repugnant men became to her. She had hated herself, she said, because she could not love her father and her brothers as she loved her mother. She suffered excruciating remorse, but her revulsion only increased.

At the age of eighteen she had accepted an offer of marriage in the hope that a long engagement might help her grow accustomed to a man and cure her of her "disease." It turned out a ghastly failure and nearly drove her insane. She could not face marriage and she dared not confide in her fiancé or friends.

She had never met anyone, she told me, who suffered from a similar affliction, nor had she ever read books dealing with the subject. My lecture had set her free; I had given her back her self-respect.

As sexual relations became freer, so did the attempt to grasp them at their core. "The modern woman's great distress has been the discovery of the dissimilarity between her own erotic nature and that of man," said Ellen Key. "The feeling of motherhood is the most thoroughly sensuous and therefore the most thoroughly soulful of emotions . . . [woman] is sensuous, so to speak, from head to foot and chronically, whole man is so only acutely and locally. . . . With women love usually proceeds from the soul to the sense and sometimes does not reach so far; that with man it usually proceeds from the senses to the soul and sometimes never completes the journey—this is for both the most painful of the existing distinctions between man and woman."

Gilman predicted the day "when women no longer make their living out of their loving." Then, she said, "the prostitute, and that more successful specialist, the mercenary wife, will leave the world. The reduction of sex-attraction from its present fever-height to a normal level, and the perfect freedom for true marriage resultant upon right distribution of property, will take away the cruder and more violent forms of sexual sin, and give us pure monogamy at last."

True sexuality, added Goldman, "will not admit of conqueror and conquered; it knows but one great thing: to give of one's self boundlessly, in order to find one's self boundlessly, in order to find one's self richer, deeper, better. That alone can fill the emptiness and transform the tragedy of woman's emancipation into joy, limitless joy."

Kids' Power

Basic to the attack on the family was a new consciousness of youth.

A generation had been born into a world completely alien from that of their parents. Randolph Bourne, one of its spokesmen, welcomed "The Century of the Child"—

School discipline, since the abolition of corporal punishment, has been almost nominal; church discipline is practically nil; and even home discipline, although retaining the forms, is but an empty shell. The modern child from the age of ten is almost his own master. The help-lessness of the modern parent face-to-face with these conditions is amusing.

The old order—youth dominated by age—was being flipped over. "We insist on worshipping the God of our fathers," complained Gilman. "Why not the God of our children? Does eternity only stretch one way?"

Children were not only a separate class, she said, they were the dominant class. "Mankind has been continuous upon earth for millions of years; children have been equally continuous. . . . The children outnumber the adults three to two."

The child, added Key, "even at four or five years of age, is making experiments with adults, seeing through them, with marvellous shrewdness making his own valuations and reacting sensitively to each impression. . . . Parents . . . have as little power or right to prescribe laws for this new being as they possess the power or might to lay down paths for the stars."

As for the school system, it was the reason there were "so

many clever children and so many stupid adults." Constipated teachers lecturing rows of ordered, numbered students was "soul-murder."

After the revolution schools would be "surrounded by gardens." There would be "no classrooms at all, but different halls with ample material provided for different subjects and, by the side of them, rooms for work where each scholar will have a place assigned to him for private study."

"Youth rules the world," shouted Bourne, "but only when it is no longer young. It is a tarnished, travestied youth that is in the saddle in the person of middle age."

In the new age of the twentieth century, "anything is likely to happen"—a new world demanded youth. "Old men cherish a fond delusion that there is something mystically valuable in mere quantity of experience. Now the fact is, of course, that it is the young people who have all the really valuable experience. It is they who have constantly to face new situations, to react constantly to new aspects of life. . . . Most older men live only in the experience of their youthful years. . . . The ideas of the young are the living, the potential ideas; those of the old, the dying, or the already dead. . . . Must the younger generation eternally wait for the sign? The answer, of course, is that it will not wait."

Furthermore, as humanity liberated itself economically and spiritually, old age itself would disappear. "Getting old is no necessity," wrote Key. "It is only a bad habit."

"The real enemy of youth," said Bourne, was "not doubt but convention," convention that killed the spirit, that the old imposed on the young "by economic pressure to force him to conformity." Society was "one vast conspiracy for carving one into the kind of a statue it likes, and then placing it in the most convenient niche it has." It forced young people to choose between "the routine of a big corporation" and "the vicissitudes of small business," neither of which was exciting, satisfying, or truly productive.

Real youth knew its home was "not the niche but the open road, with the spirit always travelling, always criticising, always learning, always escaping the pressures that threaten its integrity."

Anyone who wanted to be young had better create his own choices and stay radical. The struggle for liberation was an end in itself, and "the strength and beauty of the radical's position is that he already to a large extent lives in that sort of world which he desires."

Days of Magic

Bourne was a crippled young man from middle-class Bloomfield, New Jersey. His sharp eyes, "hunched back, ungainly hands, and too prominent brow, together with the long cape he sometimes wore" gave him the air of a true extraterrestial. His sharp mind, strong spirit, and constant refusal to conform to official taste made him the first hero of the emerging youth culture.

Bourne's world arrived in *Bohemia* and came alive in the dawn of the Aquarian Age. The Bohemian lifestyle was that of the poor but free gypsy artist—

The medieval French believed that Gypsies came from the Central European fields of Bohemia. They called these Gypsies Bohemians, and when the age of romanticism touched French literature this name was exaltingly used to denote the penniless and carefree writers, poets, journalists, artists, actors, sculpture, and other members of that wide group which later the French and Russians so aptly labelled "intellectual proletariat."

Bohemian circles could be traced in America at least to Edgar Allan Poe and the "Pfaffians" who frequented Pfaff's restaurant at 633 Broadway. Later the circle included Walt Whitman, and at the turn of the century there were Maria's, the Bohemian Club in San Francisco, and the Bismark Cafe in Austin, Texas, where William Sydney Porter (O. Henry) published a magazine called *The Rolling Stone*.

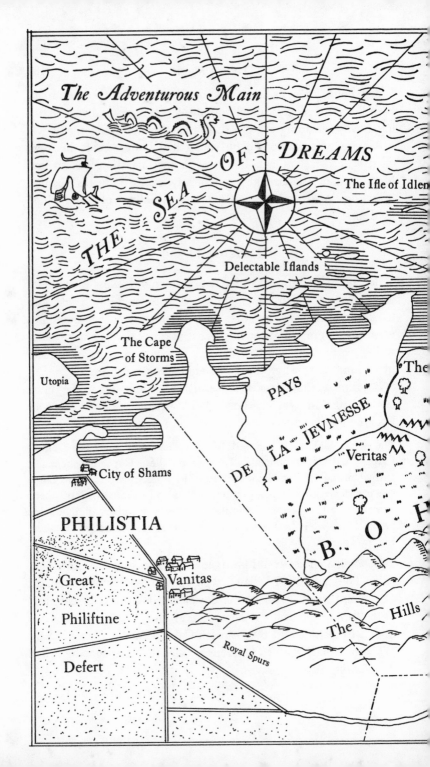

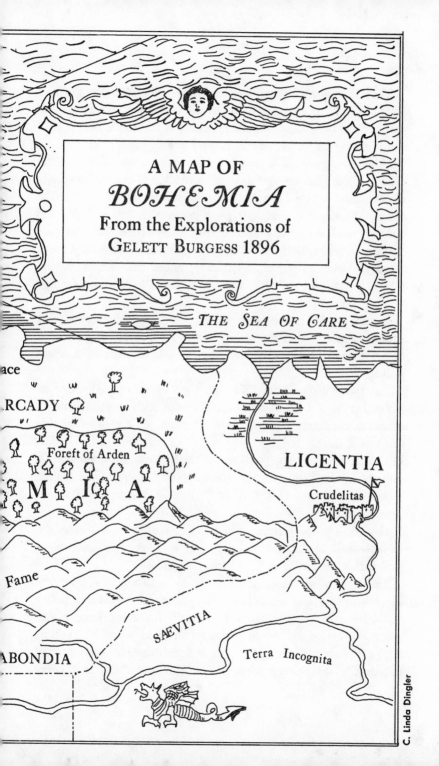

A MAP OF
BOHEMIA
From the Explorations of
GELETT BURGESS 1896

THE SEA OF CARE

ace

RCADY

Foreft of Arden

M I A

LICENTIA

Crudelitas

Fame

SAEVITIA

ABONDIA

Terra Incognita

C. Linda Dingler

The Greenwich Village area in New York was literally and figuratively on the border between the ghettoes to the south and east and the baronial stores and mansions to the north. Before 1910 the Washington Square environs were largely populated by social workers and political reformers. But in its days of magic the area had low rent, cheap food, and a quiet, self-contained village atmosphere. Artists began to pour in and spring up out of the square. Broken-down stables were renovated into studios, and galleries and workshops materialized everywhere. The low-rent flats and cheap restaurants filled with painters, reformers, writers, revolutionaries, sculptors, dilettantes, anarchists, actors, adventurers, poets, and dancers of all varieties, all of whom seemed to know each other.

In January 1911, a cooperatively owned magazine called *The Masses* began publishing in the Village. As a right-wing Socialist organ it was dull and dogmatic, and by late summer 1912 it was falling apart.

But the staff got Max Eastman, then teaching philosophy at Columbia, to be the new editor. Eastman and a friend went to dinner at the mansion of Mrs. O. H. P. Belmont, "the indefagitable duchess of the Gilded Age" who had divorced William K. Vanderbilt. Mrs. Belmont coughed up $2,000 because Eastman was "a militant." John Fox, a writer who happened to be at the dinner, threw in another $1,000. Thus, wrote Eastman, "our super-revolutionary magazine owed its send-off to a leader of New York's 400—to the fortune of old Public-be-Damned Vanderbilt, in fact—and to a southern gentleman with as much interest in proletarian revolution as I had in polo ponies."

The first new issue had a two-page cartoon depicting the capitalist press as a whorehouse. The magazine's editorial policy could be called left-Socialist, but its rhythm came from a vast vicarious energy and freedom from sectarian ideology. The editors kept a "steady objection to dogma and insistence on experimental thinking." The guiding ideal, wrote Eastman, "was that every individual should be made free to live and grow in his own chosen way. That was what I hoped might be achieved with all this distasteful palaver about politics and economics."

Somehow, the magazine came together. It focused the Bohemian community and gave it an identity and direction. Its poetry, cartoons, fiction, jokes, political theory, reportage of the class war, and discussions of sexuality were the voice of a young community that had taken to the air. The magazine was "kicked off the subway stands in New York, suppressed by the Magazine Distribution Company in Boston, ejected by the United News Company of Philadelphia, expelled from the Columbia University library and bookstore, stopped at the border by Canada, and swept out of colleges and reading rooms from Harvard to San Diego," all of which buoyed the spirits, if not the finances, of the staff. "*The Masses* has a sense of humor," they proclaimed. "Enjoy the revolution."

An occasional drawing by Pablo Picasso and Robert Henri and regular work by John Sloan, Art Young, George Bellows, Boardman Robinson, Stuart Davis, and Robert Minor appeared in the magazine. Carl Sandburg contributed a poem denouncing Billy Sunday and regular writing was done by John Reed, Louis Untermeyer, Arturo Giovannitti, and Floyd Dell. Dell was the managing editor and the only one besides Eastman who got a salary, but many of the staff made money by selling the magazines on the street.

Typical of the writers was Harry Kemp, the "tramp poet," a large hobo whose burly presence in the Village was made famous by the newspaper reporters he attracted "simply by appearing in public without a hat—which seemingly no other male of the time dared to do." He wrote this to Rudyard Kipling—

> Vile singer of the bloody deeds of empire,
> And of the bravery that exploits the poor,
> Exalter of subservience to masters,
> Bard of the race that bound and robbed the Boer.

At Last—a Perfect Soldier

Robert Minor, *The Masses*, July 1916

We note your metaphors that shine and glisten
But underneath your sounding verse, we see
The exploitation and the wide corruption
The lying, and the vice, and misery.

Your people lay upon the back of others—
The bullet, and the prison, and the rod,
Wherwith ye scourge the races that subserve you,
And then blaspheme by blaming it on God.

Meanwhile, Emma Goldman and Alexander Berkman published
Mother Earth on the Lower East Side; then came *The Seven Arts*
of Randolph Bourne, Waldo Frank, and James Oppenheim, and,
in late 1914, *The New Republic.*

On MacDougal Street there was the Liberal Club, frequented
by Lincoln Steffens, Upton Sinclair, Sinclair Lewis, and Henrietta
Redman, the free-love advocate. One floor down was Polly's
restaurant, run by Polly Holladay, an anarchist from Evanston,
Illinois. The cook at Polly's was Hippolyte Havel, a friend of
Emma Goldman who sneered "bourgeois pigs!" in the face of new
customers. Everywhere "there was talk, endless talk, but it gave
a new direction to our thoughts, and we felt tremendously awake
and open-eyed."

    Yet we are free who live in Washington Square,
    We live as uptowners wouldn't dare.

In late 1912 a well-to-do Socialite named Mabel Dodge returned
from a heady European acquaintance with Gertrude Stein. She and
her husband took a large apartment in the Village and at the urging
of Lincoln Steffens opened it for community discussions—some
open, others planned—on topics ranging from social revolution to
the new science of psychoanalysis.

The idea of someone opening a private home for community
meetings was so novel that it was covered in newspapers across
the country. "Looking back upon it now," wrote Mabel Dodge,
"it seems as though everywhere, in that year 1913, barriers went
down and people reached each other who had never been in

touch before; there were all sorts of new ways to communicate, as well as new communications."

In February 1913 the burgeoning circle of rebel artists rented the armory of the 69th Regiment for a huge show to celebrate "the new spirit." Modernists, cubists, expressionists, fauvists, and neoimpressionists from Paris and New York displayed over 1600 pieces of art, free of the National Academy, in a show that drew huge crowds, high excitement, and bitter criticism. The symbol of the exhibition was the pine-tree emblem of the American Revolution, and its highlight came to be Marcel Duchamp's *Nude Descending a Staircase*, which Theodore Roosevelt branded "degenerate," a product of "the lunatic fringe." The painting was dubbed elsewhere as "Staircase Descending a Nude" and "an explosion in a shingle factory." One art magazine ran a contest to "find the nude in *Nude Descending a Staircase*."

The show as a whole was attacked as a "harbinger of universal anarchy," and the riot police were called out to control the giant crowds waiting to get in. When the collection showed in Chicago, students at the Art Institute hung Brancusi and Walter Pache in effigy and burned imitations of paintings by Matisse, whom they also hung in effigy. By the time the show's national tour was over more than 300,000 people had seen it.

In Provincetown the theater group came under the direction of young Eugene O'Neill, who eventually moved the show to Greenwich Village. There were Bohemian colonies of sorts in every city and in Carmel and Monterey, Taos and Santa Fe. In Chicago the colony was pioneered by Thorstein Veblen. Writers and artists rented stores on the south side that had serviced the 1893 Exposition. There was a circle at the apartments of Floyd Dell (who moved to the Village) and Margery Currey. Harriet Monroe's *Poetry* published early works of Carl Sandburg, D. H. Lawrence, Robert Frost, Vachel Lindsay, Amy Lowell, Tagore, William Butler Yeats, Hart Crane, Ezra Pound, and T. S. Eliot. In 1914 the livelier *Little Review* made its debut. It was put out by a flighty woman named Margaret Anderson and was supported in large part by Frank Lloyd Wright. Anderson occasionally lived in a tent on the shores of Lake Michigan, where she hosted a circle that included Ben Hecht, Maxwell Bodenheim, Theodore Dreiser, and Sherwood Anderson.

But the heart of the culture was in the Village. One night at the Dodge house Bill Haywood, Elizabeth Flynn and Carlo Tresca, Emma Goldman, Alexander Berkman and Ben Reitman, Walter Lippmann, Frank Tannenbaum, Amos Pinchet, John Reed, Eastman, Steffens, and others gathered to talk revolution. Haywood, Flynn, and Tresca were then working in the IWW silkworkers strike in Paterson, across the river in New Jersey. At least one striker had been killed, and there were 20,000 workers out. But the newspapers had completely suppressed coverage, and no one but the Wobblies and anarchists even knew the strike was going on.

After hearing Haywood speak, John Reed went to cover the strike for *The Masses*. Reed was "the fair-haired boy of the Village," a tall, energetic ex-cheerleader from Harvard who looked like "an overgrown hero of a high school football team." He was "young and irrepressibly in love with life," a portrait of vigorous innocence.

Reed was arrested in Paterson. When booked he listed "poet" as his occupation and was promptly crammed into a tiny cell with eight strikers.

The spirit of the Paterson strike was as high as Lawrence, and the prison rocked with song and laughter. Four days later Reed's friends bailed him out. "You'll be back," a cellmate told him as he left.

Reed returned to New York and wrote an amazing series of first-person accounts. Then he and Mabel Dodge set about organizing a pageant to dramatize the strike for a New York audience and raise funds for the union. They raised enough money to rent Madison Square Garden for one night, and then they and the union put together an eight-act pageant to portray the lives of the silk workers and the progress of the strike.

The night of the show somebody set up a huge red neon "IWW" on top of the Garden that shone all over the City while frantic police tried to shut off the power.

Fifteen thousand people, most of them workers, came to see the show. The cheap seats sold out first and after holding the show for about an hour the doors were opened and the Garden filled up for free—

Fifteen thousand spectators applauded with shouts and tears the great Paterson Strike Pageant at Madison Square Garden. The big mill aglow with light in the dark hours of early winter morning, the shrieking whistles, the din of machinery—dying away to give place to the "Marseillaise" sung by a surging crowd of 1,200 operatives, the fierce battle with the police, the somber funeral of the victim, the impassioned speech of the agitator, the sending away of the children, the great meeting of desperate hollow-eyed strikers—these scenes unrolled with a poignant realism that no man who saw them will forget.

The emotional peak came with the reenactment of the funeral of Valentino Modestino, a striker killed by police. "Pallbearers carried a coffin down the center aisle of the Garden through the audience. Over 1000 strikers followed, singing 'The Funeral March of the Workers.' Sitting in a box seat, Mrs. Modestino became hysterical when the funeral procession reached the stage. The cast of strikers heaped red carnations and evergreen boughs on the bier and Haywood, Tresca, and Gurley Flynn repeated the speeches they had made at Modestino's graveside. Many in the audience wept."

"For a few electric moments," said Mabel Dodge, "there was a terrible unity between all those people. They were one."

The show was a psychic success but a financial catastrophe. Reed and Dodge sailed to Europe, to the amazement of those who expected him to become a dedicated servant of the revolution. "Revolution, literature, poetry," said Walter Lippmann, "they are only things which hold him at times, incidents merely of his living."

The Mexican Situation

Source: One Big Union Monthly

But soon Mabel complained that John "might as well have been gone from there for all he was with ME. He drank his coffee with the morning paper propped up before him, his honey-colored round eyes just popping over 'THE NEWS!' "

They came back to America, and he went to Mexico to cover the revolution. He traveled with Pancho Villa and pleaded, in vain, that Woodrow Wilson keep out of it.

Then he went to Ludlow and found "stoves, pots, and pans still half full of food that had been cooking that terrible morning, baby carriages, piles of half-burned clothes, children's toys all riddled with bullets, the scorched mouths of tent cellars."

And then to Europe again where the apocalypse was well under way. "This is not our war," he wrote again and again and in vain.

Wilson dragged the country into world war as he had dragged it into Mexico. Draft evasion and resistance skyrocketed all over the country, and a small armed rebellion broke out among Oklahoma farmers. The Socialist party took the leadership of the antiwar movement. The United States, said the conservative Akron *Beacon-Journal*, had "never embarked upon a more unpopular war. . . . The vast majority of the people [have] never been convinced that war was necessary either to sustain our honor or to protect our interests." In September 1917 the *Beacon-Journal* reported there was "scarcely a political observer whose opinion is worth much but what will admit that were an election to come now a mighty tide of socialism would inundate the midwest [and] all other sections of the country."

By 1919 the Russian Revolution had clearly succeeded. The American economy collapsed into a postwar depression. Populism came to life again in the Non-Partisan League in Minnesota and the Dakotas. While many conservative Socialists had split the party to support Wilson and the war, the young left wing turned to bolshevism and active revolution. William Z. Foster, a Communist, made big gains inside the AF of L, and a huge strike shut down most of the steel industry. The Boston police walked off their jobs. A general strike shut down Seattle. When Wilson visited there he drove through block after block after block of workers standing with their arms folded, in total silence. Four million workers walked off their jobs in 1919.

But with the agrarian left already gone under and with the working class fragmented by trade, nationality, and race, the revolutionary movement was no match for the march of the right. By 1920 it had been virtually wiped out.

For the overwhelming catastrophe of war had left the United States and the world staggered, dazed, bewildered. What had it meant? What could it possibly mean? Thirty-five million dead human beings. An entire generation of Europeans had slaughtered one another in trenches. Fields, farms, towns, and villages were gutted and drenched in blood by a cataclysm that defied even the imagination. An influenza-epidemic killed millions.

The ghastly feeling set in that "the war to end all wars" was just the beginning, that the cycle of depression, revolt, war, and materialism would repeat itself again and maybe even again, that an unimaginable worse was yet to come, soon. "Madness has entered everything," said Wilson.

The war swept up John Reed. He stormed the Winter Palace with the Russian Red Guard, wrote *Ten Days That Shook the World*, and then died; his ashes were buried in the Kremlin Wall with those of Bill Haywood. By then Jack London was dead, a suicide, and Mabel Dodge was living in Taos, the wife of a Pueblo Indian.

Under cover of war the government smashed *Mother Earth*, *The Masses*, and the entire Socialist and Wobbly press. Four printings of James Joyce's *Ulysses*, published by the *Little Review*, were confiscated and burned in public. *The New Republic* went prowar, and Max Eastman made long strides toward the right wing, while ex-Bohemian George Creel directed the government propaganda machine.

Debs and thousands of other Socialists were thrown in jail.

More than a quarter of the Socialist party local headquarters were burned, blown up, or otherwise destroyed. In 1920, Debs campaigned from his jail cell and got nearly a million votes, but by then the party was in shambles. Many Wobblies were murdered and what was left of the leadership was imprisoned. Emma Goldman was arrested and then deported along with some 600 other Russian immigrants.

Wilson sent troops and supplies into Russia to fight against the revolution. At least seventy Americans died in support of the Czarist generals.

The right-wing reign of terror here was prolonged with the red scare led by Attorney General A. Mitchell Palmer. Palmer's gestapo broke up meetings, destroyed offices, smashed into private homes, and threw thousands of radicals, suspected radicals, and immigrants in chains and marched them through the streets. Meanwhile, in the "red summer" of 1919, the worst black-white warfare since Reconstruction exploded in cities across the country.

Thus the Progressive alliance was consummated. Having ridden the wave of revolution into power, the new professional-trade-union middle class joined its baronial allies in smashing the revolutionary left. Prohibition, the Klan, and the fundamentalism of the dying farm community, the antiradical spy network in the factories and unions, the ritual murders of Sacco, Vanzetti, and the Rosenbergs, the reigns of Harding, Hoover, McCarthy, Dulles, Nixon—all were echoes of that repression.

From the World War on, American material wealth was built on physical conquest in Asia and Latin America and the two devastations of Europe. The "high standard of living" of the new middle class took its payment in the cancerous gray of "100 percent Americanism," in the immeasurable psychic dead-weight of keeping other people down all over the world.

The fifty-year winter of imperial America had set in.

CELEBRATE! CELEBRATE!

But it wouldn't last. As the First World War brought on the Russian Revolution, the Second brought on the Chinese and Indian. The door to the conquest of the Orient was shut. Two thousand years of constant westward expansion from Rome to America to the Pacific crashed on the southeast coast of Asia, and like a frustrated dying monster, the American machine thrashed its tail senselessly again and again on the land and people of Korea, Vietnam, Laos, and Cambodia.

From there it would all unravel.

For the Populists, Socialists, Wobblies, realists and naturalists, blacks, women, and Bohemians had already shattered the Calvinist-capitalist system at its core, and before the First World War people were already dancing on the Victorian coffin.

"This is the greatest place in the world!" John Reed had written his parents from New York. "You cannot imagine such utter freedom! Freedom from every boundary, moral, religious, social."

"You have no idea how exciting it was," said a Village woman, "to go to bed with a man, and know at the same time you were striking a blow for sexual freedom."

"Margaret Sanger," said Mable Dodge, "was the first person I ever knew who was openly an ardent propagandist for the joys of the flesh . . . for Margaret Sanger to attempt what she did at that time seems to me now like another attempt to release the energy of the atom. . . . She taught us the way to a heightening of pleasure and of prolonging it, and the delimiting of it to the sexual zones, the spreading out and sexualizing of the whole body until it should become sensitive and alive throughout, and complete. She made love into a serious undertaking—with the body so illuminated and conscious that it would be able to interpret and express in all its parts the language of the spirit's pleasure."

In the spring of 1914, Dodge and some friends conducted an Indian peyote rite—

Raymond went out and found a green branch to make the arrow and he found the eagle feathers. For a "fire" he laid a lighted electric bulb on the floor with my Chinese red shawl over it, and for the Mountain of the Moon—I forgot what he did about that—but the Peyote Path was a white sheet folded into a narrow strip, running towards the east along the floor.

The evening we were to engage ourselves to experiment with consciousness, none of us ate any dinner. . . . At nine o'clock we extinguished the lights and sat on the floor in a crescent shape with the Peyote Path running eastward out of our midst.

Raymond, who constituted himself the Chief, sat at the foot of the path behind the fire, an arrow in one hand, and a few lovely eagle feathers in the other. . . . He looked so somber sitting there crosslegged I was filled to bursting with sudden laughter. I was thrilled and delighted and amused. . . .

The PEYOTE lay in a little heap in the center of the space before him. It looked like small, dried-up buttons with shriveled edges, and it had a kind of fur on the upper side. . . .

Suddenly Raymond seized a piece of the PEYOTE and popped it into his mouth and began to sing. At last he raised his chin and began to howl like a dog. . . .

Then we all, in our different fashions, reached out and took the PEYOTE and put it into our mouths, and began to chew upon it. But it was bitter! Oh, how it was bitter! I chewed for a little while and watched the others. They all seemed to be chewing away, too. Everybody chewed.

But after a while, as I swallowed the bitter saliva, I felt a certain numbness coming over me in my mouth and limbs. But it was only over my body.

My brain was clearly filled with laughter, laughter at all the others there. Laughter, and at the same time a canny, almost smug discretion took possession of me. . . .

Everyone seemed ridiculous to me—utterly ridiculous and immeasurably far away from me.

Far away from me, several little foolish human beings sat staring at a mock fire and made silly little gestures. Above them I leaned, filled with an unlimited contempt for the facile enthrallments of humanity, weak and petty in its activities, bound so easily by a dried herb, bound by its notions of everything—anarchy, poetry, systems, sex, and society.

Bobby! Look at Bobby's beard! Like a Persian miniature of a late period, not well drawn, inexpressive, he rolled subjugated eyes, increasingly solemn as he viewed the changing colors rolling before him. And Hutch! Good heavens! Hutch looked like a Lutheran Monk! Genevieve stared continually at a spot on the rug before her, her eyes enormous now, the whites showing all round them in an appalled revelation of something. . . .

And always there was the music, black music, ragtime. The beat came from Congo Square in New Orleans, where Afro-American drummers beat out the rhythms of VODUN, a cult of the Dahomean tribe, which the slaves brought with them from Africa.

Congo Square was destroyed in 1885, but the cult permeated Louisiana and the South and its music was New Orleans. "King" Buddy Bolden, a trumpeter with a gigantic following, formed the first jazz band and then went insane. The music mixed with rural blues and spread up the Mississippi, carried by black musicians like Scott Joplin and countless others to St. Louis, Chicago, then New York.

It was basic, powerful, inescapable sound "that demanded physical response, patting of the feet, drumming of the fingers, or nodding of the head in time with the beat. The barbaric harmonies, the audacious resolutions, often consisting of an abrupt jump from one key to another, the intricate rhythms in which the accents fell in the most unexpected places, but in which the beat was never lost."

New York, said the *Nation* in 1915, was "a city gone mad over the fox trot and the white lights."

Third Heartbeat from the Sun

All Indians must dance, everywhere, keep on dancing. Pretty soon in next spring Great Spirit come. He bring back all game of every kind. The game be thick everywhere. All dead Indians come back and live again. They all be strong just like young men, be young again. Old blind Indian see again and get young and have fine time. When Great Spirit comes this way, then all the Indians go to mountains, high up away from whites. Whites can't hurt Indians then. Then while Indians way up high, big flood comes like water and all white people die, get drowned. After that, water go way and then nobody but Indians everywhere and game all kinds thick. Then medicine man tell Indians to send word to all Indians to keep up dancing and the good time will come. Indians who don't dance, who don't believe in this word, will grow little, just about a foot high, and stay that way. Some of them will be turned into wood and be burned in fire.

—Wovoka, the Paiute "Ghost Dance" Messiah

At Wounded Knee and elsewhere throughout the west, the "Gay Nineties" brought horrifying massacres of the last free Native American settlements. The warrior chieftains Metacom (King Philip), Joseph Brant, Little Turtle, Osceola, Pontiac, Black Hawk, Tecumseh, Crazy Horse, Sitting Bull, Geronimo, Captain Jack; the supremely articulate Chiefs Joseph and Seattle, Lone Wolf and Cochise, Powhatan and Logan, Canassatego and Satanta, Little Crow and Black Elk, Red Cloud and John Ross; the master agronomist Nipmucks, the brilliant constitutionalist Iroquois, the literate technologist Cherokee, the pacifistic Hopi, the spiritualist Lakota, the fierce Seminole, who were never really conquered—all slowed and changed the rampage of European society across the American continent, but never really stopped it.

By 1900 the "frontier" was officially dead and the U.S. government was deep in the business of conquering other nations. All but a few tribal enclaves had been dispersed or locked into reservations, where they would greet a new century laden with poverty, disease and racial bigotry parallel to that heaped upon the refugees of southern slavery.

Since 1492 the whites had approached native culture with profound schizophrenia. One segment of the European mind, in the Calvinist spirit, saw the Indians as agents of the Devil, subhumans to be exterminated or to be expunged of their independent identity. As late as 1988, President Ronald Reagan, whose career had been built in part by killing Indians (he played General George Armstrong Custer in the movies) could tell a global media audience that it may have been a "mistake" to put Native Americans on reservations. "Maybe we should not have humored them in wanting to stay in that kind of primitive life style."

Reagan's remarks were prompted by a delegation of Native Americans that had travelled to the Moscow summit hoping to meet with the President there because he had refused to do so at home.

Reagan thus epitomized five centuries of mainstream white blindness to the cultural complexity and ecological sophistication of native America. The actual slaughter of whole Indian nations formed the tragic backdrop for modern America's birth pains.

But another portion of the European soul found in the native culture a source of unmatched instruction and inspiration. The earliest Pilgrims could not have survived without them. Benjamin Franklin published translations of dozens of speeches by native chieftains. He and Edmund Burke widely praised the Iroquois League, which kept peace between six nations for more than 200 years. He, Jefferson and Thomas Paine drew on native ideas for the federal Constitution, the Declaration of Independence and the incendiary "Common Sense."

In the face of the new industrial machine, as their Ghost Dances mourned the passing of an ancient way of life, the Indians also left a clear legacy for the century to come. Its core was wrapped in the oneness of the natural and human ecologies. "The earth and myself are of one mind," said Chief Joseph. "The measure of the land and the measure of our bodies are the same."

"The shining water that moves in the streams and the rivers is not just water but the blood of our ancestors," said Chief Seattle—

"We know that the white man does not understand our ways. One portion of land is the same to him as the next, for he is a stranger who comes in the night and takes from the land whatever he needs.

"He treats his mother, the earth, and his brother, the sky, as things to be bought, plundered, sold like sheep or bright beads. His appetite will devour the earth and leave behind only a desert.

"Every part of this earth is sacred to my people. Every shining pine needle, every sandy shore, every mist in the dark woods, every clearing and humming insect is holy in the memory and experience of my people. The sap which courses through the trees carries the memories of the red man.

"The air is precious to the red man, for all things share the same breath: the beast, the tree, the man, they all share the same breath.

"Teach your children what we have taught our children, that the earth is our mother. Whatever befalls the earth befalls the sons of the earth. Man did not weave the web of life, he is merely a strand in it.

"Whatever he does to the web, he does to himself."

Conservative and even progressive whites generally dismissed the native speeches as of marginal interest, and viewed their extermination as an unfortunate necessity. The full context of that tragedy was perhaps best encapsulated in the career of General Nelson A. Miles, who commanded troops at the Wounded Knee Massacre, then led them against the American Railway Union during the 1894 Pullman strike, then helped defeat Aguinaldo's rebels fighting for independence in the Philippines.

That war was precursor to the American nightmare in Vietnam. Its chief prosecutor was Theodore Roosevelt, whose racist diatribes on native America were laced with violence. When it came to the land, Roosevelt was identified with progressive "conservationism," but that credo was more about long-term resource management than an organic connection with the earth.

In opposition, a critical segment of white society took to heart much of the native word and spirit. At its forefront was John Muir, a pioneer ecologist whose concerted and often bitter battles to save some of America's most beautiful landscapes led to the 1910 founding of the Sierra Club. Two years prior, Roosevelt gave San Francisco permission to dam the magnificent Hetch Hetchy Valley in Yosemite National Park. The city had other sources of water available, but convinced TR it was "cheapest" to sacrifice the Hech Hetchy. Muir was heartbroken. The sun, he said, "shines not on us, but in us—

"Garden- and park-making goes on everywhere with civilization, for everybody needs beauty as well as bread, places to stay and pray in, where Nature may heal and cheer and give strength to body and soul. It is impossible to overestimate the value of wild mountains and mountain temples as places for people to grow in, recreation grounds for soul and body.

"They are the greatest of our natural resources, God's best gifts, but none, however high and holy, is beyond reach of the spoiler.

"These temple destroyers, devotees of ravaging commercialism, seem to have a perfect contempt for Nature, and instead of lifting their eyes to the mountains, lift them to dams and town skyscrapers."

Among the Bohemian sub-culture—and later among the hippies of the 1960s and the New Age/holistic movement beyond—the native/ecologist worldview was a romantic inspiration that took tangible form in the "back-to-the-land" lifestyle.

At the turn of the century, Bolton Hall, a friend of the "Mother Earth" circle, urged families to leave the cities and take up small-scale intensive farming. In THREE ACRES AND LIBERTY (1907) he told readers that "the amount that a single well-managed, well-tilled acre will produce in a season is simply incredible." A family of five could raise enough vegetables for itself (exclusive of potatoes for winter) on a plot 150 × 100 feet. A three-acre farm was enough for a family's independence and could lay the foundation for a new way to live. "You raise more than vegetables in your garden," he said. "You raise your expectation of life."

There were a raft of similar books—TEN ACRES ENOUGH, THE CALL OF THE LAND, THE NEW EARTH, HOW TO LIVE IN THE COUNTRY—all carrying the same essential message: the cities and the large single-owner farms had failed. Every family should have a little land on which to raise its own food. Under intense cultivation, with goats or a milk cow, a garden, and perhaps an orchard, a small farm could support a family. "Most of us have children," wrote Hall, "and we all know how we love and treat them. Treat the land in the same manner, feed it, and keep it clean, and you will have no cause to complain."

But as the populists well knew, there was one immense barrier to the small-farming ideal—the money system controlled the land. Land prices were still "cheap," but the people who needed it had no money at all. "Mortgages are hard to get in the East, and loans to help in building are hardly to be had at all," Hall complained. As a result "land is either held intact as large farms or is sold entire to speculators who hold it until it can be divided into city lots."

The need to merge organic self-containment with urban growth took form in the "garden city" plans of Ebenezer Howard, an Englishman. Howard's idea was to guide urban expansion into a series of planned communities that would contain the industries in which the people worked. The towns would be surrounded by an irreducible "green belt" of farms and would be filled with parks, playgrounds, orchards and gardens. They would function as communal units.

The need to unify natural function with urban expansion was expressed in America in aspects of the park planning of Frederick Law Olmstead and in the organic architectural designs of Louis Sullivan, Frank Lloyd Wright, and the Chicago School. Wright was also the first major architect to introduce Oriental design to America, the result of a trip to Japan in 1905.

Meanwhile Socialists, single-taxers, anarchists and others began to build "the new society within the shell of the old" in the form of utopian communities. The history of utopias in America was already a long one, including the efforts of Labadists, Ephratians, Rappites, Zoarites, Shakers, Eben-Ezers, Inspirationists, Owenites, Oneida Perfectionists, Bethelites, Aurorians, Icarians, and many others.

In the nineties there were two major efforts by Socialists: one on several thousand acres of land at Cave Mills, Tennessee, the other on the Kaweah River in California.

The Cave Mills commune was financed by "The Coming Nation" of Greensburg, Indiana, the precursor of the "Appeal to Reason." In June 1897 the colony opened Ruskin College of the New Economy, the world's first Socialist college. But the community fell apart two years later, largely due to internal dissension.

The commune at Kaweah was fairly successful, but the government, in a rare burst of conservationist zeal, decided to turn the area into Sequoiah National Forest.

The single-taxers had colonies at Fairhope, Alabama, and Arden, Pennsylvania. A group of Christian Socialists founded the Christian Commonwealth in Muscogee County, Georgia, which lasted from 1896 to 1900. Upton Sinclair used the royalties from THE JUNGLE to start Helicon House in New Jersey, but the house burned down.

Most of the colonies were relatively shortlived for reasons of internal conflict and financial woes which, of course, always made the internal problems worse.

But while they often didn't last long, people like H. D. Lloyd could argue that "only within these communities has there been seen in the wide borders of the United States, a social life where hunger and cold, prostitution, intemperance, poverty, slavery, crime, premature old age, and unnecessary mortality, panic and industrial terror have been abolished. If they had done this only for a year, they would deserve to be called the only successful 'society' on this continent, and some of them are generations old!

"They are little cases of people in our desert of persons," he added. "All this has not been done by saints in heaven, but on earth by average men and women."

Lloyd felt the "separate successes" of the communes should continue, but that they would be short-lived until society solved its problems "by all, for all."

He and others also felt that the best basis for a utopian community was not politics but religion.

Revolutionary politics did merge with religion in the Christian Socialist movement, which centered in the nineties in the Brotherland of the Co-Operative Commonwealth. There were revolutionary priests all over the country. Herbert Casson of the Labor Church of Lynn, Massachusetts, told his congregation that "many a church is nothing but a spiritual opium joint." In 1886 Father Edward Mc-Glynn of New York endorsed single-taxer Henry George for mayor. He was summoned to Rome, and excommunicated when he refused to go. Two years later the press attacked him for quoting Cardinal Manning's statement that "necessity knows no law, and a starving man has a right to his neighbor's bread."

In 1904 the nationally-known preacher and theologian George D. Herron nominated Debs for president as a Socialist. The mainstream clergy, charged Herron, lived off "the ghastly philanthrophy of men who have heaped their colossal fortunes upon the bodies of their brothers." They were like the scavenging priests who "accompanied the pirate ships of the sixteenth century, to say mass and pray for the souls of the dead pirates for a share of the spoil."

But "commercial tyranny and social caste are a war against God," preached Herron. Christ was a revolutionary, and "the Gospel of Jesus to the poor was the democracy of the people . . . Men are equal in the love of God. No soul is of less worth to God than another soul. . . . OUR father means a democracy in the production and distribution of wealth."

While the attack escalated on the established church and the

'HE STIRRETH UP THE PEOPLE'

JESUS CHRIST

THE WORKINGMAN OF NAZARETH
WILL SPEAK
AT BROTHERHOOD HALL
— SUBJECT —
— THE RIGHTS OF LABOR —

Art Young, *The Masses*, December 1913

established wealth behind it, the country was swept by a religious revival. William James noted in 1906 "a wave of religious activity, analogous in some respects to the spread of early Christianity, Buddhism, and Mohammedanism." Revivalist Billy Sunday toured to gigantic crowds wherever he went. There was a rebirth of fundamentalism in the farm community, of the Muslim faith in the black community, the spread of a liberal-Protestant "social gospel" in the middle class, and a flippant interest in Eastern religion among the Bohemians—

> In the summer
> I'm a nudist
>
> In the winter
> I'm a Buddhist

The secular counterpart of the religious revival was the debate over "human nature." The progressive view was that one part of the mind—the intellect—and one part of society—the intellectuals—should take control of the rest and reshape it. After liquefying him in the melting pot, progressive technocrats would remake Man into a "better" model, presumably one more tastefully white-Anglo-Saxon-Protestant, patriotic, middle class, and consumer-oriented.

The anarchists took a different view. Deeply influenced by the lives and writings of the Russians Leon Tolstoy, Peter Kropotkin and Mikhail Bakunin, American anarchism gained notoriety after Chicago's 1888 Haymarket bombing. The real statement of law, said Albert Parsons, one of the eight anarchists convicted after that lethal explosion, was "obey the rich." Law was the "tool of thieves" whereby "the great mass of people who inhabit our planet have been robbed of their equal right to the use of the soil and of all other natural opportunities. In the name of [statute law] large sections of our race have been bought and sold as chattels; by it the vast majority of the human race are today held in the industrial bondage of wage slavery."

And in that context, they argued, much-publicized attempts to "improve human nature" reeked of hypocrisy. As Emma Goldman put it: "freedom, expansion, opportunity, and, above all, peace and repose, alone can teach us the real dominant factors of human nature and all its possibilities."

In 1892 Goldman's lover, Alexander Berkman, shot Henry Frick, the baron of coke, in anger over Frick's role in breaking the bloody Homestead strike near Pittsburg. Nine years later another anarchist, Leon Czolgosz, killed William McKinley, the third U.S. president to be assassinated in 36 years.

At timber yards and factories throughout America, the syndicalist-anarchist I.W.W. spread a free-wheeling guerrilla ideology that demanded an end to all fetters on human nature. "Anarchists hold that it is wrong for one person to prescribe what is the right action for another person, and then compel that person to obey," said Parsons. Humankind would find its true self only in "a free society where there is no concentration of centralized power, no state, no king, no emperor, no ruler, no president, no potentate of any character whatsoever."

The libertarian decentralist views of the anarchists wrote an ideological bottom line to the era, where secular humanism and a belief in the inseparability of Humankind and the natural planet thoroughly intertwined. "God, the state, and society are nonexistent," wrote Goldman. "There is no conflict between the individual and the social instincts, any more than there is between the heart and the lungs."

As Muir and the ecologists assimilated the native belief in the inseparability of humankind and nature, the anarchists and Christian Socialists put into a Twentieth Century framework the Transcendentalist faith in the oneness of all people, and the human value of all manufactured material. In Kansas City labor organizer Mary "Mother" Jones "told the great audience that packed the hall that when their coal glowed red in their fires, it was the blood of the workers, of men who went down into black holes to dig it, of women who suffered and endured, of little children who knew but a brief childhood. 'You are being warmed and made comfortable by human blood,' " she said.

Thus there was no escape from the demands of ecological harmony or social justice. "When I see suffering around me, I myself suffer," said Debs. "So when I put forth my efforts to relieve others, I am simply working for myself."

"Every human life is interlocked with the destiny of every other life, past, present and to come," said Herron. "In the last analysis of salvation, no man is wholly saved, and God himself is not wholly saved from the consequences of human sin, until all men are saved."

The real meaning of Christianity, added Charlotte Perkins Gilman, was "not only that God is one . . . but that MAN is one—

"All noble and beautiful emotions . . . all the distinguishing abilities, the power and skill and ingenuity we call 'Human' are social and immortal.

" 'I' am born, grow up and die. 'I' am a transient piece of meat, enjoying food and sleep and mating, hunting, and fighting.

"But 'we' are more than that. 'We' together constitute another 'I,' which is Human Life. That was born gradually, many ages back, and is now slowly growing up. In that human life, that common, mutual, social life are all things that make us human.

"When we enter consciously into that great life we are indeed immortal, 'saved' indeed, from primeval limitations of the animal ego."

So basic an act as eating offered daily proof. Even the rich, she wrote, were "never satisfied" because anyone with food would invariably feel the hunger of those without, and would try to give "a thousand dinners to himself to quench that hunger."

"We have been taught," Gilman added, "in tattered remnants of worn-out faiths, to despise human nature. . . . We have been taught in later days, by half-seeing students of science, that we were but beasts, and must fight it out as they did, our progress lying in the slow, painful process of survival."

But Social Darwinism and its Calvinist parent constituted an unholy marriage of primitive superstitions. "The love for human beings," she said, "is not a dream of religion, it is a law of nature, bred of human contact, of human relation, of human service; it rests on identical interest and the demands of a social development which must include all, if it will permanently lift any."

Ultimately it was love that powered revolution. Humanity might for a time deny its most basic desire, its highest joy, but human nature, like water, would ultimately find its own level. "Free love?" asked Goldman—

"As if love is anything but free. Man has bought brains, but all the millions in the world have failed to buy love. Man has subdued bodies, but all his armies could not conquer love. Man has chained and fettered the spirit, but he has been utterly helpless before love. High on a throne, with all the splendor and pomp his gold can command, man is yet poor and desolate, if love passes him by.

"And if it stays, the poorest hovel is radiant with warmth, with life and color. Thus love has the magic power to make of a beggar a king. Yes, love is free; it can dwell in no other atmosphere. In freedom it gives itself unreservedly, abundantly, completely. All the laws on the statutes, all the courts in the universe, cannot tear it from the soil, once love has taken root."

With love's final triumph, added Gilman, the mind of humanity would open to "happiness such as we have never been able to conceive in our little ego-stunted brains."

The new century would test that vision to the fullest. A Second World War would follow the First, and then stalemate and quagmire defeat in Korea and Vietnam.

Each war would be followed by intense reaction. The Red Scare after World War I, McCarthyism and the Cold War for World War II and Korea, the Nixon-Agnew era during the Vietnam War.

Each cycle also had its time of bread-and-circus materialism: the Jazz Age Twenties, the fat, complacent Fifties, the sharp-edged, cynical era of the "Me Decade" 1970s.

But each also brought its years of upheaval, its days of hope and magic. With the Crash of 1929 came a second Roosevelt, and a New Deal that incorporated pieces of the old Populist and Socialist platforms. The movements for labor, farm, civil and women's rights all thrived in the 1930s, as did a folk radicalism reminiscent of the old Bohemian spirit.

In the 1960s, John Kennedy and Lyndon Johnson brought in a revived New Deal in the form of the New Frontier and Great Society. Most of that drowned in the bottomless Vietnam pit. But it was also overwhelmed by a cultural explosion that embodied all the egalitarian, feminist and ecological energies of the turn of the century, and then some, as if Watson and Debs, DuBois and Marcus Garvey, Scott Joplin and the Ashcan School, Emma Goldman and Margaret Sanger, Mabel Dodge and John Reed, the IWW and Iroquois League had all been reborn in the bodies of a new generation, born with the atom bomb, armed with computers and electric guitars and the astonishing power of the global media.

By the 1960s Vietnam was making it all too clear that the fifty-year global dominance of the American Empire, outlined by Brooks Adams and initiated by Theodore Roosevelt, had run its course. As it unravelled in southeast Asia, the Middle East and Central America, it brought with it the downfall of Richard Nixon, the first American president to resign under fire.

In his wake would come yet another cycle of history, initiated with the weak liberal revivalism of Jimmy Carter and the birth of an anti-nuclear pro-solar movement, shipwrecked on the shores of an Iranian hostage crisis, then followed by eight years of reaction and materialism with Ronald Reagan.

But through the entire century some vectors have remained constant.

One has been the inevitability of detente among the major powers, a force even the ultimate Cold Warriors would find impossible to resist. In the midst of his prosecution of the Vietnam War, it was none other than Richard Nixon who opened the door to China, and sold soft drinks to the Soviets. Then, in the twilight of his bread-

and-circus eighties, while sinking into the abyss of a drug-tainted counter-revolution in Central America, it was Ronald Reagan who signed on with Mikhail Gorbachov to the official opening of the era of nuclear disarmament.

As he did, the pendulum swung back not only leftward, but out into a whole new plane. For despite all the technological progress, despite astonishing advances in science, engineering, communications, medicine, information processing and all forms of mechanical wizardry, the basic questions raised by the populists and socialists, Bohemians and Wobblies way back in the 1890s remained unanswered.

A cynical, hectic age had once again layered over the human issues of social justice and ecological sanity. In the late 1980s, our increasingly crowded planet, so laden with genius, also bears an escalating nightmare of desperate poverty and lethal environmental contamination. *"The measure of the land and the measure of our bodies are the same,"* warned Chief Joseph, and the plagues of AIDS and cancer, of drug addiction and random violence, of omnipresent filth and unbalanced weather gave daily reminders that one cannot exploit other people, or pollute the planet without infecting every corner of one's own life. *"Whatever befalls the earth befalls the sons of the earth,"* said Seattle. *"Man did not weave the web of live, he is merely a strand in its web. Whatever he does to the web, he does to himself."*

All the intellectual keys to human liberation and ecological holism were beautifully articulated at the turn of the century. Through each cycle of our history, the movements have come back in new forms.

As each successive cycle grows shorter and more intense, the lessons of the previous age, of prior idealists and ecologists, fighters for justice and poets of the new dawn, all make themselves felt. *"Even little children who lived here and rejoiced here for a brief season will love these somber solitudes, and at eventide they greet shadowy returning spirits,"* said Chief Seattle—

"And when the last Red Man shall have perished, and the memory

*of my tribe shall have become a myth among the White Men, these
shores will swarm with the invisible dead of my tribe.*

"*And when your children's children think themselves alone in the
field, the store, the shop, upon the highway, or in the silence of the
pathless woods, they will not be alone.*

"*At night when the streets of your cities and villages are silent
and you think them deserted, they will throng with the returning
hosts that once filled and still love this beautiful land.*

"*The White Man will never be alone.*"

But the question remains: in an atomic age, facing ecological
disaster and human chaos, will we have the selfless wisdom, the
greatness of spirit, to digest the lessons of our incredibly fertile past,
and to choose life? Said Seattle:

"*Tribe follows tribe, and nation follows nation, like the waves of
the sea. It is the order of nature, and regret is useless.*

"*Your time of decay may be distant, but it will surely come, for
even the White Man whose God walked and talked with him as
friend with friend, cannot be exempt from the common destiny.*

"*We may be brothers [and sisters] after all.*

"*We will see . . .*"

Notes

The following citations indicate where quoted material can be found. Most of these sources are available in paperback editions.

Prologue

I was born . . . breathe; Dee Brown, *Bury My Heart at Wounded Knee* (1971), p. 242.

I could see . . . penned up; John G. Neihardt, *Black Elk Speaks* (1961), p. 221.

The Robber Barons

Gold is the . . . paradise; Walter Raleigh, *The English Voyages of the Eighteenth Century* (1910), p. 28.

God gave me my money; Matthew Josephson, *The Robber Barons* (1934), p. 318.

In time you . . . valuable; *Ibid.*, p. 50.

The mainstream explanations for the causes of the Civil War generally skirt the question of why the Union wouldn't let the Confederacy secede. Perhaps the following statements from Lincoln, Stephan A. Douglas and Richard P. Bland add some light—

Separate our common country into two nations, as designed by the present rebellion, and every man of this great interior region is thereby cut off from some one or more of the outlets. . . . The outlets . . . are indispensible to the well-being of the people.

—Abraham Lincoln, 1862.

We can never acknowledge the right of a State to secede and cut us off from the Ocean and the world, without our consent.

—Stephen A. Douglas, 1860.

The people of the West and Northwest took up arms in the late civil war more than all else, for the purpose of forever securing to themselves free navigation of the Mississippi River and its tributaries, that their produce might find easy, cheap, and ready transportation to the markets of the globe.

—Richard P. Bland, Democrat of Missouri. From William Appleman Williams, *The Roots of the Modern American Empire* (1969), pp. 102, 185, and 190.

A National Blessing!; Josephson, *Barons*, p. 57. Accounts of Morgan's gun deal also appear in Gustavus Myers, *History of the Great American Fortunes* (1937), and in Frederick Lewis Allen, *The Great Pierpont Morgan* (1949). According to Allen, Morgan's return on a six weeks' investment of $20,000 was $5,400.

Continue growing richer . . . closes; Josephson, *Barons*, p. 59.

Estimates of total land grant acreage vary. The figure of 200 million acres appears in Thomas C. Cochran and William Miller, *The Age of Enterprise* (1961), p. 133. Most estimates run between 130 and 150 million acres. Part of the variance is due to the difference between total area granted and that actually collected. The statistics on the Credit Mobilier case come from John D. Hicks, *The American Nation* (1946), p. 77. An account of the bribery surrounding the passage of the Pacific Railway Act appears in Robert E. Riegel, *The Story of the Western Railroads* (1926), p. 74.

Whenever his keen . . . rates; Josephson, *Barons*, p. 13.

Drove his men . . . party; *Ibid.*, p. 14; and William Augustus Croffut, *The Vanderbilts and the Story of Their Fortune* (1886), p. 45.

Vanderbilt was one . . . nail; Myers, *Fortunes*, p. 295.

No hardships or . . . meetings; Josephson, *Barons*, p. 19.

Monument at once . . . enterprise; Charles Francis and Henry Adams, *Chapters of Erie* (1871), p. 5.

At ten o'clock . . . fog; *Ibid.*, p. 30.

A standing army . . . hotel; *Ibid.*, p. 42.

Cultivating a thorough . . . high; *Ibid.*, p. 54.

Vanderbilt allus told . . . light; Croffut, *Vanderbilts*, p. 95.

There was a . . . smokestack; Josephson, *Barons*, p. 139. *See also* Adams, *Chapters*, p. 155.

Let everyone carry . . . corpse; Josephson, *Barons*, p. 148.

Just as a . . . "trusts"; *Ibid.*, p. 115. (From J. A. Hobson, *The Evolution of Modern Capitalism.*)

These intimate conversations . . . life; *Ibid.*, pp. 48–49.

Wilkerson and Company . . . screw; *Ibid.*, p. 268. Rockefeller considered competition "idiotic, senseless destruction—

Competition had existed for generations. In all lines of industry, history had repeated itself over and over, in cycles every ten or twelve years. Excessive production, followed by loss with failure and bankruptcy to the weaker concerns. The strong ones, the survivors, finding themselves in control of the trade, remembering those losses they had suffered, took advantage of the opposition to recoup themselves by changing higher prices, and also picked up the wrecks along the shore, buying out the ruined competitors. For a while, business was good and profitable. Presently outsiders, seeing the prosperity, set up new competition, and once more the experience was repeated, with consequent loss and bankruptcy.

—Mark Sullivan, *Our Times*, II (1927), pp. 279–280.

I tried to . . . cooperate; Josephson, *Barons*, p. 266.

He advertised that . . . city; Cochran and Miller, *Enterprise*, p. 149.

There is a good account of the 1895 gold crisis in Ray Ginger, *The Age of Excess* (1967), p. 171.

Who invoked the . . . factories; Jack London, *The Iron Heel* (1907), p. 80.

The old competitive . . . abolished; Sullivan, *Times*, II, p. 354.

Commercial expansion greater . . . Seattle; Josephson, *Barons*, pp. 434 and 442.

Two certificates of stock . . . difference; *Ibid.*, p. 450.

A complete account of the corporations tied into the Morgan-Rockefeller community of interest can be found in the Pujo Commission Report of 1912. The $22 billion represented in the various holdings was roughly the dollar-value equivalent of all assessed property in the twenty-two states west of the Mississippi River, or twice that of all assessed property in the thirteen states of the South.

Harriman's Asian dealings are discussed in Ginger, *Excess*, p. 215.

It was simple . . . fortress; William Allen White, *Autobiography* (1946), p. 150.

The same monopolies . . . party; Ginger, *Excess*, p. 107.

A joint-stock company . . . concern; Cochran and Miller, *Enterprise*, p. 167.

Shall the railroads . . . this?; Robert V. Bruce, *1877: Year of the Violence* (1959), p. 320.

Everything to the . . . it; Ginger, *Excess*, p. 32.

Is somebody out . . . ones; Harold Zink, *City Bosses in the United States* (1930), p. 83.

The policy in Philadelphia . . . involved; *Ibid.*, p. 211.

Practically every house . . . boss; *Ibid.*, p. 83.

Wholesale frauds were . . . hands; Hicks, *Nation*, p. 87.

The existing coalition . . . money; Adams, *Chapters*, p. 97.

The Commission, as . . . corporate lawyer; Cochran and Miller, *Enterprise*, pp. 132–133.

I can hire . . . half; Leo Huberman, *We the People* (1947), p. 235.

The class I . . . estate; Frederick Townsend Martin, *The Passing of the Idle Rich* (1911), p. 148.

At a dinner . . . dollars; Charles and Mary Beard, *The Rise of American Civilization*, II (1941), pp. 392–393.

WE have made . . . system; Josephson, *Barons*, p. 202.

An account of the spike-driving incident appears in the American Heritage *New Illustrated History of the United States*, X (1963), p. 834. A hearsay account, picked up in an Ann Arbor coffeehouse, portrayed the first spike-driving executive as having broken his shin with the sledge-hammer.

Fatality and injury statistics are from James Weinstein, *The Corporate Ideal in the Liberal State* (1968), p. 40; and Cochran and Miller, *Enterprise*, p. 231.

A considerable number . . . age; Joyce Kornbluh, ed., *Rebel Voices: An I.W.W. Anthology* (1964), p. 159.

Taking the cost . . . value; Weinstein, *Corporate*, pp. 26–27.

The difference between . . . towns?; Beard, *Rise*, I, pp. 693–694.

Men are cheap . . . place; Huberman, *We*, p. 223.

The farmer was . . . industry; White, *Autobiography*, p. 400.

Sometimes he must . . . wanderer; William J. Ghent, *Our Benevolent Feudalism* (1902).

Some are built . . . brick; Cochran and Miller, *Enterprise*, p. 251. Statistics on urban crowding are on p. 264. *See also* Barry Weisberg, *Beyond Repair: The Ecology of Capitalism*.

Almost all of . . . engines; *Ibid.*, p. 134.

The effects of . . . railroading; Riegel, *Railroads*, p. 178.

The builders had . . . anywhere; John Moody, *The Railroad Builders* (1919), p. 10.

Two dirt-ballasted . . . pile; Riegel, *Railroads*, p. 311.

By the 1880's . . . bankruptcy; Josephson, *Barons*, pp. 292–293.

A huge organization . . . lower prices; Louis Brandeis, *Other People's Money* (1967), pp. 102–103.

Willard King's; statistics are cited in Myers, *Fortunes*, p. 91. They were used by the U.S. Commission on Industrial Relations, 1916, which added that "the actual concentration has, however, been carried very much further than these figures indicate. The largest private fortune in the United States, estimated at $1 billion, is equivalent to the aggregate wealth of 2.5 million of those who are classed as 'poor,' who are shown to own the average about $400 each." Charles Spahr's statistics are cited in Cochran and Miller, *Enterprise*, p. 261. An early reviewer of this manuscript has criticized the portrayal of the average American family as living at "bare subsistence" level by pointing out that an income of $1000 then was roughly the 1970 real equivalent of $6000. On that basis, the average family income of $380 computes to $2280 a year, which corresponds to the federal poverty level. Even a family that grows its own food can hardly live on that.

American Factories are . . . ours; Claude G. Bowers. *Beveridge and the Progressive Era* (1932), p. 69. There are many complex explanations for the activities of American troops overseas. It would be false to say that economic considerations were the only important ones for everybody involved. But one can hardly separate or ignore them—

We went to Nicaragua in 1910, I believe. In my judgment we never had any sufficient reason for going. Nevertheless, we sent our marines there, landed them, took possession of the country, marched to the capital, killed some 200 Nicaraguans, and placed in control, as the nominal President of Nicaragua, a clerk or employee of a corporation of Pittsburgh.
—Senator William Borah of Idaho (in Huberman, *We*, p. 252).

I spent thirty-three years and four months in active service as a member of our country's most agile military force—the Marine Corps. I served in all commissioned ranks from a second lieutenant to major-general. And during that period I spent most of my time being a high-class muscle-man for Big Business, for Wall Street, and for the bankers. In short, I was a racketeer for capitalism. . . .
Thus I helped make Mexico and especially Tampico safe for American oil interests in 1914. I helped make Haiti and Cuba a decent place for the National City Bank boys to collect revenues in. . . . I helped purify Nicaragua for the international banking house of Brown Brothers in 1909–1912. I brought light to the Dominican Republic for American sugar interests in 1916. I helped make Honduras "right" for American fruit companies in 1903. In China in 1927 I helped see to it that Standard Oil went its way unmolested. During those years I had, as the boys in the back room would say, a swell racket. I was rewarded with honors, medals, promotion. Looking back on it, I feel I might have given Al Capone a few hints. The best he could do was

operate his racket in three city districts. We marines operated on three continents.

—Major General Smedley D. Butler (in Huberman, *We*, pp. 252–253).

Growth rate statistics from Lewis Corey, *The Decline of American Capitalism* (1934), p. 33.

Active, capable men . . . outsiders; Vernon L. Parrington, *The Colonial Mind, 1620–1800* (1927), p. 18. It seems to me that the roots of modern Western fascism can be found in Calvinism.

Calvinist election to heaven was indicated by an exertion of the will paralleling the will of God. The surest sign of election was to imitate him, and he was a symbol of Fear—all-powerful, wrathful, violent. His "chosen" were likewise, to the point of "damning" other people to hell—slavs, gypsys, Jews, Indians, Quakers, Nonconformists, non-whites in general.

The struggle to achieve immortality—to escape death—took the form of an unending magnification of the ego. Calvinist God-consciousness was a machine vision of total power operating within a finite, strictly defined universe.

Its logical secular-scientific offspring was the Nietzschean superman and master-race. Compare Cotton Mather's "pre-millionialism," for example, with the vision of the Thousand-Year Reich—

Christ will physically appear, the earth will be refined but not consumed by fire, and for a thousand years paradise will reign. (In Perry Miller, *The New England Mind* (1953), p. 187.)

On the material level, fascism, and modern Western imperialism, can be seen as the final, decayed expression of the Lutheran Reformation.

Luther's revolt was born in the decayed corpse of Catholic feudalism of which Louis XIV and Philip II were the last full expression.

The Lutheran challenge marked the break-up of the old feudal order and the rise of the capitalist middle class. As systematized by Calvin, the revolt took the form of a new assertion of the old church-state tyranny. This time, though, power had passed from the feudal lords to the bankers and merchants:

Calvin did for the Bourgeoisie of the sixteenth century what Marx did for the proletariat of the nineteenth. . . . The doctrine of predestination satisfied the same hunger for an assurance that the forces of the universe are on the side of the select as was to be assuaged in a different age by the theory of historical materialism.
—R. H. Tawney, *Religion and the Rise of Capitalism* (1954), p. 99.

The Lutheran middle class threaded the needle between the Catholic feudal lords on top and the agrarian and emerging industrial masses below.

With the religious revolution came an accompanying one in industry and commerce. The triumph bore its final fruit in the British Empire, the American empire, and German fascism.

What comes next?

A joint-stock corporation . . . today; Samuel Eliot Morison, *Builders of the Bay Colony* (1930), p. 65.

There is a two-fold . . . you; Parrington, *Mind*, pp. 48–49.

Tolerate all views . . . error; *Ibid.*, pp. 101–102.

Heresy, Prophaness & . . . Worship; Miller, *Mind*, p. 176.

Projected caste distinctions into eternity; Parrington, *Mind*, p. iv.

The Execution of . . . mee; *Ibid.*, p. 110.

Mather also embraced . . . slave; Thomas Jefferson Wertembaker, *The Puritan Oligarchy* (1947), p. 198.

Religious exaltation flowered . . . cosmic; Parrington, *Mind*, p. 108.

The growth of . . . God; Richard Hofstadter, *Social Darwinism in American Thought* (1967), p. 45.

The laws of . . . God; *Ibid.*, p. 151.

Get rid of . . . blessedness; Ghent, *Feudalism*, pp. 135–136.

To the struggle . . . generations; Hofstadter, *Darwinism*, p. 61.

It is constantly . . . offered, Cochran and Miller, *Enterprise*, p. 263.

There may be . . . sin; William G. McLoughlin, *The Meaning of Henry Ward Beecher* (1970), p. 150.

Niggers are lazy . . . people; Moody, *Railroad*, p. 188.

The most beautiful . . . be; Ginger, *Excess*, pp. 233–234.

Objections to the . . . tried; in H. Wayne Morgan, ed., *The Gilded Age: A Reappraisal* (1967), p. 25.

We shall keep . . . be; Ginger, *Excess*, p. 114.

Divine right to . . . property; Bowers, *Beveridge*, p. 317.

The outline of . . . sight; Henry Adams, *The Education of Henry Adams* (1961), pp. 499–500.

The lawyer's place . . . salary; Richard Hofstadter, *The Age of Reform* (1955), p. 160. This book is fine in dealing with the Progressives, but its treatment of the Populists is one of the seminal tracts in Newspeak.

Our time, our . . . prostitutes; Ghent, *Feudalism*, p. 146.

New structure of . . . communities; Robert Wiebe, *The Search for Order, 1877–1920* (1967), pp. 249–251. *See* Henry Adams, *Democracy* and Jane Addams, *Twenty Years at Hull House.* Christopher Lasch's *The New Radicalism in America* deals well with Jane Addams' search for her place in society. Wiebe's book is an excellent general study of the mind and politics of progressivism. See also Weinstein's *Corporate Ideal* and Gabriel Kolko's *Triumph of Conservatism*, and George Sherman, *Infinity's Trial* (Cornell, unpublished).

Working with college . . . free; Frederick Howe, *The Confessions of a Reformer* (1967), pp. 249–251.

McKinley won because . . . property; White, *Autobiography*, p. 285.

The billions of . . . church; Weinstein, *Corporate*, p. 10.

What we need . . . itself; Richard T. Ely, *The Strength and Weakness of Socialism* (1894), p 240. Ely complained that society tended to raise wages but not salaries.

As higher education . . . power; Edward A. Ross, *Social Control* (1901), p. 88.

A method that . . . inward; *Ibid.*, p. 428–429.

The administrative mind . . . steel; in Daniel Aaron, *Men of Good Hope* (1961), pp. 271–272.

One of the key institutions of the Progressive technocracy, if not its center, was the universities. Through the Gilded Age, and even more so at the turn of the century, the barons poured money into the universities, many of which still bear their names. The baronial endowments were often hailed in the press as shining examples of enlightened philanthrophy.

> John D. Rockefeller
> Wonderful man is he
> Gives all his spare change
> To the U. of C.
> He keeps the ball a-rolling
> In our great varsity.
> —Josephson, *Barons*, p. 325.

Many, however, weren't quite so enthusiastic. The Populist *New Era* told farmers that "when you grease your old wagon or light your lamp tonight you ought to remember you are contributing of your ten cent potatoes to the support of the Chicago University." (Norman Pollack, *The Populist Response to Industrial America* (1966), p. 81.)

You've got to . . . farm; Weinstein, *Corporate*, p. 202.

The law of . . . things; W. T. Cunningham, *The Gospel of Work* (1902), p. 16.

On the thorough . . . without; Theodore Roosevelt, *Fear God and Take Your Own Part* (1916), pp. 56–57.

We shall guard . . . bloodshed; Richard Hofstadter, *The American Political Tradition* (1948), pp. 218–219. A grandchild of the Progressive attitude toward civil liberties was McCarthyism in the 1950s. See Michael Rogin, *McCarthy and the Intellectuals*.

This country needs . . . Spanish dead!; Hofstadter, *Tradition*, pp. 212–215. Roosevelt referred to his troops as "born adventurers in the old sense of the word" in *The Rough Riders* (1899).

During the past . . . rapid; Theodore Roosevelt, *The Winning of the West*, I (1905), pp. 1–4.

In every instance . . . no!; Hofstadter, *Tradition*, pp. 212–213.

He [Grant] never forgot . . . reigns; Bowers, *Beveridge*, pp. 68–76. McKinley was somewhat hesitant to take the Philippines. "I walked the floor night after night," he said,

and I am not ashamed to tell you gentlemen, that I went down on my knees and prayed Almighty God for light and guidance more than one night. And one night it came to me this way—I don't know how it was, but it came. . . . There was nothing left for us to do but to take them all, and to educate the Filipinos, and uplift and civilize and Christianize them, and by God's grace do the very best we could by them as our fellow-men for whom Christ also died. And then I went to bed, and went to sleep and slept soundly.

In a less emotional moment McKinley noted the annexation of the Philippines as a "commercial opportunity to which American statesmanship cannot be indifferent. It is just to use every legitimate means for the enlargement of American trade."

Andrew Carnegie, who was known as an "anti-imperialist," envisioned the day "when five hundred millions, every one an American, will dominate the world—for the world's own good." (Both quotes from Beard, *Rise, II*, pp. 205, 375–376).

The Revolt of the Farmers

It is quite . . . room; Frederick Jackson Turner, *The Frontier in American History* (1920), pp. 19–21.

American democracy was . . . frontier; Henry Nash Smith, *Virgin Land* (1950), p. 253. The quote is from a speech by Turner. For the struggle over the Constitution *see* Charles A. Beard, *The Economic Origins of the Constitution*; Elisha P. Douglass, *Rebels and Democrats;* Staughton Lynd, *Anti-Federalism in Dutchess County*; and Jackson Turner Main, *The Anti-Federalists.* "The Federal Constitution has served the American people in the same way that their national monarchies served the peoples of Europe." A. Lowell, quoted in Herbert Croly, *Progressive Democracy.*

God made this . . . it; Smith, *Virgin*, p. 228. O. E. Rolvaag's *Giants in the Earth* gives an overwhelming portrait of the struggle to settle the Great Plains. The book is an awesome experience, as is Mari Sandoz' *Old Jules.* An interesting first-person account of pioneering pre-Civil War Illinois is Rebecca and Edward Burland, *A True Picture of Emigration*, an 1830s account (recently published).

John D. Hicks, in *The Populist Revolt* (1961), says one farmer in ten got free land; Fred A. Shannon, in *The Farmer's Last Frontier* (1968), says it was one in eight or ten.

Only a little . . . generations; Hicks, *Nation*, p. 239.

It is no . . . American; Riegel, *Railroads*, p. 288.

Mortgage statistics are from Shannon, *Frontier*, pp. 95 and 306.

To talk of . . . acres; *Ibid.*, p. 170 Shannon quotes an English observer who wrote in 1882 that it was "plain to everyone that the virgin soils of the western prairie are wasting under a false system of agriculture and would eventually give out." For a current statement on that prediction *see* Floyd Allen, "A Farm Renaissance Comes to North Dakota," in *Organic Gardening and Farming Magazine* (April 1972).

Figures on farm income are from Shannon, *Frontier*, pp. 176 and 295–303, and from Cochran and Miller, *Enterprise*, p. 231. Someone will no doubt point out that in absolute terms railroad freight rates were declining. Food prices, however, also declined while the value of the dollar tripled.

An army of . . . with; William A. Peffer, *The Farmer's Side* (1891), p. 59. The debate over whether or not the Populists were "revolutionaries" bores on. On the basis of careers like that of Ben Tillman and post-1900 Tom Watson, historians and newspapers have taken to labeling a wide variety of reactionary politicians as "Populists."

Many of the pops did follow tortured paths after 1896. Mary Lease became a Socialist, then a Hanna Republican. Ignatius Donnelly withdrew in bitter confusion. Watson and many of the southerners, like so many other embittered rebels from so many other crushed revolts, became violent racists and callous power-brokers.

Essentially the Populist movement was dead after 1896. Before that it was broad-based but overwhelming anti-imperialist, democratic, and antiracist. Its seminal document—the document on which its politics should be judged—was the 1892 Omaha platform. Its spirit was much like that of an earlier rebellion, captured in a pre-1800 newspaper interview.

I inquired of an old plough-jogger the cause and aim of the people of that assembly [Shays' march on the Springfield armory].

He said to get redress of grievances. I asked what grievances. He said we have all grievances enough, I can tell you mine; I have labored hard all my days, and fared hard; I have been greatly abused; been obliged to do more than my part in the war; been loaded with class-rates, town-rates, province-rates, continual rates, and all rates, lawsuits, and have been pulled and hauled by sheriffs, constables, and collectors, and had my cattle sold for less than they were worth; I have been obliged to pay and nobody will pay me; I have lost a great deal by this man, and that man, and t'other man; and the great men are to get all we have; and I think it is time for us to rise and put a stop to it, and have no more courts, nor sheriffs, nor collectors, nor lawyers; I design to pay no more; and I know we have the biggest party, let them say what they will.
—Carl Taylor, *The Farmers' Movement, 1620–1920* (1953), p. 41.

Human happiness is . . . wealth; in Edward A. Martin, *History of the Grange* (1873), p. 431.

The Grange is . . . himself; *Ibid.*, p. 470.

We hold, declare . . . cost; Resolutions of the Springfield, Illinois, Farmers' Convention, April 2, 1873. See H. S. Commager, ed., *Documents of American History*, II (1958), p. 78.

The adoration of . . . so; George B. Tindall, ed., *A Populist Reader* (1966), p. 109.

The people are . . . now; Hicks, *Revolt*, p. 103.

Those who controlled . . . coroprations; *Ibid.*, p. 136.

Tenancy figures from Ghent, *Feudalism*, p. 51.

Wall Street owns . . . beware!; Taylor, *Movement*, p. 283.

To say that . . . produced; Tindall, *Reader*, pp. 13–17.

What is life . . . one; Norman Pollack, *The Populist Response to Industrial America* (1966), pp. 19, 26–27.

Like the thunder . . . belongs; Garraty, *Nation*, p. 612.

The Government will . . . man; Hicks, *Revolt*, pp. 196–198.

We must have . . . earth; Taylor, *Movement*, p. 275.

At the conclusion . . . hurricane; Hicks, *Revolt*, p. 228.

The American people . . . march; Tindall, *Reader*, pp. 60–73.

The system is . . . commodity; Huberman, *We*, p. 163.

The narrowness of . . . whatsoever; Philip Bruce, *The Rise of the New South* (1905), p. 427.

Say or write . . . rebellion; Kenneth Stampp, *The Peculiar Institution* (1956), p. 211. For a general account of slave resistance, *see* Herbert Aptheker, *American Slave Revolts*. For a short account of the Texas slave insurrection, *see* Richard Hofstadter and Michael Wallace, *American Violence* (1971). The many books of Ulrich B. Phillips and Eugene Genovese's *Political Economy of Slavery* are examples of the traditional view of the slave.

Looked for many . . . squatters; Hicks, *Nation*, p. 2.

Forty acres of . . . vote; Lerone Bennett, *Black Power: The Human Side of Reconstruction* (1967), p. 40.

For a general account of violence during Reconstruction, *see* Hofstadter and Wallace, *Violence*, pp. 101–103; Stewart Landry's *Battle of Liberty Place* (1955) tells the story of the New Orleans coup d'etat from an "unreconstructed" point of view. *See also* C. Vann Woodward's *Reunion and Reaction* for an account of the 1876–1877 "election."

The South is . . . iron; C. Vann Woodward, *Origins of the New South* (1951), p. 115.

A new race . . . manufactures; *Ibid.*, p. 151.

I was the . . . *Ibid.*, p. 128.

Probably the most . . . history; *Ibid.*, p. 118.

The government at . . . Honduras; *Ibid.*, p. 72.

Essentially two classes . . . south; Shannon, *Frontier*, p. 99.

The persecutions of . . . filth; Woodward, *Origins*, p. 214.

A new capitalistic . . . money; *Ibid.*, p. 179. *See also* Roger W. Shugg's essay in Staughton Lynd, ed., *Reconstruction* (1967).

When one of . . . allow; Alex Arnett, *The Populist Movement in Georgia* (1922), p. 206.

A tenant offering five bales of cotton was told, after some owl-eyed figuring, that his cotton exactly balanced his debt. Delighted at the prospect of a profit this year, the tenant reported that he had one more bale which he hadn't yet brought in. 'Shucks,' shouted the boss, "Why didn't you tell me before? Now I'll have to figure the account all over again to make it come out even.

—In Huberman, *We*, p. 195.

A bitter and . . . class; Woodward, *Origins*, p. 251.

Men of the . . . wrong; C. Vann Woodward, *Tom Watson: Agrarian Rebel* (1963), p. 173.

Like cutting off . . . eye; Woodward, *Origins*, p. 244.

It is needless . . . corruption; *Ibid.*, p. 262.

The baccanalia of . . . ballots; George H. Knoles, *The Presidential Campaign and Election of 1892* (1942), p. 191.

The feeling of . . . protection; Woodward, *Watson*, p. 223.

Though the people . . . people; Ginger, *Excess*, p. 114.

I take my . . . o'clock; Williams, *Roots*, p. 370.

We have reached . . . fight; Woodward, *Origins*, p. 270.

You may call me an anarchist, a socialist, or a communist. I care not, but I hold to the theory that if one man has not enough to eat three times a day and another man has $25,000,000, that last man has something that belongs to the first.

—Mary Lease.

Buried under a . . . deep; Hicks. *Revolt*, p. 339.

We propose to . . . House; Arnett, *Georgia*, p. 133.

This country is . . . capital; William DuBose Sheldon, *Populism in the Old Dominion: Virginia Farm Politics, 1885–1900* (1935), p. 107.

Will prefer government, . . . spheres; Pollack, *Response*, p. 124.

Not a Populist . . . dream; O. Gene Clanton, *Kansas Populism* (1969), p. 193. G. C. Clemens was Mark Twain's cousin.

There must be . . . good; Pollack, *Response*, pp. 106–107.

"The men who now corner gold, would, under their administration, also corner silver."

—Topeka *Advocate*

"What is government to me if it does not make it possible for me to love! and provide for my family! The trouble has been, we have so much regard for the rights of property that we have forgotten the liberties of the individual. We have had some illustration of that in the great strike at Chicago and a number of other illustrations. I claim it is the business of the government to make it possible for me to live and sustain the life of my family. If the government doesn't do that, what better is the government to me than a state of barbarism?"
—Lorenzo Lewelling, Populist governor of Kansas (in Tindall, *Reader*, p. 149.)

For God's sake . . . gifts; Hicks, *Revolt*, p. 358.

Elect Bryan and . . . President; Arnett, *Georgia*, p. 198.

Free silver is . . . ruin; Woodward, *Watson*, p. 281.

A line of graves; *Ibid.*, p. 289. The speaker is H. D. Lloyd. Jones promised the convention that Bryan would drop Sewall. *See* Paolo Coletta, *William Jennings Bryan; Political Evangelist, 1860–1908* (1964).

If one believes there are "crucial decisions" in history, then

Debs' decision to back Bryan was by far the most important of the period. Had he fought for and won the Populist nomination, the People's party would have merged the mass of the left of both the farm and labor communities for the first (and only) time.

The scenario works both ways. The blame for the election of McKinley would then have been right on Debs' door, offering consensus historians a whole new approach to proving radicalism doesn't pay. Furthermore, Debs was not yet a Socialist and it is impossible to say what shape his thoughts might have taken had he been the nominee.

Nonetheless, given the benefit of hindsight, a Debs-Watson campaign might have been the only real opportunity the Populists had to weather the 1896 campaign and to bring the radical wings of the farm and labor communities together on a national scale.

Probably no man . . . Bryan; Hicks, *Nation*, p. 272.

At no time . . . crisis; Robert F. Durden, *The Climax of Populism: The Election of 1896* (1965), p. 145.

Mules, swine and . . . States; Pollack, *Response*, p. 129.

Populists, Anarchists and . . . anarchist; Durden, *Climax*, pp. 150 and 141; and Coletta, *Bryan*, pp. 172 and 143.

Food and clothes . . . death; Hicks, *Nation*, p. 267.

Named William Jennings . . . Bryan; Coletta, *Bryan*, p. 175.

No crown of . . . victory; *Ibid.*, p. 155.

Destined for a . . . it; White, *Autobiography*, p. 292.

I have always . . . occasions; Durden, *Climax*, p. 145.

There was no . . . country; *Ibid.*, p. 138.

The last week . . . Avenue; Coletta, *Bryan*, p. 187.

We have escaped . . . commune; Pollack, *Response*, p. 130.

Like a squad . . . mob; Aaron, *Men*, p. 261.

Do you think . . . them; Coletta, *Bryan*, p. 195. Rosewater's statement to Roosevelt is on p. 283.

We propose to . . . fanaticism; Coletta, *Bryan*, p. 171.

A sham and . . . regiment; Woodward, *Watson*, p. 305.

The southern delegates . . . belong; *Ibid.*, p. 310.

I confess that . . . at; Woodward, *Origins*, p. 288.

We have conceded . . . Populism; Woodward, *Watson*, p. 311, 328.

I told them . . . ourselves; C. Vann Woodward, *The Strange Career of Jim Crow* (1957), p. 61. *See also Origins*, p. 288.

The nucleus around . . . people; Durden, *Climax*, p. 156.

Go behind the . . . prostitution; Clanton, *Kansas*, p. 207.

Our party as . . . it; Woodward, *Watson*, p. 329.

All our high-blown . . . future; Durden, *Climax*, p. 162.

Politically I was . . . be; Woodward, *Watson*, p. 331. After 1896, Watson dropped out of politics. When he returned in 1904 he was a changed man—a virulent racist and anti-Semite. "The white people dare not revolt so long as they can be intimidated by the black vote," he said. "I am a state Socialist through and through . . . but the lines of division between public utilities and private property are just as plainly discernible as are the lines between murder and arson. . . . Like a sheet of flame from Hell, Socialism would devour the Home, and all that is purest and best in Christian civilization—reducing all women to the same level of sexual depravity . . . [it would never] make a white woman secure from the lusts of the negro. (*Watson*, p. 405). In 1910 he joined the Democratic party.

Some of our . . . election; Woodward, *Origins*, p. 348. *See also* Hofstadter and Wallace, *Violence*, pp. 230–236. In 1900 in Kentucky a radical candidate for governor named William Goebels challenged the election by staging a mass march on the capitol building. The Louisville and Nashville Railroad brought in a thousand gunmen; Goebels was shot and killed.

All those who . . . them; Woodward, *Origins*, pp. 330–336.

Year	Number of farms (in millions)	Farm Population (in millions)	Percentage of Population	Acres (in millions)
1900	5.7	39.5	52.0	838
1920	6.5	31.9	30.1	956
1940	6.3	30.5	23.2	1061
1970	2.9	9.7	4.8	1121
1985	2.3	5.4	2.2	1014

(From *Statistical Abstract of the United States*, 1970 & 1987)
Song "I Ain't Got No Home in This World Anymore" reproduced by permission of Ludlow Music.

The Revolt of the Workers

"*Proletariat*: Derived originally from the Latin *proletarii*, the name given in the census of Servious Tullius to those who were of value to the state only as the reares of offspring (*proles*); in other words, they were of no importance either for wealth, or position, or exceptional ability." Jack London, *The Iron Heel*, p. 33.

"The rights and interests of the laboring man will be protected by the Christian men to whom God in His infinite wisdom has given the property interests of the country." George Baer, President of the Anthracite Coal Trust, 1902 (*Ibid.*, p. 68).

Drive a rat . . . you; Bruce, *1877*, p. 67.

The man, his . . . father; Jacob Riis, *How the Other Half Lives* (1957), p. 35.

Complete and absolute . . . interests; *Ibid.*, p. 83.

When soldiers did . . . fatal; Irving J. Sloan, *Our Violent Past* (1970), p. 180.

We must have our property; Bruce, *1877*, p. 142.

But one spirit . . . corporations; *Ibid.*, p. 183.

There is a . . . rebuke; *Ibid.*, p. 164.

(They have) declared . . . country; *Ibid.*, p. 232, and Philip Foner, *History of the Labor Movement in the Unites States* (1947).

There is no . . . master; John A. Garraty, *The American Nation* (1966), p. 525, and Norman J. Ware, *The Labor Movement in the United States, 1860–1890* (1964), p. xv.

A small but . . . world; Stephen Thernstrom, *Poverty and Progress: Social Mobility in a Nineteenth Century City* (1964), p. 158.

Substantial saving by . . . community; *Ibid.*, p. 162.

Sometimes black despair . . . ambitions; Samuel Gompers, *Seventy Years of Life and Labor*, I (1925), p. 138.

Without a word . . . activity; *Ibid.*, p. 96–97.

We are living . . . evolution; Louis Reed, *The Labor Philosophy of Samuel Gompers* (1930).

Labor leaders in . . . fees; John S. Gambs, *The Decline of the I.W.W.* (1932), pp. 49–50.

The most unscrupulous . . . new; Kornbluh, *Rebel.*

Long-haired, wild-eyed . . . pay; Garraty, *Nation*, p. 484.

I have often . . . public; Henry David, *The History of the Haymarket Affair* (1963), pp. 191–192.

Even if they . . . lawlessness; *Ibid.*, p. 181. Parsons did throw around some pretty violent language. In 1885 he wrote,

Dynamite! Of all the good stuff, that is the stuff! Stuff several pounds of this sublime stuff into an inch pipe (gas or water pipe), plug both ends, insert a cap with fuse attached, place this in the immediate vicinity of a lot of rich leaguers who live by the sweat of other people's brows, and light the fuse. A most cheerful and gratifying result will follow.
—In Louis Adamic, *Dynamite: The Story of Class Violence in America* (1958), p. 47.

Like many other leftists, Parsons seems to have talked a lot of violence and committed little. The right, on the other hand, seems to say little and do a lot of killing.

Brutality and unheard-of . . . known; David, *Haymarket*, p. 404.

An account of the 1887 Louisiana sugar strike appears in Hofstadter and Wallace, *Violence*, p. 139.

A reward that . . . dividends; in Daniel Aaron, ed, *America in Crisis* (1952), p. 141.

We had to . . . Italia; Josephson, *Barons*, pp. 371–372. Berkman spent thirteen years in prison following the attempted killing. His *Prison Memoirs of an Anarchist* contains a description of the assassination attempt and an account of his life in jail.

Paralyzes arms and . . . skin; Mary Jones, *The Autobiography of Mother Jones* (1925), p. 133.

An account of the New Orleans general strike appears in Woodward, *Origins*, p. 231.

Simplicity itself, we . . . labor; Stanley Buder, *Pullman: An Experiment in Industrial Order and Community Planning, 1880–1930* (1967), p. vii.

The company owns . . . bodies; *Ibid.*, p. 99. Robert Todd Lincoln, son of Abraham, succeeded Pullman as president of the corporation, which became a part of the Morgan-Rockefeller empire.

We can handle ... out; Joseph G. Raybeck, *A History of American Labor* (1959), p. 144.

I feel that . . . resistance; Ray Ginger, *Eugene V. Debs: A Biography* (1962), p. 144.

If it takes ... delivered; Sloan, *Violent*, p. 197.

Thugs, thieves, and ex-convicts; Raybeck, *Labor*, p. 203.

Innocent men and . . . fire; Ginger, *Debs*, p. 154.

There seemed to ... count; Sloan, *Violent*, p. 200.

Men have been court; Ginger, *Debs*, p. 149.

Done its best ... other; *Ibid.*, p. 162. The refusal of Gompers and the AF of L to support the strike was crucial. It was never clear whether Gompers viewed the union as friends or as competition. The AF of L also refused to support the IWW Lawrence strike of 1912 because, in Gompers' words, it was a "class conscious industrial revolution . . . a passing event that is not intended to be an organization for the protection of the immediate rights or promotion of the near future interests of the workers." In Kornbluh, *Rebel*, p. 160.

If Grover Cleveland . . . name; Woodward, *Watson*, p. 261.

I am a ... it; Ginger, *Debs*, p. 167.

Conspiracy from the . . . thought; McAlister Coleman, *Eugene V. Debs: A Man Unafraid* (1930), p. 184.

A necessary conflict . . . demagogues; Ginger, *Debs*, p. 55.

Not because I ... power; Coleman, *Debs*, p. 184.

The issue is ... change; Ginger, *Debs*, p. 204.

Revolutionary activity consisted . . . formulas; Paul F. Brissenden, *The I.W.W.: A Study of American Syndicalism* (1919), p. 241.

Our conduct is ... hard; Ginger, *Debs*, p. 295.

Every hint at . . . government; *Ibid.*, p. 247.

Opposed and strongly . . . produced; *Ibid.*, p. 453.

I don't want you to follow me or anyone else. If you are looking for a Moses to lead you out of this capitalist wilderness, you will stay right where you are. I would not lead you into the promised land if I could, because if I could lead you in, someone else could lead you out.
—Debs, in Michael Harrington, *The Accidental Century* (1971), p. 116.

If I rise . . . imagine; Coleman, *Debs*, p. 106, and William A. Williams, *The Contours of American History* (1966), p. 388.

Socialism is coming . . . Party; David A. Shannon, *The Socialist Party of America* (1955), p. 4.

He never felt . . . meaning; Clarence Darrow, *The Story of My Life* (1932), p. 68.

The picture of . . . Debs; Coleman, *Debs*, p. 249.

The growth of . . . past; Ginger, *Debs*, p. 289.

A large minority . . . States; Weinstein, *Corporate*, p. 170.

Tell Roosevelt to . . . that; Adamic, *Dynamite*, p. 137. Mother Jones hated Mitchell, who was a close associate of Gompers and a member of the National Civic Federation. "Mr. Mitchell died a rich man," she said, "distrusted by the working people whom he once served." In *Autobiography*, p. 160.

We always believed . . . situation; Adamic, *Dynamite*, p. 126.

The Caucasians are . . . others; Gary B. Nash and Richard Weiss, eds., *The Great Fear* (1970), p. 115.

Everything is quiet . . . miners; Adamic, *Dynamite*, p. 139.

A man must . . . yourself; David Brody, *Steelworkers in America: The Nonunion Era* (1969), p. 84.

Shop keepers were . . . immune; Jones, *Autobiography*, p. 109.

Visionary politician . . . box; Brissenden, *I.W.W.*, pp. 94–129. *See also* James Weinstein's *The Decline of Socialism in America, 1912–1925.* The standard explanations for the collapse of American socialism lay heavy emphasis on the factional disputes. No doubt the expulsion of the IWW from the Socialist party in 1912 was important, as was the friction during and after the war between pro- and antiwar Socialists, Communists, the Foster movement in the AF of L, the IWW left and right, and so on.

Factionalism is a part of all movements, as is repression. The repression surrounding the First World War, however, is almost incomprehensible. A movie director was sentenced to ten years in prison for making a movie about the American Revolution that apparently slurred the British, who were now allies. A man was given a ten-year sentence for verbally criticizing the government and a woman was given ten years for criticizing the YMCA. People were actually jailed for carrying banners that bore quotations from Woodrow Wilson's *New Freedom.* Books containing the slightest pro-German sentiment (including one, fittingly enough, by Albert Beveridge) were banned from libraries, and others, like *Ulysses*, were burned.

Needless to say, it wasn't too healthy even to be known as a Socialist. It is also true that jailing half an organization tends to bring about splits and faction-fighting just from the difficulties in communications and the overwhelming differences in consciousness between a person inside a jail and one on the outside. This is not to say that factionalism wasn't a key factor in bringing the breakdown of American socialism. But nothing happens in a vacuum.

Another standard explanation for the breakdown of the Socialist movement is that the American people as a whole simply didn't want it, and that those who did were the "marginal, alienated" elements of society to begin with.

The history of the country before the First World War doesn't bear this out. Socialism was acknowledged as a legitimate, if not universally embraced, ideology, and the presence of the Socialist party and of the IWW was accepted as a regular, healthy part of American life. The partisans of the left seemed to feel that, as with any new idea, time would tell.

But repression closed in before anyone had figured. It was a small minority of the country that took part in the stamping out of formal socialism. That the majority looked on with indifference, or perhaps unwillingness to risk body and job, is another question. What is true is that "the end of ideology" came about not by a general vote, but largely by a conscious violent campaign of politicians and businessmen to stamp out a clear alternative to the status quo.

As for the concept of "marginal, alienated" elements of society, and the now-standard practice of psychoanalyzing rebels, there is little to be said except "Who's calling whom what?" Professional historians, physicians, politicians, and other labeled experts have taken upon themselves the task of measuring all deviants by their own presumably perfect android credentials. Their insistence on "objectivity" and "normality" is another expression of the Puritan-Progressive-machine nonconsciousness that continues to plague humanity with its insistence on cramming everyone into a metal box while at the same time denying the life of our common humanity. Who needs it?

Arouse ye slaves! . . . guns; Eugene V. Debs, *Life, Writings and Speeches* (1908).

Who never did . . . trade; Wayne Broehl, *The Molly Maguires* (1964), p. 355.

Well, if I . . . principle; Adamic, *Dynamite*, p. 233.

If you want . . . masters; Coleman, *Debs*, p. 252.

Children were clubbed . . . Farm; Elizabeth Gurley Flynn, *I Speak My Own Piece* (1955), p. 128.

The miners accept . . . morality; Adamic, *Dynamite*, p. 261. West

Virginia was in a state of war for a pretty long time. Mother Jones described conditions in 1902—

Men who joined the union were blacklisted throughout the entire section. Their families were thrown out on the highways. Men were shot. They were beaten. Numbers disappeared and no trace of them found. Storekeepers were ordered not to sell to union men or their families. Meetings had to be held in the woods at night, in abandoned mines, in barns. In *Autobiography*, p. 63.

We have been . . . militia; Howard Zinn, *The Politics of History* (1971), p. 88.

There were very . . . at; *Ibid.*, p. 92.

If those deputies . . . butchered; Adamic, *Dynamite*, p. 262.

Murder by deputy . . . monotonous; *Ibid.*, p. 263.

The preamble, songs, and otherwise unnoted Wobbly material can be found in Joyce Kornbluh's *Rebel Voices: An IWW Anthology*, without which this book couldn't have been written. "Solidarity Forever" was written by Ralph Chaplin; "Pie in the Sky," by Joe Hill; "Bread and Roses," by James Oppenheim. The Wobbly culture had its deepest roots in the "jungles" which were home for thousands of hoboes. Their communal fires could be seen in every railyard and all across the plains. Harry Kemp, the hobo poet who wrote for the *Masses* in Bohemian New York (see next chapter), described the jungles as "often a marvel of cooperation.

Discarded tin cans and battered boilers are made over into cooking utensils and dishes. Each member contributes to the common larder what he has begged for the day. There is usually in camp someone whose occupational vocation is that of cook, and who takes upon himself as his share of the work, the cooking of meals.

Stews are in great favor in trampdom and especially do they like strong, scalding coffee. Usually the procuring of food in such a camp is reduced to a system such as would interest economists and sociologists. One tramp goes to the butcher shop for meat, one goes to the bakers for bread, and so forth. And when one gang breaks up, its members are always very careful to leave everything in good order for the next comers. They will even leave the coffee grounds in the pot for the next fellow so that he can make "seconds" if he needs to. These things are a part of tramp etiquette, as is also the obligation each new arrival is under to bring, as he comes, some wood for the fire. In Kornbluh, *Rebel*, p. 67.

The Wilson war administration catered to trade-union labor. Wages and bargaining privileges went up, Gompers was welcomed into the government. Typical of the propaganda issued by the government was an American Alliance pamphlet by John R. Commons entitled "Why Workingmen Support the War," which read in part—

This is an American workingman's war, conducted for American workingmen, by American workingmen. Never before has democracy for wage-earners made so great progress. . . . If this continues, American labor will come out of this war with the universal eight-hour day, and with as much power to fix its own wages by its own representatives as employers have.

Unfortunately, precisely the opposite followed war's end. With a crashed economy, high unemployment rate, and absence of wartime pressures, the government and factory owners attacked the trade unions as viciously as they did the labor radicals. Many unions were broken in the strikes of 1919 with a violence and vengeance that recalled the nineties.

What did follow in the twenties were attempts at "profit-sharing" and company unions—"welfare capitalism"—as a method of uprooting labor discontent. The most basic form of paternalism took shape under Henry Ford. He upped wages to an unheard-of $5 a day but then installed a spy system in his factories so thorough that workers communicated with each other only in the "Ford whisper."

By the thirties Ford's wages were no longer good enough and

the violent strikes at his plants—like those at Homestead and Pullman—announced another failure in the efforts of a "benevolent" factory owner. *See* Bernstein, *The Lean Years*.

Days of Magic

It could probably . . . Congress; Mark Twain's last years were plagued by misfortune and tragedy. His wife and two of his three daughters died, and his finances were badly fouled up. But his spirits stayed high much of the time, which he attributed to his basic temperament. He played a lot of billiards.

Every time in twenty-five years that I have met Roosevelt the man a wave of welcome has streaked through me with the hand-grip; but whenever [as a rule] I meet Roosevelt the statesman & politician I find him destitute of morals & not respect-worthy. It is plain that where his political self and party self are concerned he has nothing resembling a conscience; that under those inspirations he is naively indifferent to the restraints of duty & even unaware of them; ready to kick the Constitution into the backyard whenever it gets in his way. . . . But Roosevelt is excusable—I recognize it & [ought to] concede it. We are all insane, each in his own way, & with insanity goes irresponsibility. Theodore the man is sane; in fairness we ought to keep in mind that Theodore, as a statesman & politician, is insane and irresponsible.
  —In Albert Bigelow Paine, *Mark Twain*, III (1912), p. 1231.

We have pacified . . . Power; Paine, *Twain*, III, p. 1164.

During twenty-three . . . you?: Mark Twain, *Letters from the Earth* (1964), pp. 42–44.

In Man's heaven . . . name; *Ibid.*, pp. 17, 46, and 34.

As I look . . . alive: Joan London, *Jack London and His Times* (1939), pp. 288, 301. Like Meyer Berger and a few other Socialists,

Jack London was a racist. "I am first of all a white man," he said, "and only then a Socialist." In 1904 he wrote an essay entitled "The Yellow Peril" that would have thrilled Dean Rusk. He supported the Mexican strongman Huerta and traveled the country preaching revolution while attended by a Korean valet. The older he got, the more he moved toward national, rather than democratic, socialism. He supported American entry into the World War in terms that epitomized the times.

I am with the Allies life and death. Germany today is a paranoiac. She has the mad person's idea of her own ego, and the delusion of persecution. She thinks all nations are against her. She possesses also the religious mania. She thinks that God is on her side. These are the very commonest forms of insanity, and never before in history has a whole nation gone insane.

I believe the World War so far as concerns, not individuals but the entire race of man, is good.

The World War has compelled man to return from the cheap and easy lies of illusion to the brass tacks and iron facts of reality.

The World War has redeemed from the fat and gross materialism of generations of peace, and caught mankind up in a blaze of the spirit.

The World War has been a pentacostal cleansing of the spirit of man."

—Jack London, *London*, p. 370.

Watch out next . . . throttled; Jack London, *Heel*, p. 167.

A whole generation . . . it; Richard O'Connor, *Jack London* (1964), p. 248.

Had published an . . . Scott; Upton Sinclair, *American Outpost* (1927), p. 73. Sinclair authored nearly a hundred books in his long career. In the thirties he ran as a Socialist for governor of California and came very close to winning. He was also deeply interested in extrasensory phenomena. His book *Mental Radio* deals with experiments in telepathy conducted by him and his wife. His story *The Overman* (Little Blue Book #594) deals with the transcendence of the human mind into another level of consciousness.

White-faced and . . . family; Upton Sinclair, *Autobiography* (1962) p. 112.

What Uncle Tom's Cabin . . . chicken; Sullivan, *Times*, II, pp. 472 and 541. Though London and Sinclair were closely connected as Socialist writers, they were worlds apart personally. When the swashbuckling London met the relatively straightlaced Sinclair one night in New York, London decided to "have his fun" by blowing Sinclair's mind with "tales of incredible debauches; tales of opium and hashish, and I know not what other strange ingredients; tales of whiskey bouts lasting for weeks." In O'Connor, *London*, p. 242—from Sinclair's *Mammonart*.

"There is an ecstasy that marks the summit of life," London wrote in *Call of the Wild*, "and beyond which life cannot rise. And such is the paradox of living, this ecstasy comes when one is most alive, and it comes as complete forgetfulness that one is alive." Kerouac and Cassidy.

The white men . . . side; T. Thomas Fortune, *Land, Labor and Politics in the South* (1884), pp. 239–242.

But one hope . . . character; Booker T. Washington, *The Future of the American Negro* (1899), p. 132. *See also Up from Slavery*. Get some property . . . lost; *see* August Meier, *Negro Thought in America, 1880–1915* (1963), p. 146.

Few political appointments . . . consent; W. E. B. Du Bois, *Autobiography* (1968), p. 239.

Feel in conscience . . . them; W. E. B. Du Bois, *The Souls of Black Folk* (1965), pp. 50–54. Du Bois was first a Socialist, then a Communist in his long, amazing career. In his early days at least he advocated disfranchising the "ignorant" of both races, and Marcus Garvey accused him of promoting a "caste aristocracy." He also supported American entry in World War I.

A type of . . . corporation; Meier, *Thought*, p. 148. *See also* Gilbert Osofsky, *Harlem: The Making of a Ghetto*; and Allan Spear, *Black Chicago*.

Interesting coincidence that . . . vote; Woodward, *Origins*, p. 324.

I don't go . . . Indian; Richard Hofstadter, *Tradition*, p. 212. On Josephine Daniels, *see* Woodward, *Jim Crow*, p. 77.

Literacy statistics from Leonard Broom and Norval Glenn, *Transformation of the Negro American* (1967), p. 83. The left-wing of the Socialist party passed numerous resolutions for black equality. Debs opposed them, saying "The Negro does not need them, and they serve to increase rather than diminish the necessity for explanation. When the working class have triumphed in the class struggle and stand forth economic as well as political free men, the race problem will forever disappear." In 1905, Du Bois predicted a race war in which blacks and Asians would overwhelm whites.

Felt leap within . . . pottage; James Weldon Johnson, *The Autobiography of an Ex-Colored Man* (1912). Jack Johnson was heavyweight champion until 1915. At the time he was acknowledged by many—many grudgingly—as the greatest fighter ever. He was, however, hounded by the authorities and went to Europe, where he was greeted more hospitably. In 1915 he fought Jess Willard, an ex-cowboy, in Havana. He didn't bother to train for the match.

The fight itself amounted to little. For twenty-two rounds Willard and Johnson milled about under the scorching Cuban sun, without either delivering a blow with real force behind it. Then in the twenty-third round something happened, opinions differ as to what—whether a blow by Willard, or a sun-stroke, or whatever. At all events Johnson was seen to sink slowly to the canvas floor of the ring, stretch himself out at full length—and raise his arms as if to shade his eyes from the sun!

In Sullivan, *Times*, V, p. 604.

Johnson returned quietly to his home on the south side of Chicago and never fought again. In 1933 he conducted his own jazz orchestra.

All the divine . . . Americans; C. Eric Lincoln, *The Black Muslims in America* (1966), pp. 50–52.

Would accost white . . . domination; *Ibid.*

We have good . . . ourselves; Andrew Sinclair, *The Emancipation of the American Woman* (1966), p. 37.

Women with skins . . . point; Hicks, *Nation*, p. 248.

Up the mountain . . . in; Jones, *Autobiography*, p. 35.

If she had . . . discontent; Flynn, *Speak*, p. 99.

When the strike . . . pay; *Ibid.*, p. 107.

Bourgeois, middle-class . . . conviction; Aileen S. Kraditor, *The Ideas of the Woman Suffrage Movement, 1890–1920* (1965), p. 252.

A better Christian . . . State; Emma Goldman, *Anarchism and Other Essays* (1910), p. 203.

The women of . . . ladies; Jones, *Autobiography*, pp. 203–204.

With its great . . . soul; Goldman, *Anarchism*, p. 223.

She had no . . . fed; Charlotte Perkins Gilman, *Women & Economics* (1966), pp. 61–63.

The wife who . . . embrace; Goldman, *Anarchism*, p. 193.

Women have ceased . . . men; Rheta Childe Dorr, *What Eight Million Women Want* (1910), p. 4.

To unite man . . . bread-winner; Ellen Key, *Love and Marriage* (1911), p. 16.

Only cohabitation . . . morality; *Ibid.*, pp. 16–17.

Not to remain . . . attachment; Flynn, *Speak*, p. 140.

The most influential . . . generation; Kraditor, *Ideas*, p. 97.

A source of . . . waste; Charlotte Perkins Gilman, *The Home: Its Work and Influence* (1913), p. 73.

We pay rent . . . with; *Ibid.*, p. 118.

Revel in fat-soaked . . . growth; *Ibid.*, pp. 134–142.

With citizen's rights . . . indulgence; *Ibid.*, p. 335.

Almost every child . . . care; Ellen Key, *The Renaissance of Motherhood* (1914), p. 112.

The custom of criminal; Goldman, *Anarchism*, p. 178.

The men and women . . . self-respect; Emma Goldman, *Living My Life* (1932), pp. 555–556. Reprinted by permission A. A. Knopf.

The feeling of . . . woman; Key, *Love*, pp. 95–99. The feeling was prevalent at the time that enfranchising women would discourage war. "She knows the history of human flesh; she knows its cost; he does not." Clive Schriener, *Woman and Labor* (1911), p. 178.

When women no . . . last; Charlotte Perkins Gilman, *Human Work* (1904), p. 371. "Work, modern work, has no sex-connotation whatsoever. Moreover, modern science has shown that the female, instead of being inferior, is, if anything, the more important of the sexes." *Ibid.*, p. 214.

True sexuality will . . . joy; Goldman, *Anarchism*.

School discipline, since . . . amusing; Randolph Bourne, *Youth and Life* (1913), p. 33.

We insist on . . . way; Gilman, *Home*, p. 51.

Mankind has been . . . two; *Ibid.*, p. 230.

Even at four . . . stars; Ellen Key, *The Century of the Child* (1909).

So many clever . . . adults; *Ibid.*, p. 248.

Surrounded by gardens . . . study; *Ibid.*, p. 264.

Youth rules the . . . age; Bourne, *Youth*, p. 14.

Old men cherish . . . dead; *Ibid.*, pp. 12–15.

Must the younger . . . wait; Randolph Bourne, *History of a Literary Radical* (1920), p. 126.

Getting old is . . . habit; Key, *Child*, p. 179.

The real enemy . . . conformity; Bourne, *Youth*, p. 279.

A vast conspiracy . . . has; *Ibid.*, p. 287.

Not the niche . . . integrity; *Ibid.*

Hunched back, ungainly . . . wore; Christopher Lasch, *The New Radicalism in America, 1889–1963* (1967), p. 74. This is the book that led me to write this section.

The medieval French . . . proletariat; Albert Parry, *Garrets and Pretenders, A History of Bohemianism in the United States* (1933), p. ix.

Our super-revolutionary . . . ponies; Max Eastman, *The Enjoyment of Living* (1948), p. 404.

Steady objection to . . . it; *Ibid.*, pp. 418–420.

The kinship of *The Masses* and the early *Liberation News Service*/underground press is very real. Basic to each was the wild young energy and magic of Bohemia in 1914 and hippiedom in 1967.

Among the questions that linger are: "Why did Max Eastman

join the right wing?" and "Why did Marshall Bloom kill himself?" Better to ask "Why do fools fall in love?"

Simply by appearing . . . do; Allan Churchill, *The Improper Bohemians* (1959), p. 32. A typical organizational debate took place at the *Masses* when Floyd Dell called for a vote on whether or not to run some poetry in the magazine. Hippolyte Havel, visiting from *Mother Earth* screeched "Voting! Voting on poetry! Poetry is something from the soul! You can't vote on poetry!"

Dell replied that even the editors of *Mother Earth* voted on what material to run. "Yes," responded Havel, "but we don't abide by our decisions." *See ibid.*, p. 108.

Vile singer of . . . God; *Ibid.*, p. 97.

There was talk . . . open-eyed; *Ibid.*, p. 70.

Yet we are . . . dare; John Reed, *A Day in Bohemia*.

Looking back upon . . . communications; Mabel Dodge Luhan, *Movers and Shakers* (1936), p. 39.

For a general discussion of the Armory show and the art of the period, *see* Barbara Rose, *American Art since 1900*.

An overgrown hero . . . team; Churchill, *Improper*, p. 73.

Fifteen thousand spectators . . . forget; Luhan, *Movers*, p. 205.

Pallbearers carried a . . . wept; Kornbluh, *Rebel*, p. 202.

For a few . . . one; Luhan, *Movers*, p. 204. Mabel was by no means a political revolutionary. Her autobiography reeks of class prejudice, and blacks may not have been welcome at the discussion evenings except at appointed times. The much-vaunted evenings had an extremely elitist air about them. But in the never-ending continuum of historical paradox, Mabel found happiness married to Tony Lujan, a Pueblo Indian.

Revolution, literature, poetry . . . living; Granville Hicks, *John Reed* (1936), p. 176.

Might as well . . . NEWS!; Luhan, *Movers*, p. 233.

Stoves, pots and . . . mouths; Richard O'Connor and Dale L. Walker, *The Lost Revolutionary: A Biography of John Reed* (1967), p. 130. Eastman also went to Colorado. *See Enjoyment*, pp. 449–454. According to him, full-scale American intervention in Mexico was largely prevented by the American Union against Militarism, a peace group organized by his sister Crystal. Had it not been for pressure from that group, he said, Wilson would have continued a policy that "would have meant a war that would end only in the occupation of every square mile of Mexico by American soldiers!"

A source of much copy for historians has been the postwar struggle over the League of Nations. Billed as an "idealistic" attempt by Wilson to build a structure for world peace, the plan was attacked by a strange assortment of leftists and rightists who have since been lumped together as "isolationists" and, somehow, been loaded with part of the blame for World War II.

In fact, the Fourteen Points and the League were explicitly racist and were aimed at building an imperial alliance of western European powers that more resembled the Holy Roman Empire and Congress of Vienna than the modern United Nations. The League charter was more a general pact among the industrial nations for the division of the third world than it was a plan for peace.

For a general history of American foreign policy, *see* William Appleman Williams, *The Tragedy of American Diplomacy*; David Horowitz, *The Free World Colossus* and *Containment and Revolution*; and Gar Alperovitz, *Atomic Diplomacy: Hiroshima and Potsdam*.

Never embarked upon . . . country; Weinstein, *Corporate*, p. 235.

"I should like to have socialism," wrote Jack London in 1901, "yet I know that socialism is not the very next step; I know that capitalism must live its life first. That the world must be exploited to the utmost first; that first must intervene a struggle for life among the nations, severer, intenser, more wide-spread, than ever before. I should much more prefer to wake tomorrow in a smoothly running socialistic state; but I know I shall not; I know that a child must go through its child's sicknesses ere it becomes a man. So always remember that I speak of the things that are, not of the things that should be." Jack London, *London*, p. 333.

"Our civilization is still in a middle stage, scarcely beast, in that it is no longer wholly guided by instinct; scarcely human, in that it is not yet wholly guided by reason." Theodore Dreiser, *Sister Carrie*.

You have no . . . freedom; Churchill, *Improper*, p. 160.

Was the first . . . atom; Luhan, *Movers*, pp. 69–71.

Raymond went out . . . something; Luhan, *Movers*, p. 265–269. Mabel and a few others in the circle only took one peyote button, while Raymond and two others took more. When Mabel came down she got very uptight about the three people still tripping in her living room and prayed that they would leave, whereupon someone returned and threw them out of the house. It was a bad trip. One of the women had a breakdown, and Mabel and her friends had to wire the woman's father to come get her.

When the Bohemian scene broke up immediately before and during the war, Mabel went to Taos and fell in love with Tony Lujan, who fed her a lot of peyote. Her descriptions of her trips in *At the Edge of Taos Desert*, the final volume of her autobiography, are on a par with Leary's.

One of the preoccupations of the Progressive intellectuals was their search for "reality." They looked for it in war and found one kind; Mabel found the other.

That demanded physical . . . lost; Johnson, EX-COLORED. See Ben Sidran, BLACK TALK (1971), pp. 47–49 and footnote.

A city gone . . . lights; Henry F. May, THE END OF AMERICAN INNOCENCE (1964), p. 338. This book has a good account of the Chicago Bohemian scene.

All Indians must . . . fire; Dee Brown, BURY (1971), p. 416.

Maybe we should . . . style; The Associated Press, "Remarks on 'Humoring' Indians Bring Protest from Tribal Leaders," in the NEW YORK TIMES, June 1, 1988, Section A, page 13.

Some superb talks by the tribal leaders mentioned, and more, can be heard on a cassette called GREAT AMERICAN INDIAN SPEECHES (Caedmon: 1976). They are read by Vine Deloria, Jr., and Arthur Junaluska. BLACK ELK SPEAKS is also highly recommended.

For a general survey of native culture and its leaders, see Alvin M. Josephy, Jr.'s THE INDIAN HERITAGE OF AMERICA (1969) among a host of others.

For a discussion of the impact of native American thought on the Founding Fathers, see Bruce E. Johansen, FORGOTTEN FOUNDERS (1981).

The earth and . . . same; Brown, BURY, p. 316.

The shining water . . . himself; all quoted material from Chief Seattle appears in Virginia Irving Armstrong (ed.), I HAVE SPOKEN (1971) and in a beautiful poster produced by the Silicon Valley Toxics Coalition, 760 N. First-Second Floor, San Jose, California, 95112.

Shines not on us . . . skyscrapers; John Muir, LET ALL THE PEOPLE SPEAK AND PREVENT THE DESTRUCTION OF THE YOSEMITE PARK (1908) and John Muir and Ansel Adams, YOSEMITE AND THE SIERRA NEVADA (1948).

The amount of . . . life; Bolton Hall, THREE ACRES AND LIBERTY (1907), pp. 20, 371.

Most of us . . . complain; Ibid., p. 123. Edmund Morris, TEN ACRES ENOUGH (1907); Harvey W. Wiley, THE LURE OF THE LAND (1915); W. S. Harwood, THE NEW EARTH (1906); E. P. Powell, HOW TO LIVE IN THE COUNTRY (1911).

Mortgages are hard . . . lots; Hall, LIBERTY, p. 381.

Only within these . . . women; Caro Lloyd, HENRY DEMAREST LLOYD (1912), P. 67.

Many a church . . . joint; Henry F. May, PROTESTANT CHURCHES AND INDUSTRIAL AMERICA (1967), p. 248.

The ghastly philanthropy . . . wealth; Ibid., p. 251, and George D. Herron, THE CHRISTIAN SOCIETY (1894), pp. 90–132.

A wave of . . . Mohammedanism; William James, THE MORAL EQUIVALENT OF WAR AND OTHER ESSAYS (1971), p. 47.

In the summer . . . Buddhist; Churchill, IMPROPER, p. 255. Joe Gould wrote the lines. Interest in Eastern religion was sparked in part by the visit of an Indian holy man named Vivikenanda to the 1893 World Exposition. He criticized the West for its materialism and is mentioned in Paramahansa Yogananda's AUTOBIOGRAPHY OF A YOGI.

Obey the rich . . . slavery; Lucy Parson (ed.), FAMOUS SPEECHES OF THE EIGHT CHICAGO ANARCHISTS (1969), pp. 103–105. Compare what happened to the Chicago Eight of '86 with the Chicago Eight of '68.

Freedom, expansion, opportunity . . . possibilities; Goldman, ANARCHISM, p. 68.

God, the state . . . lungs; Ibid., p. 58.

Told the great . . . blood; Jones, AUTOBIOGRAPHY, pp. 195–6.

Every human life . . . saved; Herron, CHRISTIAN, p. 88.

Not only that God . . . any; all quotes from Charlotte P. Gilman in this section are from WORK, pp. 120–121, 145, 368–372, 388, and HOME, p. 345.

Free Love? . . . . root; Goldman, ANARCHISM, p. 242.

"I hate soldiers," said John Reed. "I hate to see a man with a bayonet fixed on his rifle, who can order me off the street. I hate to belong to an organization that is proud of being a caste of superior beings, that is proud of killing free ideas, so that it may more efficiently kill human beings in cold blood. They will tell you that a conscript army is democratic, because everyone has to serve; but they won't tell you that military service plants in your body the germ of blind obedience, or blind irresponsibility, that it produces one class of commanders in your state and your industries, and accustoms you to do what they tell you even in times of peace."

Thunderbunny's Mistory Book
   Full Moon in Aquarius, 1972
   Summer solstice, 1988
      Good Luck, again and again.

Books from

Algren, Nelson. **NEVER COME MORNING.** pb: $7.95

Anderson, Sherwood. **THE TRIUMPH OF THE EGG.** pb: $8.95

Brodsky, Michael. **X IN PARIS.** pb: $9.95

Brodsky, Michael. **XMAN.** cl: $21.95 pb: $11.95

Codrescu, Andrei, ed.
AMERICAN POETRY SINCE 1970: UP LATE.
cl: $23.95 pb: $12.95

Dubuffet, Jean.
ASPHYXIATING CULTURE AND OTHER WRITINGS. cl: $17.95

Howard-Howard, Margo (with Abbe Michaels).
I WAS A WHITE SLAVE IN HARLEM. pb: $12.95

Johnson, Phyllis, and Martin, David, Eds.
**FRONTLINE SOUTHERN AFRICA:
DESTRUCTIVE ENGAGEMENT.**
cl: $23.95 pb: $14.95

Null, Gary.
**THE EGG PROJECT:
GARY NULL'S COMPLETE GUIDE TO GOOD EATING.**
cl: $21.95 pb: $12.95

Santos, Rosario, ed.
**AND WE SOLD THE RAIN: CONTEMPORARY FICTION
FROM CENTRAL AMERICA.**
cl: $18.95 pb: $9.95

Sokolov, Sasha. **A SCHOOL FOR FOOLS.** pb: $9.95

Wasserman, Harvey.
HARVEY WASSERMAN'S HISTORY OF THE UNITED STATES.
pb: $6.95

Weber, Brom, ed.
**O MY LAND, MY FRIENDS:
THE SELECTED LETTERS OF HART CRANE.**
cl: $21.95 pb:$12.95